RIGHT MAN
RIGHT PLACE
WORST TIME

Commander Eric Feldt
His Life and His Coastwatchers

BETTY LEE

Copyright © 2019 Betty Lee

This book is copyright. Apart from any fair dealing for the purpose of private study, research, criticism or review, as permitted under the Copyright Act, no part may be reproduced by any process without written permission. Enquiries should be addressed to the publisher.

All rights reserved.

Disclaimer: The author/editor and publisher gratefully acknowledge the permission granted to reproduce the copyright material in this book. Every effort has been made to trace copyright holders and to obtain their permission for the use of copyright material. The publisher apologises for any errors or omissions in the book and would be grateful if notified of any corrections that should be incorporated in future reprints or editions of this book. While every effort has been made to ensure that the information contained within this book is accurate and up to date, the Author and Publisher makes no warranty, representation or undertaking whether expressed or implied, nor does it assume any legal liability, whether direct or indirect, or responsibility for the accuracy, completeness, or usefulness of any information.

Published by:
Boolarong Press
38/1631 Wynnum Road
Tingalpa Qld 4173
Australia.
www.boolarongpress.com.au

First published 2019

A catalogue record for this book is available from the National Library of Australia

ISBN: 9781925877267 (paperback)

Cover painting by Barbara Fea
Cover image of Commander Eric Feldt from *The Coast Watchers*
Cover design by Boolarong Press
Typeset in EB Garamond 12pt by Boolarong Press
Image: *Hand-drawn binoculars* by Freepik.com

Printed and bound by Watson Ferguson & Company, Tingalpa, Australia

DEDICATION

Dedicated to all those who took part in the Battle for Australia.

AUTHOR'S NOTE

I am neither a professional writer nor an historian. This book is not an authorised biography or an in depth research work. It was written in the hope that more everyday Australians would come to know of Eric Feldt and the Coastwatchers and feel proud and grateful that he and his men existed.

However, given the wealth of material left by Eric Feldt in his 1946 book, *The Coast Watchers*, and his oral history, plus research contained in Peter Jones' *Australian Argonauts*, and him graciously allowing the use of this, together with information from books and articles about and by other Coastwatchers; I had a treasure trove from which to chose what to include in this story.

With 2019 being the 80th anniversary of the inception of the Coastwatchers, physically by Eric, and of the beginning World War II, this book is also meant as a tribute and thank you to him and all those involved in WWII in Australia and the Pacific.

Betty Lee

CONTENTS

Dedication		iii
Author's Note		v
Acknowledgements		ix
Prologue		xi
Chapter 1:	Peter, Gussie and the Feldt Family 1876-1913	1
Chapter 2:	The Naval College Years 1913-1916	21
Chapter 3:	World War I and Post War Navy 1917-1923	37
Chapter 4:	New Guinea Pre World War II: 1923-1927	61
Chapter 5:	New Guinea Pre-World War II: 1928-1939	83
Chapter 6:	The WWII Coastwatchers: The Beginning	113
Chapter 7:	The Fall of Rabaul and the Aftermath	131
Chapter 8:	The Coastwatchers and the Japanese Invasion of the N.E. Area	179
Chapter 9:	The Coastwatchers of Bougainville, Guadalcanal and other Solomon Islands	207
Chapter 10:	The Coastwatchers – Townsville, the *Paluma*, and Papua New Guinea	239
Chapter 11:	The Coastwatchers – Guadalcanal, Bougainville and Illness	265
Chapter 12:	Post War Life	285
Bibliography		301
Endnotes		303

ACKNOWLEDGEMENTS

My thanks go to many people who have helped to make this book possible. First and foremost among these is my Aunt Brenda 'Penny' Tait. She sparked an interest in family history which had lain dormant in me. This rekindled an interest in my Great Uncle Eric Feldt and the Coastwatchers that had begun when I first read his book *The Coast Watchers* in my late teenage years.

Penny has also contributed significantly to much of the information in this book. This includes the transcription of *Gussie's Story* that she hand-wrote, which was typed and produced in booklet form by Susan Reye. Penny also provided me with Enid Critchton's version of *Gussie's Story*. Several of the photographs came from Penny's collection.

The next person I wish to thank is Vice Admiral Peter Jones. It was from reading his masterpiece *Australia's Argonauts: The remarkable story of the first class to enter the Royal Australian Naval College*, that I learnt what a truly remarkable person Eric Feldt was. I am also grateful to Peter for providing information and help from his wonderful store of knowledge.

A special thanks goes to an amazing character, James Burrowes, The Last Coastwatcher, whom I greatly admire. Jim is in his mid-nineties and together with his son Robert has a marvellous website called *The Last Coastwatcher* which is dedicated to trying to keep the memory of the Coastwatchers alive.

I thank my family for their support and tolerance during the time I have spent compiling and writing. To my partner, Mike Robson, my son Jason Lee, daughter Melissa Lee, my step-daughter Fiona Robson and step-son Chris Robson go my sincere thanks and appreciation.

I acknowledge a debt of gratitude to my Great-grandmother Ausgusta 'Gussie' Feldt for writing *Gussie's Story* and to Eric himself for recording his oral history and for writing *The Coast Watchers*. In doing so, they provided me with a wealth of information which otherwise would not have been available. I can only hope that this book will is some small way pay tribute to them both.

Other relatives whom I wish to thank for their help are Alison Early, Mardi Spencer, Susan Peatfield and James Mitchell.

To my editor, Stephen Thompson goes my appreciation for his fine efforts in sorting out my many spelling, typing and grammar mistakes and for structuring the manuscript into a cohesive story. For finding Stephen and giving me support (after an earlier misadventure with the manuscript) I am very thankful to Pat Noad. I thank Dr William Heaslop for acquainting me with Connal Gill's presentation to the Royal Historical Society of Queensland. To my publishing team, Dan Kelly, Bill Adrisurya and Tara Shaw at Boolarong Press go my sincere thanks for all the help and support they have provided. I am very grateful to Gail Cartwright for her excellent indexing and to Barbara Fea for her beautiful cover painting. My thanks also go to the Genealogical Society of Queensland Writing Group for their help in many practical aspects of writing.

I acknowledge the following sources of information: the State Library of South Australia for granting me permission to publish from *Reminiscences of Commander Eric Feldt*; The National Film and Sound Archive of Australia (NFSA) and Amalgamated Wireless of Australasia (AWA) for allowing me to hear the recording made by Rupert Long of his interviews with Coastwatchers and other officials who attended the opening of the Coastwatchers Memorial in Madang in 1959; and the Australian War Memorial for permission to publish several photographs.

I wish to state that any errors in this book are my own.

Most of all I want to acknowledge and thank Eric Feldt and the Coastwatchers for their bravery and selflessness and for the contribution they made at a time of Australia's greatest need.

PROLOGUE

Enemy air raids were still occurring at Tulagi as Acting Commander Eric Feldt lay in his bed in Tulagi Naval Hospital in the Solomon Islands in March and April 1943. He was sleeping a lot. Was the morphine he was being given to ease the bouts of chest pain making him drowsy, or was it due to exhaustion from a year of overwork and stress, or a combination of both?

What had been his thoughts since 20 March, when on a plane taking him from Guadalcanal to Auki on Malatia in the Solomon Islands he was struck by the most severe pain he had ever felt? The pain, in the middle of his chest, behind his breast bone, was heavy and crushing and radiated down his left arm, making him feel short of breath.

Eric Feldt was a man who generally kept his emotions in check. An exception was his tendency to justified (in his opinion) outbursts of anger when things did not go as he wanted for his loyal band of Coastwatchers.

On the morning of 20 March, the pilot had turned the plane around at Auki without disembarking his important passenger and rushed the Head of the Coastwatchers to Tulagi. The hospital doctor diagnosed a coronary thrombosis, a heart attack, and ordered complete rest for Eric.

As he lay in his hospital bed, Eric had plenty of time to look back on the events that had brought him to this hospital in the Pacific War Zone in World War II. His thoughts and memories would have turned to his parents and how their struggle to succeed in a strange new country had ultimately resulted in his birth. He would be greatly missing Nan, his wife of 10 years, who had provided much needed support for him in Townsville in 1942, when the tumultuous and testing time had led Eric to seriously overwork and endure enormous stress.

Eric would have thought of his years as one or the members of the very first Australian Naval College and the friends he had made there, especially Rupert Long and Hugh Mackenzie. With them, he had made up the tremendous trio of Naval Intelligence and Coastwatcher leaders. He would have recalled his years in the battleships in the North Sea in World War1; his eventual resignation from the Navy; the failure of his attempted new career; how this had led him to a new life in the Mandated Territory of New Guinea; his role in the Coastwatchers; and the friends he had made along the way. He would have wondered if he would ever see his family, friends and comrades again. Would another heart attack or an enemy bomb carry him off?

Perhaps most of all he may have been wondering if he and the Coastwatchers had done enough to help turn the tide in favour of the Allies in the Pacific War. The year 1942 had been a most important year in Australia's history. The young nation was facing an imminent threat as the Japanese were drawing ever closer to Australian shores and virtually knocking on the front door. There really could have been little doubt in Eric's mind that the contributions made by the Coastwatchers had greatly outweighed their numbers. While their endeavours were varied and numerous, some were more significant than others:

1939 Sep–Dec. Eric Feldt enlists and strategically places the Coastwatchers.

1942 Jan. Eric requests Keith McCarthy investigate the aftermath of the Fall of Rabaul.

Feb. Mar. Apr. Keith McCarthy et al., 'Blue' Harris et al. and Hugh Mackenzie et al., rescue 350 Australian soldiers sacrificed by Australia, left to perish after the fall of Rabaul.

May. Jack Read's and Donald Kennedy's sightings of Japanese war ships confirms their presence near Bougainville and Solomon Islands and aids readiness for the invasion of Tulagi and the Battle of the Coral Sea.

Jul. Don Macfarlan and Snowy Rhoades send message that Japanese have nearly completed a vital airfield near Lunga, propelling the Allies to bring invasion of Guadalcanal forward to early August.

Aug. Dick Horton and Henry Josselyn go in with US Marine invasion forces to Tulagi as guides.

Aug. Paul Mason and Jack Read on Bougainville warn of Japanese planes approaching Guadalcanal and ensuring the Allies invasion is successful.

1942 Aug.-1943 Mar. Hugh Mackenzie sets up Coastwatchers on Guadalcanal. Mason and Read and other Coastwatchers in the Solomons continue giving vital warnings of planes flying over and ships sailing down 'The Slot'. This contributes greatly to the Allies being able to hold Guadalcanal and eventually defeat the Japanese. Coastwatchers rescue hundreds of downed airmen and shipwrecked sailors.

1942 Nov. Lyndon Noakes in New Guinea sends signals of each new Japanese location as they try to set up a posts on the Mambare River. Bombing of locations by the Allies prevents a potential attack by Japanese on the Allies' flank at Buna and also stops the Japanese from sending supplies to Buna.

Nov. Dec. Coastwatcher ship *Paluma* marks a safe passage from Milne Bay to Buna, allowing small ships to carry tanks, cannons and other heavy artillery needed to defeat the Japanese, who are dug in at Buna.

It had all come at a cost. Many Coastwatchers were ill, missing or dead, including Eric's best friend, Bill Kyle, and Eric had come close to joining him.

CHAPTER 1

PETER, GUSSIE AND THE FELDT FAMILY 1876-1913

The Year 1899 was a significant one in Australia's history for it saw the birth of 28 male infants destined to become the very first cadet-midshipmen of the Royal Australian Naval College in 1913. The Australian nation was just twelve-years-old when its Naval College came into being. Pride and interest in the activities of the cadet-midshipmen was high. They became known as the Pioneer Class, and their progress was frequently reported in the newspapers of the day. Born on 3 January 1899, Eric Augustas Feldt was first of these to make an entrance into the world.

When the young thirteen and fourteen-year-old boys arrived at the Royal Australian Naval College, Geelong, it would have been impossible to predict the importance this step would become in the outcome of one of Australia's darkest hours.

The training and education given to Eric was strict and demanding, but it helped to make him the man he became. Although this is the story of one man, who was the right man at the right place during the dark days of World War 2, it also records the vital contributions of other men about whom the same could be said. Two of these were also to come from the Pioneer Class.

Eric was born to pioneering parents Peter and Augusta 'Gussie' Feldt at the family home, *Norland*, situated in Victoria Estate, in the sugar cane country near Ingham, North Queensland. His birth certificate has his middle name spelt as Augustas, while in his naval records it is spelt Augustus.

Eric's parents had been born in rural areas near Helsingborg, Southern Sweden. Peter Nilsson Feldt was born in Frillestad, Malmohus, Skane on 11 October 1853, the son of a soldier turned farmer, Nils Persson Feldt. Peter's mother, Johanna Botilla Alm, died in April 1864, shortly after childbirth when Peter was 10-years-old. Nils Feldt remarried in December 1865. Peter's two younger brothers, Anders 'Andrew', born in 1857; Carl 'Charles', born 1860; and half-sister, Johanna, born 1867, would eventually join him in Queensland.

Augusta Blixt was born in Hjarnap, Malmohus, Skane on 27 April 1862, the daughter of Sven Peter Blixt and Bothilda Lundberg. Her grandfather, Petter Per Larsson Blixt, had been a corporal in the Scanian Hussar Regiment. When Sven Peter died in 1880, he left a family consisting of his wife, Bothilda; Gussie; a son, August, born in 1864; and 2 little daughters, Carolina born in 1875 and Anna Maria in 1878.

Fortunately for her descendants, Eric's mother left a memoir called *Gussie's Story*, which she wrote in one of Eric's old naval college exercise books. Members of the family have made hand-written and typed copies, which are held and treasured by the family. While not long or detailed, it provides a valuable record of the challenges Eric's parents had to face in a strange new land.

The pioneering life of Peter and Gussie Feldt was not one to draw attention. Their story began in Sweden in about 1876–77. Gussie was 14 when she first met Peter, who was 22. She was staying in a boarding house while going to Lutheran confirmation classes and saw him every day for six months. Peter wrote her a poem for her Confirmation Day.

In 1878 Peter left Sweden, embarking on 22 June on the sailing ship *Friedeburg*, leaving from Hamburg and bound for Brisbane,

Australia, via Rio, Brazil. Unfortunately there was an outbreak of typhoid fever on board. After arriving in Moreton Bay on 16 October, passengers and crew were quarantined on Peel Island in Moreton Bay. Some were released on 18 November, others finally set foot in Brisbane on 27 November.

Peter's first work was in Bowen, North Queensland. He was employed to mind sheep on an outstation, where he had a small bush hut and was provided with a shepherd's ration of flour, sugar, tea and salt beef. By 1881 Peter had made enough money to send to Anders and Carl. With help from Queensland's assisted immigration scheme, the brothers arrived in Cooktown on 19 November 1881.

Meanwhile, Gussie was growing up in Sweden, eventually finding work she loved in a glamorous theatre restaurant in charge of the buffet refreshments.

It is not known how many letters Peter sent to Gussie, however one day early in 1882 a letter arrived from him which took Gussie by surprise. It contained a photo of him sporting a long beard, a money order and a proposal asking her to come to Australia and marry him. Facing the most difficult decision of her life, Gussie gave careful consideration to the pros and cons, discussing it with family and friends. She spent sleepless nights wondering if she should leave her native land and travel across the sea to a strange new land on the other side of the world to make a new life with a man she had not seen for four years. Gussie recalled the time she had spent with Peter as being exciting, and she thought he was trustworthy, however leaving her family, friends and way of life would not be easy. While theatre life was glamorous, Gussie could see that behind the scenes the actors suffered from poverty and hardship, conditions that existed for many people in Sweden at that time. She saw Australia as offering opportunities for prosperity and for owning plenty of land. Gussie's mother, Bothilda, was very upset by the thought of losing her daughter. Her husband had died and her son August was missing at sea, but she was planning to remarry. For Gussie, the loss of close family members had lessened reasons for her to stay in Sweden.

She sought to reassure her mother and herself by saying that if life in Australia with Peter did not work out as hoped she would work to raise money and return to Sweden. On the other hand, if all went well, Bothilda and family could come out to Australia, where there was a chance of a better life for the little girls.

Finally, Gussie, who had turned 20, mustered up her courage and decided to go. She set out with a travelling companion, leaving Helsingborg on the Danish steamer *Dagmer* bound for London. After a few days in London, they caught a train to Plymouth and embarked on the *SS Almora* on about 28 November 1882. The Queensland assisted immigration scheme sponsored their passage.

For Gussie the trip was wonderful. There was music and dancing on board every night, and she was chosen as Captain of the Mess for the Danes and Swedes.

The *Almora* arrived in Townsville on Sunday 14 January 1883 and anchored off shore as there was no harbour at that time. Standing on deck, Gussie watched the lighter, which had come to take passengers ashore, draw closer. She scanned it, looking for Peter. Surely he would have come to meet her. Her throat tightened in fear when she could see no sign of him. Suddenly she saw a hand waving and a voice saying, "*Gussie hur star de till?*" (Gussie how are you?).[1] Fear gave way to disappointment, a feeling they both shared. Gussie's 'Prince Charming' looked to her more like 'the wild man from Borneo.' His fair curly beard had grown longer than in his photo and he was not wearing a coat. In the heat of the tropics that was normal, but Gussie had not expected this; in cold Sweden wearing a coat was the custom.

Tall, blond, blue-eyed and well-developed, Peter had imagined his 'Cinderella' would have grown up to be tall, slender and curvaceous. Instead, dark-haired Gussie had remained short in stature and more on the chubby side than on the curvy. Their personalities also differed. Peter was reserved and work oriented while Gussie was outgoing and socially inclined. Despite their differences and disappointment at reality not meeting their expectations, and after some reflection, the betrothed decided to go ahead with the wedding and were married on 23 January. Peter's brother Anders came in from the country to be best man.

The newlyweds travelled separately to their destination near Ingham, on the Herbert River, 90 miles north of Townsville. Peter and Anders went overland with their horses. 'They were to make a house ready for the bride'. Ten days later Gussie left on a small steamer called *Victory*.

The Feldt brothers and Gussie spoke only Swedish when they arrived in Australia. By the time she boarded *Victory*, Gussie thought she could understand most of the English that was being spoken. It seemed friendly and she wished she could reply. When *Victory* arrived at Lucinda Point, the small port on the Herbert River, about 20 miles from Ingham, it was mid-afternoon. Gussie viewed the settlement with dismay. The port consisted of a few ramshackle humpies.

Peter had arranged for a boatman to take Gussie up the river to a landing at Gairloch, but she had to wait in the boatman's hut for the tide to turn at 2 o'clock the next morning. There were only two men and Gussie in the little rowing boat. The journey in the dark was dreary, with only the swishing of the oars punctuating the silence. Mosquitoes descended in droves, seeking Gussie's soft European skin.

It was afternoon when the boat reached the landing. Anders was there to meet her. He told her that her new home was only a five minutes walk away. Then he broke the news that Peter had been unable to get a house and they would have to temporarily live in what Anders called a tropical residence.

Peter was waiting at the dwelling, which had a grass thatched roof. Gussie called their humpy a bush house and described it as 'a sort of barn with a small room at the end, partitioned off as a bedroom'. Peter had been busy making a bedstead from rough timber. Outside was a smaller shelter that housed a primitive kitchen containing two iron bars supported on stones, with billy cans for boiling water and a camp oven for baking bread and roasting meat.

Peter said houses were scarce, but although it meant they would have to live there for the time being, once he had finished a contract they could look for somewhere else. Gussie saw the humorous side of her situation and laughed. Her new home bore no resemblance to the castles in the air she had imagined for her new life.

Their bush house was situated on a sugar plantation and was half a mile from the mill. There were a few houses on the plantation — a two storey one for the manager and a nice cottage for the officers at the mill — but the workers had only humpies.

She soon began to enjoy her new life, so different from her previous one. She watched the South Sea Islanders (known as Kanakas then) cutting sugar cane with large shiny steel knives as she wandered through the plantation. She saw horse drays taking cane to the mill and huge bullock teams pulling logs across the river. The small town of Ingham, 4 miles away, had no more than 50 inhabitants but was developing, with a school, hospital, post office, church and police station being built.

Letters arrived from her family and friends in Sweden telling of how they were missing her. They also brought news that her brother, August, had returned safely from sea, ironically on the *Dagmer*, the very same ship that had taken Gussie to England. While relieved that August was safe and well, Gussie thought that Fate had played a hand, because if he had returned a week earlier she might not have embarked for Australia. This was perhaps the very first time that Fate had intervened to insure the future existence of Eric Feldt.

On some Sundays, Peter and Gussie rode out to the bush and looked at a place called The Selection, where Peter had bought land. This was to be where they were to have a home once the contract work was finished. Gussie was not impressed. 'It seemed like a dreadful place: not a house to be seen for miles.'

Gussie continued her walks around the planation, and one day Fortune smiled on her when she met a little six-year-old girl called Minnie, whose family lived in a weatherboard cottage nearby. It was from Minnie that Gussie learnt to speak English. 'She was a blessing for she spoke a child's English'. Minnie's mother let her daughter visit Gussie every day, and they formed a friendship that lasted a lifetime.

For the first time in her life Gussie became acquainted with snakes. Some nights, after Peter and Gussie had lit the kerosene lamp, snakes slithered in on the floor. Gussie was terrified and climbed up on the table calling to Peter to join her. There were times during the day when two long black snakes would climb up and crawl along the inside of the grass roof. One day, when Minnie was with her, Gussie suddenly saw the two snakes very close at hand. Petrified, she grabbed Minnie by the hand and ran outside. During the wet season Gussie felt she lived in terror day and night.

Peter and Anders worked hard, building fences and clearing the bush. The money was good and when one contract ended they took on another.

A postmaster and doctor arrived in Ingham. Gussie was thankful for the latter as she and Peter were expecting their first child towards the end of the year. With the doctor and Minnie's mother in attendance, Gottfried Anton Feldt (Gotty) was born on 18 November 1883 in the middle of a thunderstorm.

Motherhood awakened Gussie to a new sense of responsibility and she implored Peter to provide a proper house. Her terror of snakes became magnified by fear for the safety of her baby.

She asked about the promised home on The Selection. Peter said he would build it in two to three months' time. In the meantime he went out every weekend to build the kitchen from saplings so there was somewhere to live when they moved out.

At the end of January 1884 they rode to The Selection, Gussie clutching her baby close to her chest. Peter and Anders carried the luggage on the backs of their horses. The men were soon busy cutting down timber, making a floor from the slabs. They made shutters for the windows and added a galvanised iron roof. Gussie was delighted to have a house with a real floor. All was well for about four months, but then the money started to run out. The property could not support them and there was no nearby work. Peter and Anders had no choice but to go back to the plantation to find work. Gussie's dread of snakes made her decide to stay.

She soon deeply regretted her decision. She was alone and lonely all week with her baby until the men returned on Saturday evening. Dingoes howled all night long, the small terrier kept rushing under the house fearful of being attacked by the wild dogs, and the grey horse tramped noisily around the house trying to avoid mosquitos. Alone in the dark, she was terrified that Aborigines might appear and do harm to her and her baby. The sounds of the night added to her fears and Gussie often did not fall sleep until daybreak. She held out for a few weeks. In the end there was nothing for it but to go back to the humpy … and the snakes. Once there, she dared not place baby Gotty on the ground.

Gussie could no longer laugh about her accommodation, and her bright, happy nature was giving way to despondency, so when she found she was expecting another baby she once again told Peter she must have a home.

It was a great relief when Anders offered to buy The Selection and Peter was able to purchase land in the township of Ingham. He set about building a rough weatherboard cottage with four rooms, a small front veranda and a detached kitchen at the back. The timber had to be pit-sawn so there was not much money left for 'trimmings, but it was a house with real windows. It was a treat!'

Peter and Anders continued doing contract work and roadmaking. Gradually Gussie added a few pieces of furniture in time for the arrival of the next baby. Mabel Christina was born on 8 June 1885.

Peter got a job as a foreman on the Shire Council, a position he held for three years. They were happy years for Gussie, with her infants, a boy and a girl, and a real home. The town was progressing and, from time to time, concerts, dances and balls were held, which Gussie loved.

Their third child, a second daughter, was born on 3 March 1888 and was named Violet Augusta. By now Gussie and Peter could speak English well enough to be understood, and this contributed to an easier life.

When the council work ended, Peter decided to make a move out to the Halifax district on the Lower Herbert River, where he rented a sugar cane farm. Halifax had been established on the Lower Herbert in the 1870s by William Ingham. Peter had sometimes taken Gussie there when she had first arrived. She had been pleased to find people who spoke her native language. She was happy to be returning to Halifax, this time to live.

The Colonial Sugar Refining (CSR) Company had come to the Herbert River in 1883. It had built large quarters for both the white and black workers and lay down a narrow-gauge railway to transport both the cane and the refined sugar. One day, in CSR's first year, Peter called out to Gussie to come and see a large black cloud. It looked very menacing as it drew nearer. They stood still, silently watching as it passed over their heads and settled on the ground around them and in the cane fields. Millions of grasshoppers began munching away at the young sticks of cane, devasting the crop and leaving very little for CSR to crush that year.

When Peter and Gussie moved to the farm, they needed help with the labour. CSR had indentured South Sea Islanders and sublet them to farmers. Peter was able to hire two Pacific Islanders who proved to be very good workers.

In 1886 Peter's half-sister Johanna arrived from Sweden. Gussie was pleased to have her company and her help with the children. Peter worked hard on the farm and Gussie in the home. She cooked for her family and for the two South Sea Islanders. Mosquitos were so prevalent that smoke buckets had to be kept going most of the time and were always placed beside the table at meal times.

The employment of the Melanesian labourers was being questioned in the community. Although some of the workers had been voluntarily recruited and had come in search of a better life, others had been kidnapped and brought against their will. This practice was known as "blackbirding". Regardless of how they arrived, the Pacific Islanders were required to do physically hard work and were paid a considerably lower wage than their white counterparts. While on one side concern was being raised about the treatment of the Islanders, on the other side members of the sugar cane industry were convinced that without black labour profit would not be possible.

Peter and the two South Sea Islanders toiled to clear the scrub, prepare the land and plant cane. In March 1890, when the stalks had grown tall, they were hit by a cyclone. The children were put to bed and fell asleep, but Peter stayed up on watch. Gussie, seven months pregnant with their fourth child, and Johanna tried to sleep but found it impossible as the house shivered and shook and the wind howled around them. About midnight there was a loud crash as the kitchen collapsed. The children were awakened and the family sat in readiness to leave at any moment. About 4am the house leaned dangerously to one side. Peter decided it was time to go. The front door was jammed so they had to climb out through a window. No sooner had they crossed the paddock to the cowshed when they heard an enormous crash and turned to see the house falling like a pack of cards.

As day dawned they sought safety elsewhere. They mounted the frightened horses, but the spooked animals refused to face the ferocity of the storm so the family had to walk to the nearest neighbour two miles away. They linked arms and, each carrying a child, strode out into the wild wind and rain. The two Melanesian men went with them, helping to carry the children, especially across the gullies where water was rising.

They reached the neighbour's house and were grateful for the shelter and cups of hot tea. When the cyclone abated about 4 pm, they thanked their neighbour and set out to walk the mile to town. Here they found others sheltering in a large sugar store owned by CSR. The storekeeper, who knew Gussie well, insisted she and her family stay in his house.

The rain that accompanied the cyclone caused flooding, and in places the water was two feet over the road.

As they had leased the farm for three years, they had no option but to carry on. First, Peter, with the help of another man, set about building a replacement house. It was another humpy, this time with a floor. After Gussie and the children returned to the farm, Peter's attention turned to the flattened cane fields. He and the South Sea Islanders worked to clear the ruined cane that had been meant to provide them with a living.

Their family was growing. Their third daughter, Emma Caroline, was born on 13 May 1890. The next crop of cane was successful, but as their lease drew to an end they needed to decide whether to renew. They found that after their three years of hard work and facing many difficulties their financial situation had not improved. This realisation left Gussie feeling rather depressed and she wondered whether they would have been better off if they had never traversed the thousands of miles to seek a better life. Her disappointment and doubt were buffered by her ambition and determination for Peter and herself to succeed. Gussie recalled how she would look lovingly at her children and with her tiny hands clenched murmur, "We mustn't fail!"

The question of the viability of sugar farms should the Melanesian labour force be withdrawn was of concern. All things considered, Peter and Gussie decided not to renew the lease and returned to Ingham in 1891. Peter found work at a tin mine about 30 miles away, but after three months the firm went broke and he returned to Ingham.

Just as he was wondering what to do, the CSR company, worried by the looming loss of the South Sea Islander workers, decided to divide up their plantation, Victoria Estate, and offer the subdivisions for sale to white settlers.

Peter put in for an allotment and was able to obtain a good one. Anders was on The Selection but their other brother, Carl, now known as Charlie, acquired land on the same side of the plantation as Peter. The terms of the sale were that the farmers were to pay interest on the value of their land, but if misfortune befell them they could pay the following season or, failing that, when they were able.

There were no houses on the plots of land, but Charlie, who was also married with children, bought a little iron house that he and Peter dismantled and re-erected on Charlie's parcel of land. Gussie and the children continued living in Ingham, where the older children were going to school. Peter joined the family on weekends. A fourth daughter, Ada Bothilda, arrived on 26 June 1892.

The brothers and the Pacific Islanders ploughed the land and planted the cane. They grew fruit trees and there was plenty of fruit, milk and eggs for the children due to their chickens and cows. Yet another daughter was born on 7 October 1894 and named Minnie Juliet after Gussie's little friend of her first years in Australia. Just as things seemed to be looking up, a terrible tragedy struck. An epidemic of whooping cough swept through Ingham. Three-month-old Minnie caught the dreadful disease and died on 12

January 1895. Gussie was grief-stricken. All the hardships she had endured were nothing compared to this heart-wrenching loss. She knew she had to carry on for the sake of her other children, and this she did, keeping constantly busy to help numb her sorrow.

The farm was doing well, and when Charlie indicated that he would like to leave and go to Ingham, Peter agreed to buy him out. This decision turned sour when the year's crop was so small that they could only pay the men's wages. Peter negotiated terms with CSR to pay compound interest.

When Charlie left, Gussie decided to go and live on the farm and to buy ponies for the oldest children to ride the three miles to school in Ingham. The iron humpy was to be their home until they could afford a better house.

The farm had fields cultivated with sugar cane and grazing paddocks for horses and cattle. It was bounded on one side by Palm Creek, which supplied permanent water. Brown rushes fringed its edges, and water lilies, with exquisite blue flowers, studded the surface of the water. The property was centrally located and a narrow-gauge railway ran right through it to the mill.

At night, when the children did their homework, Peter and Gussie, although tired after their day's work, joined them to learn more of the English language, culture, customs and history. Gussie decreed that the language of her adopted country was the only language to be spoken by their children, so English was the language spoken in the home and none of the Feldt children ever learnt to speak Swedish.

In order to help the sugar industry, the government had decided to allow the South Sea Islanders already present in Australia to stay until the time their indentures expired. The language spoken by the Melanesians, and their employers with them, was Pidgin English. Gussie thought that the Pacific Islanders were happy and many did not wish to be returned to the islands.

The year 1896 saw the family grow, with the addition of a sixth daughter, Lucy Victoria, on 29 January. By 1898 life had improved for the Feldts. Peter had built a nice house, they named *Norland*, which had six rooms and a veranda all the way round. They even had their own buggy.

Gussie was ambitious for her children. When Gotty turned 14, Gussie worried that there was no secondary school for him to attend. The local postmaster, Mr. Simpson, needed a boy to work in the post office and enquired at the school. He chose Gotty for the position, which involved office work and learning the telegraph code. Gotty commenced work at the post office and did well.

Their next child, Mabel, was intelligent, studious and had a good memory. She finished the school course at the age of 12 and wanted to be a teacher. A vacancy arose in the teaching staff and young Mabel was given the opportunity to teach. This she did for 12 months without payment. She was a child teaching other children, including her sisters.

Peter started to take an interest in local affairs and became a member of the hospital committee and other local committees, as well as being chairman of the school for many years.

Gussie tried to start a ladies' social group in the Victoria Estate settlement but did not succeed because the housewives were too busy in the day and too tired in the evening.

The Feldts' situation steadily improved. Their orchard flourished, they made a tennis court and, with their two eldest children working in respectable occupations, Gussie thought they were 'the aristocrats in the settlement'.

Then another devastating catastrophe befell them. Their second daughter, Violet Augusta, became critically ill. The doctor came and did what he could, but to no avail. Her short life of 10 years sadly came to an end on 16 November 1898. In later years, Gussie was to think that appendicitis, which was unknown in those days, was the cause of Violet's death.

The family's grief was profound. Violet had been a beautiful girl with large brown eyes and a sweet nature, and they had all been devoted to her. Gussie's grief was such that for the rest of her life not a day went by that she did not think of her beloved Violet.

Her immeasurable sadness was not lifted by the fact that she was expecting another baby. After eight weeks of sorrow and distress, Gussie gave birth to their eighth child, a son, on 3 January 1899. They named him Eric Augustas.

Gussie recorded: 'Peter was very pleased, having a son after six daughters. I still felt that nature was unkind. Why could I not be allowed to have them all, instead of losing some and having to replace them? A small voice said, "Don't you grumble for the late-comers might be a great blessing". And so it turned out to be.'

Peter and Gussie were proud of the farm and pleased with their progress. They liked to sit on the veranda, Gussie with baby Eric on her knees, and behold the fruits of their labour. They enjoyed watching Peter's pride and joy, his horses, in superb condition, frolic in the paddocks.

October 1899 saw the beginning of the Boer War. Australia raised troops to send to South Africa to help the British in the fight. Gotty, who was a few weeks shy of 17, was keen to go, but was too young. He began working on a punching bag to build up his chest muscles, hoping that might make him look older.

Patriotic fervour saw concerts being held to raise money for the cause. In the Ingham district, concern was high for the sieges in the South African towns. 'At last we got the news that Mafeking had been relieved from the siege, and then our little town went nearly mad with joy.'

To celebrate, the townspeople built a huge bonfire and people came from all around to watch it burn on a cold Saturday evening in May 1900. Speeches were made and everyone enthusiastically joined in singing *Rule Britannia*.

Sadly, despite the warmth of the fire, the postmaster, Mr Simpson, got a chill, developed pneumonia and died before the week was over. The town felt the blow, for Simpson had been a popular and cheerful man who had organised many of the town gatherings.

The new postmaster arrived, but he had an alcohol problem. This was hard on Gotty, who had to shoulder the responsibility of the office as well as manage the telegraph.

As the Boer War turned in favour of the British Empire, the British government put out a call for telegraph operators to relieve the officers in various towns in South Africa in order to substitute the English language code for the Dutch. Gotty applied and was accepted.

It is possible that Gotty had put his age up by a year. The passenger list for the ship, *Medic,* departing from Sydney on 22 March 1901, shows G. Feldt aged 18 headed for The Cape.

Gussie was not sorry to see Gotty go as she thought there might be more opportunity in South Africa and she herself had been young when she had gone to another land.

In South Africa, Gotty was given the role of town guard for the village of Rosmead. His rank was that of sergeant and his duties included drilling soldiers.

The farm continued to prosper.

In 1901 the government passed legislation that enabled the enforcement of the White Australia policy. The majority of the South Sea Islanders were to be deported back to their homelands by 1906. The void they left was filled by Italian immigrants. The higher wages paid to the Italian labourers meant that the farmers could not afford to employ them all year round, so they employed a greater number of men for a shorter period of time. Then the cane cutters moved on to another farm. Peter busied himself building larger accommodation for the men.

The younger Feldt children were growing up and Gussie thought they should have some music in the home, and a piano, though expensive, was added to the household. The girls practised the piano regularly. On Sunday afternoons visitors came to the farm and the girls played their music and served afternoon tea on the veranda. Gussie thoroughly enjoyed these visits. This was more like the social club she had earlier hoped for.

Young Eric thrived. With four sisters and devoted parents he was assured of plenty of attention. He grew up speaking English and South Sea Islander Pidgin English, and not Swedish.

Mabel became a fully qualified teacher and married Archibald Frederic Crichton in Ingham on 26 April 1905. They moved south to live in a cooler climate, in Allora on the Darling Downs.

After the Boer War ended in 1902, Gotty decided to stay in South Africa and work as a trader. As time went by, Gussie became less happy about his being so far away. She wrote to him suggesting he come home, saying that they were in a better financial position and his father could do with some help on the farm. Gotty replied that he had decided to stay until he had made enough money for a deposit on a property of his own. Then he would return, perhaps within a year.

Interesting letters came regularly from Gotty telling how he would go to a small trading post called Molepolole, on the edge of the Kalahari Desert, where, besides working, he enjoyed seeing and hunting the African wildlife.

In April 1907 a letter arrived, but it wasn't the sort of letter a parent ever wants to receive. A patrol officer had written from Molepolole to regretfully inform them that Gotty had become ill with a fever and after 11 days had died on 28 March. His passing had been fairly quick. He was unconscious for two hours before the end. Everything that could possibly be done had been done. His grave was being properly cared for. It was fenced in and a cross had been erected.

This was the blackest of all sorrows for Gussie and Peter, made worse because they had not been able to be with Gotty during his illness and as he took his last breath. In shock and deep sorrow, Gussie was unable to leave her bed for a week. Peter just sat, silent and listless, drawing on his pipe as he mourned the loss of his first-born son.

Somehow their life went on. They had each other, and their remaining children needed their care and attention.

At some point in time, the Feldt children took on nicknames that, between themselves, were to remain for the rest of their lives. Emma became 'Lassie', Ada was 'Paddy or Pat', Lucy chose 'Tommy' and Eric was 'Kruge'. The reason behind the nicknames is unknown. It has been suggested that 'Tommy' came from *Tommelise*, the Danish name for Hans Christian Anderson's *Thumbelina*, and 'Kruge' from Paul Kruger the South African Boer leader. Possibly they played a childhood game where the adopted names represented various countries: Lassie for Scotland, Paddy/Pat for Ireland, Tommy for England and Kruge for South Africa.

Why Eric chose this nickname is open to conjecture. On the face of it, it seems strange for him to choose the name of an enemy leader, especially when the foe was one his brother had been actively involved in opposing. Perhaps something in the achievements of Kruger appealed to Eric. Having received little education as a child, Kruger had risen to be both a military and political leader. Did Gotty's death in Africa have an influence on Eric as a boy? Did he read about the country where his brother's life had ended? Did he search for a hero or role model and, finding none who appealed to him in the British hierarchy, turned instead to a leader of the opposing side?

Gussie believed that all her children were bright. She thought that Mabel and Eric were the most intelligent of her brood and that both possessed excellent memories. In 1910 Eric, who was under age, sat for the Queensland State Scholarship Examination. Although he achieved a good percentage result, he did not attain a scholarship. Not wanting her clever son to miss out for a second time, in 1911 Gussie sent Eric to stay with Mabel for about six months. He attended Allora State School and sat for the examination there. Gussie thought a larger school might provide a higher standard of education, and Mabel, having been a teacher, could help him with his studies at night.

How much Gussie's plan or Eric's diligence contributed to the outcome will never be known, but success was achieved. Eric was one of the few lads who were granted a scholarship. This entitled him to free secondary school tuition. The Feldts were finally in a financial position where they were able to pay for one of their children to attend boarding school, and in 1912 Eric was enrolled at the Brisbane Grammar School.

He was a boarder there for a year, during which time the government began their search for suitable candidates for the new Royal Australian Naval College. Eric was offered the opportunity to apply and he decided to give it a go. Six other boys from schools around Queensland sat for the examination and underwent interviews. Three positions had been allocated for Queensland. Eric was the only one chosen and so became the state's first recipient of the Naval Scholarship. Twenty-seven other potential cadet-midshipmen were chosen from the other states of Australia. Eric's family were very proud of him, and so were the people of Ingham.

Peter and Gussie were not certain that Eric was cut out to be a sailor. However, Peter said, 'If, after a year, you don't like it and cannot fit in, I will pay the expenses of the year's education.'

Another Feldt daughter left the family home. Ada applied to the General Hospital in Brisbane to become a nurse and was accepted. Eric, when given free time while boarding at Brisbane Grammar, walked to the hospital to visit her.

The piano led Emma to discover she had a talent for music. In 1912, she attended St Mary's Convent School, Warwick, which was about 15 miles from Mabel in Allora, and passed her music examinations. Emma returned to Ingham and began working as a music teacher.

Peter developed a problem of recurrent abdominal pain. In 1913 he underwent an operation at Townsville Hospital and spent several weeks recuperating in hospital and at home. The records of his actual diagnosis are no longer in existence.

Meanwhile, Eric was far from home, experiencing the strange new world of the first Royal Australian Naval College.

CHAPTER 2

THE NAVAL COLLEGE YEARS 1913-1916

Australian waters had been under the protection of the British Royal Navy for over a century following the First Settlement in 1788. As the 19th century drew to a close lobbying began for Australia to have its own navy. The idea grew in popularity with the most vocal advocate being Captain William Creswell RN. He was later to become known as "The Father of the Royal Australian Navy". Creswell had begun his career as a 14-year-old cadet in 1865. In order to become midshipmen of the Royal Navy, potential Australian cadets had to travel to England for their training. This was the case up until the all-important year of 1913.

After Federation in 1901, the states' separate naval forces became amalgamated under the name of Commonwealth Naval Forces (CNF). In 1904 Creswell was appointed the inaugural Naval Commanding Officer of the CNF. Australian men were able to sign on as sailors but officer training remained a British domain. Efforts by Creswell and politicians of the day, particularly Alfred Deakin, saw the CNF increase in ships and servicemen. Plans for an Australian-based Naval College were proposed and discussed, including the suggestion of following the curriculum of the Royal Naval College at Osborne House on the Isle of Wight. The Australian intake of cadets was to differ from the British one in that social class was to play no part in their selection.

On 10 July 1911 King George V granted the title of Royal Australian Navy to the Commonwealth Naval Forces. On 16

November the same year, the government announced that Jervis Bay would be the site for the new Naval College. While this was under construction a temporary site would be needed. 'Osborne House, Geelong, with ready access to both rail and Port Phillip Bay, was chosen. Its identical name with the Royal Naval College of Osborne House was both a coincidence and a good omen.'[1]

Eric, like Gussie before him, took the time to leave a memoir. In June 1966, he recorded an oral history about his life from his Naval College years up until he relisted in the Royal Australian Navy in 1939. Titled *Reminiscences of Commander Eric Feldt*, it is held by the State Library of South Australia and provides good information about these decades of his life.

It was to Osborne House, Geelong, that Eric was headed in January 1913, only to have his journey delayed by a cyclone and floods that disrupted shipping. His 27 classmates arrived on 1 February 1913 and Eric joined them a few days later. Most of those already in residence were in their working uniforms. Eric was handed his, which consisted of a pair of boots, gaiters, blue denim trousers, a dark blue flannel shirt and a naval officer's cap. All the boys were fitted 'with a proper monkey jacket uniform with the cadet's little white stripe on the collar to indicate rank'. Eric felt it was indeed a strange new world but having come from boarding school it was not quite as strange to him as it was to those who had come straight from home.

The officer named as head of the Naval College was Captain Bertram Chambers, who had been loaned by the RN. To him fell the task of selecting the naval and academic staff. Lieutenant Duncan Grant RN (retired) was chosen as the Executive Officer. 'Grant had been on the staff of both Osborne and Dartmouth colleges and was a physical training instructor by specialisation. Although quite deaf, this tall, lean, energetic officer was an outstanding youth leader and became universally admired.'[2]

First Lieutenant Charles Elwell and Lieutenant Cuthbert Pope were other officers. There was a warrant officer, Mr Thomas Dix, who Eric thought was a very fine old gentleman. Engineering officers were Engineer Lieutenant Commander William Monk and Engineer Lieutenant Ronald Boddie. Among the members of the academic staff were Frederick Brown, a gifted mathematician who was the headmaster, and the Reverend William Hall RN, an expert at navigation who was the naval instructor and chaplain.

The teenage cadets gradually got to know each other and before long many had nicknames. There was 'Essy' Esdaile, 'Hungry' Getting, and 'Macka' Mackenzie. Eric's family nickname of 'Kruge' was not known and he became 'Feltie'. Rupert Long was dubbed 'Cocky' because his voice was breaking and at times gave way to a squawk not unlike that of a cockatoo. This friendly teenage teasing was destined to stay with Rupert all his life. Frank Larkins was selected as Cadet Captain.

The first lesson the newcomers had to learn was discipline, which they were not at all used to.

One night, not long after their arrival, the boys started a pillow fight after lights out. Before long they were ordered out of bed, made to get dressed and were marched round the lawn for an hour. A few nights later they tried it again. This time they were marched round for two hours. They were being taught in no uncertain terms that in the Navy an order had to be obeyed.

The most important event in the early days of the college was the official opening of the Naval College by Governor-General Lord Denman on Saturday 1 March. The Prime Minister, Andrew Fisher, and Rear Admiral Creswell also attended. The 28 cadet-midshipmen were paraded before the Governor-General.

> 'They were smartly dressed in traditional Navy double-breasted 'monkey' jackets with three brass buttons on each sleeve to denote their rank and white cord lanyards around their necks which had a boatswain call (whistle) at the end.'[3]

The speeches went for rather too long and four of the cadets, not yet used to standing to attention for lengthy periods, fainted.

> 'For the young cadet-midshipmen it had been an exciting but exhausting experience. Despite this, the day remained for them a treasured memory ...'[4]

The most surprising aspect of Eric's new environment was the class structure. It came as somewhat of a culture shock:

> The scheme of training was exactly the same as that used at Osborne in the Isle of Wight, where the British cadets were trained. The object was to produce a naval officer who was interchangeable and, in fact, so far as possible, indistinguishable from the RN officer. That was all right. That was the only way they knew how to produce a naval officer when it comes to that. But it was rather a shock to us in its social implications. For instance, the difference between an officer and someone on the lower deck was something that was, well, very strange to me anyway. Where I'd been used to the farm where every employee was called by his Christian name. I once called a steward, when I first got there, 'Jimmy', which was his name. And you'd have thought I'd called the King a dirty name by the lightning that flashed around my poor head as a result of it.

As junior officers, the cadet-midshipmen were provided with one steward per seven boys. The stewards prepared their uniforms and waited on them at meal times. The Navy viewed them as subordinates and familiarity was forbidden.

The daily college routine spared barely a moment and ran along similar lines each day. The cadets were woken by the Reveille bugle call at 7am. They got up, showered, dressed and had breakfast, followed by a short parade before classes at 9am. Lunch was at 12 noon, and after a short break the boys went back to the classroom until 4pm. Recreation, mainly sport, followed until 6pm, when they came inside, had another shower, got dressed, had dinner, had their dormitory inspected and then did an hour of homework. Their day ended with cocoa and biscuits and lights out at 9pm.

Looking back, Eric said, 'All your energy went into your living the ordinary life and carrying out the instructions that were given. It was, we realise since, a form of indoctrination'.

Punishment for misdemeanours took the form of physical drills. For very serious infringements, beatings were in order. Eric was fortunate, or well behaved enough, not to be one of the recipients of such retribution. He and the other cadets soon became accustomed to moving at the double when told to do anything and to stand to attention and say 'Yes, sir' when spoken to by a senior officer.

Eric's first year at the Naval College was mostly an unhappy time for him. The different way of life, the discipline, the lack of outside friends, feeling cut off from the outside world and feeling a certain degree of loneliness were hard to adjust to. However, he did adjust, becoming mates with others in the class, with John Collins in particular.

One highlight early in the year followed shortly after the opening by the Governor-General. This was the opening of the College Canteen. Otto Albert showed his comedic ability with his opening address to the eagerly waiting cadets:

> It is with great pleasure that I take part in this great function today (Cheers). I thank you one and all for the honour you have conferred on me in asking me to open this Canteen, which I feel assured will be of lasting benefit and a source of great happiness to you Gentlemen and myself (Loud cheers). What can be more relaxing, after a very arduous day at Studies, than to exercise our mouths by stringing out some of the glorious stick-jaw and other edibles of a similar nature that I hear is to be sold? (A voice — 'Votes for Women') Although by my ample proportions I may be judged to revel in all the nice things sold here (Loud laughter and a voice — 'So you do') I feel that you will all do justice to it ,especially on Saturdays, when your pockets are full to overflowing with money from the Paymaster's table. Not being accustomed to speech-making, Gentlemen, but like some of you, more able to enter into the pleasure of eating some of the very enjoyable edibles that I see before me, I have great pleasure in declaring this Canteen open. (Loud and prolonged cheering). I would ask you all being Sunday,

to refrain from too much shouting, which I know is the only means of relieving your pent-up feelings, due to the excitement caused by this ceremony, which will be marked, I feel sure, as an epoch in the history of this College. (A great outburst of cheering, which lasted several minutes).[5]

Otto was solemnly presented with a jam tart on a silver tray. Then a rush of jubilant youngsters hurtled towards the canteen counter eager to purchase and devour the tempting treats.

Sport was an important outlet for energy and emotions for the boys. Eric was athletic and became the first captain of the rugby team. Larkins was captain of the cricket team. Eric did not excel at cricket and only made the first XI 'because the others were worse'. In the following years he was able to relinquish his place to younger cadets.

The position of Cadet Captain was changed each quarter during the first 12 months. Newman took over from Larkins and was followed by Burnett and then by Eric. The cadets were given leave during the year, but for those whose home was too far away, like Eric, there was not time to travel there and back so their holiday was spent at the college. The Christmas leave at the end of 1913 was a welcome break and was long enough for all the boys to at last go home.

Eric was able to spend his 15th birthday, on 3 January 1914, at home with his family. When his father asked if he wanted to leave the Naval College, Eric's answer was no, because he had found 'some nice mates and one especially, Jack Collins'.

Sunday 18 January dawned bright, sunny and hot. The family had planned a day trip to Forrest Beach, which was about 10 miles away. Gussie and Peter decided not to go so Eric went with Emma, Lucy and a friend of Lucy's. The young people made the journey in two pony traps, and on arriving they went into the water to swim and cool off.

The swimming spot had been a favourite with the Feldts and other Ingham families for many years. The hot Sunday had brought other people and their dogs to the beach. The excited animals barked and romped as the waves rolled onto the sand.

Emma suggested one last dip before they had their picnic lunch. Lucy, who was 11 days shy of her 18th birthday, did not feel like going in again and sat on the beach while the others swam. After a while, she decided to wade into the sea and sat down in the shallows. A wave lapped her body and she felt something grab her right thigh. For a moment she thought it might have been Eric teasing her. She put her hand down to push him away and instead touched the slimy hard head of a crocodile. Lucy felt faint with fear and recoiled in horror.

Fortunately, just at this moment, the others were coming in. Seeing her fall backwards, they at first thought she had been knocked by a wave but Eric noticed that she suddenly seemed to shake and he was puzzled by how strange it all looked. He grabbed hold of one of her arms, and as he did so she yelled, 'Pull, pull.' Emma grabbed her other arm and together they pulled. Then a wave rolled back revealing the terrifying sight of a repulsive reptile firmly attached to their sister's right leg. They pulled, but nothing happened. It held fast with its jaw of many teeth embedded in Lucy's thigh. When another wave came, they pulled again with all their might and succeeded in dragging Lucy and the 10–12 foot monster up onto the beach. The crocodile held on for what seemed like ages. Eric was thinking he might have to try kicking it in the eye, when, perhaps disturbed by all the shouting, it finally gave way and slid back into the sea.

The greatly relieved foursome turned their attention to Lucy and the nasty gashes on her thigh. Lucy herself was cool-headed and instructed the others to tie a towel tightly around her upper thigh to staunch the blood flowing from her injuries. They placed her in the bottom of one of the traps and Emma made haste in taking her to the hospital in Ingham.

Eric and Lucy's friend packed up their belongings and hurried back to tell his parents the horrifying news that their youngest daughter had been attacked by a crocodile. In a state of shock, Gussie quickly collected a few necessities for Lucy and the trio drove to Ingham Hospital in the trap. The three miles there seemed like an eternity to Gussie as she worried about her daughter's fate and thought of the pain she must have been enduring.

They arrived at the hospital to find that Lucy was doing well and had been commended for her bravery. The location of the dramatic event meant that a considerable amount of sand had made its way into the gashes caused by the croc's teeth. The doctor and nurses had to carefully flush the grains of sand from Lucy's wounds before suturing could begin. In all, 23 sutures were required. Lucy spent a month (and her 18th birthday) in hospital. Her narrow escape from the jaws of death, literally, attracted much interest and Lucy received a lot of attention in the weeks and months after the event. Luckily, apart from significant tell-tale scars on her right thigh, she made a full recovery.

The family had never seen a crocodile at Forrest Beach before, but there were large creeks at either end of the bay which were crocodile habitats. They wondered if the barking and frolicking of the dogs earlier in the day had caught the attention of the crocodile. The creature may have been seeking smaller prey and had not expected Lucy's leg to be attached to something larger.

The story quickly made many of the Queensland newspapers and found its way into newspapers in the other states as well. However, it was not reported as an attack by a crocodile but as an attack by an alligator, as these reptiles were called in those days.

When Eric returned to the Naval College, he was unsure whether to talk about the crocodile episode so he didn't mention it to anyone except John Collins. Lieutenant Grant had, however, read

THE NAVAL COLLEGE YEARS 1913-1916

about it in the newspapers. He summoned Eric and asked him if it were true. Grant told Eric there had been talk of awarding him a lifesaving medal, but he thought that a cadet-midshipman having a medal ribbon on his uniform would look out of place. Eric stood to attention and said, 'Yes, sir', and there the matter ended.

On 11 February 1914 Eric and his classmates returned to Osborne House. An extra block had been built to house the 1914 entry cadets who had arrived the day before. Larkins and Eric were named as Cadet Captains in charge of the new arrivals, while Newman and Burnett were made Cadet Captains for the 1913 entry group.

During the previous year, the Pioneer Class had had naval experience on HMAS *Encounter* and been taken on board to view HMAS *Melbourne*. On 3 March 1914 all the cadets were given the opportunity to inspect the battlecruiser HMAS *Australia*, head of the Australian Fleet.

For the first time, the boys saw life in a gunroom, as the junior officers' mess was known. *Australia* made an impression on one of the cadets, who thought that she had 'a bonza canteen'.

Captain Chambers left to take up a sea command shortly after this occasion. His position was temporarily filled by Duncan Grant, who had been promoted to Lieutenant Commander. Grant received telegrams from Frank Albert during Easter leave saying that Otto was ill and his return would need to be delayed. He was suffering from an ear infection and had a high temperature. Grant replied that leave was granted up until the doctor certified Otto was fit to return.

Then on May 15th a telegram arrived which said, 'Otto died this morning eight o'clock meningitis send any papers you wish me to sign Frank Albert.'[6]

Grant and the cadets were stunned and shocked at the loss of this fun-loving boy who had been one of the personalities of the Pioneer Year. Included in his belongings, which were mournfully packed to be returned to his grieving family, there were five volumes of Harmsworth self-educator A *Golden Key to Success in Life*.

His parents erected a monument above his grave in Waverley Cemetery in Sydney. It was in the form of a broken black marble column, symbolising a life cut short. Inscribed on the base of the column were the signatures of all his cadet classmates.

With Otto's death, a long association between his father Frank and the Naval College began.

The College year continued, like the previous year, with studies concentrating on mathematics, physics, engineering and seamanship. Less weight was given to English, history and French among other subjects. Two of the cadets were thought to be unsuitable and left the program.

World War I broke out on 4 August 1914. Eric recalled: 'We were kids, and it seemed very romantic to all of us, and we were full of ideas of going to sea and covering ourselves with glory'. He then reflected, 'And in this, I don't think we were very far behind the adults of all countries.' Several officers from the College, including Lieutenant Commander Elwell, left to join the war effort. News arrived a few weeks later that Elwell had been killed leading a charge at the Battle of Bita Paka near Rabaul in September. It was a shock to the cadets and brought home the reality of war that someone in authority, someone they knew and liked, could be killed.

Back in Ingham, Peter and Gussie had made a significant decision. Peter had turned 60 years of age and was not as fit as in his pre-operation days, and all of the children except Lucy had moved away. The Feldts decided to put the farm on the market. In January 1915 the sale of the property was settled. It was hard for them to leave their beautiful *Norland,* which had been so much a part of them and their lives, but they hoped for an easier life in a cooler climate.

THE NAVAL COLLEGE YEARS 1913-1916

The people of Ingham gave them a big send off and presented Gussie with a tea and coffee service. Peter and Gussie each made a speech. In hers, Gussie said she had always admired English people and was very thankful to feel that she belonged and that her children had been born and raised in Australia.

Peter, Gussie and Lucy moved to Brisbane. Emma Feldt was married there to William Alexander Fleming Latimer on 20 February 1915. The Feldts busied themselves with war work. Gussie became treasurer of a branch of the Red Cross and a member of the Spinning Guild. The latter were 'mostly old ladies and we had all the wool given to us and the wheels were made of old bicycles.' After four years they had raised 900 pounds. This was donated to a hospital that had two of its wards reserved specially for soldiers.

With his parents living in Brisbane, Eric was pleased to be able to go home when on leave. Peter began buying and selling houses to make some money, so each time Eric returned to Brisbane he found himself living in a different suburb. He was apt to get lost and, rather embarrassingly, had to ask how to find his way home.

By the beginning of 1915 the permanent Royal Australian Naval College at Jervis Bay on the New South Wales south coast had been sufficiently constructed for the classes from the three years to take up residence. The 1915 class arrived on 10 February and the 1913 and 1914 students a day later. The nearest town was Nowra, 25 miles away, via a muddy dirt road. There, Eric was later to make the acquaintance of a young lady by the name of Gwen, who was to become his girlfriend.

The new college and its surroundings were a beautiful sight to behold. The centrepiece was the Quarterdeck, a large open area of green lawn framed by attractive new buildings. Kangaroos grazed contentedly on the grass, an impressive clock tower stood atop the gymnasium, bushland surrounded the college perimeter and magnificent gum trees added to the scenery. The beautiful bay itself was the jewel in the crown. There was one drawback, as Eric described:

> The design of the college was all that could be desired ... And there we were in a beautiful college, miles and miles away from everywhere. That was what was wrong with it. It was too isolated, and everybody, including the senior officers, eventually got a Jervis Bay mentality - rather feeling that the world revolved around it, which it doesn't.

Eric was made Senior Cadet Captain of the 1915 entry cadets. The newcomers had an easier time than the Pioneer Class because they had the two previous years as examples to follow and the discipline had been somewhat relaxed from the harshness that the 1913 cadets had experienced.

Jervis Bay was an excellent training place for the cadets to learn boating and sailing skills. There was good sailing water, but quite big seas, and a fair surf came in at times. The boys learnt both how to sail and how to handle a boat in the surf the only way how — by experience. 'A graduate of Jervis Bay was always pretty competent in a small boat.' They had a net and sometimes made very good hauls of fish.

In June 1915, Captain Charles Morgan took over leadership of the Naval College, but it was Grant who kept his finger on the pulse of the cadets' activities.

Later that year saw the arrival of the infamous *Franklin*, a 145ft steam yacht the Navy had acquired for steamship training and to travel to Sydney for supplies. The trouble with the *Franklin* was she had an extremely severe roll, making all the cadets seasick, with the exception of Larkins. In spite of her relentless rolling, she provided a good grounding in seamanship and simple engineering. The eventual result was that few, if any, of the cadets later suffered from seasickness.

The accommodation on the *Franklin* was another trial. It was very cramped. Instead of the regulation 18 inches between hammocks, it was 15 inches.

> ...and when the ship rolled every hammock piled up on top of the one on the down side, then swung across and piled up against the one on the other side. Consequently, we didn't even get much sleep. We were too sick to eat, and we were pretty tired from the work we had done, and when we came back, we were generally just about all in.

The first Regatta Day at Jervis Bay was held on 10 November 1915. The winners of the third year (1913) rowing race were John Collins (stroke), Horace Thompson, Harold Farncomb, James Esdaile, Eric Feldt, Eddy Nurse and Dick Cunningham (cox).

Larkins, Newman and Feldt were the Chief Cadet Captains by the end of the year, 'which was the most exalted rank one could reach as a cadet midshipman'. When the cadets returned to Jervis Bay in early 1916 for the beginning of the final year for the Pioneer Class, there was no officer for the incoming class. Eric was put in charge of them as Senior Cadet Captain.

> 'I was really doing a lieutenant's work in that respect. It wasn't so onerous, and I was so used to the job that it didn't cause any difficulty ... Incidentally, having been a Cadet Captain or a Chief Cadet Captain gave you nothing, except it might have been remembered on paper somewhere.'

It did show that Eric's leadership qualities and skills were recognised early by the Naval College and were called on for all four years of his time there. This experience would have enhanced and helped to hone his leadership ability.

On 1 April the Naval College gave a gymnastics display in the gymnasium. A variety of feats, contests and tricks were performed. Eric played his part in a group that gave displays on the horizontal bars. He and Commander Grant then had a close fought duel with sabres. In the proper order of things, Grant was the winner.

An athletics day was held on 29 April. Eric won the open broad-jump and was runner-up to Collins in the open quarter mile.

In September the first rugby match was played at Jervis Bay, against the team from the Royal Military College, Duntroon. Eric, who normally captained the Naval College team, had sustained a leg injury and could not play in this significant match. Frank Larkins took over as captain. The team had been unbeaten in its matches against Sydney school teams so there was some optimism for success. When the game came to an end, the score was Navy 20 Army 9. The victory to the Naval College was one which would rarely be repeated in years to come.

At the end of the year, colours were awarded to cadets who had shown sporting prowess. Eric received colours for rugby and athletics.

The final examinations began on 5 December. Over the four years there had been remarkable consistency in the individual rankings in the academic results. The regular high achievers were Harold Farncomb, John Collins, James Esdaile, Eric Feldt, Eddy Nurse and Dick Cunningham, and so it was with the final exam results. They were placed in the top six, which entitled them each to three months seniority if, and when, they eventually passed from sub-lieutenant to lieutenant. History and English were Eric's favourite and best subjects. He was always a keen reader, with Kipling and O. Henry being two of his favourite authors.

The passing out ceremony on Tuesday 12 December 1916 was a big affair. Five of the original group were no longer with them. The cadet-midshipmen paraded before Governor-General Sir Ronald Munro Ferguson, Admiral Creswell, politicians, other officials, families and various spectators. Sir Ronald, who couldn't pronounce his Rs, told a story about one of his wife's ancestors being the captain who brought Nelson's body back from Trafalgar in a 'bawel of wum'. The cadets found the story both entertaining and interesting.

Prizes were presented. Harold Farncomb came first, winning several prizes, as did second place achiever, James Esdaile. John Collins came third, winning the Otto Albert Prizes for both seamanship and engineering. Eric received a prize for history and English, 'the best thing that I possibly could have got: every volume of Kipling.'

When the ceremony came to an end, the cadet-midshipmen had graduated, and in their place stood 23 rated midshipmen.

The following day the midshipmen made their way to Sydney. They were met at Central Railway Station by Frank Albert and his son Alexander. Frank took the young men out to dinner and then to a show.

The following morning the midshipmen in their best uniforms assembled at the Alberts' residence. Then they took the tram to Bronte to visit Otto Albert's grave at the Waverley Cemetery. For most of them it was their first visit and they saw their signatures engraved at the base of Otto's column. They placed a wreath on his grave and had a group photograph taken next to it. The visit greatly affected both Frank Albert and the midshipmen.[7]

After lunch with the Albert family, the midshipmen headed home on leave before they embarked to go overseas to take part in the Great War, not knowing that some of their number were destined never to return.

THE PIONEER CLASS 1913

Albert, Otto Edmund
Armitage, George William Thomas
Burnett, Joseph
Calder, Norman Keith
Collins, John Augustine
Conder, Alfred Denis
Cunningham, Earnest Semple 'Dick'
Esdaile, James Claude Durie
Farncomb, Harold Bruce
Feldt, Eric Augustus
Getting, Frank Edmond
Gilling, Lloyd Falconer
Hirst, Paul Hugil
Howells, Elmer Benjamin
Kimlin, Peyton James
Larkins, Frank Lockwood
Lecky, John Valentine Stuart 'Jack'
Long, Rupert Basil Michel
Mackenzie, Hugh Alexander
Newman, Jack Bolton
Nurse, Edwin Scott
Reilly, Winn Locker
Sadleir, Cyril Arthur Roy
Showers, Henry 'Harry' Arthur
Thompson, Horace John Harold
Vallentine, Harry Bertram
Watkins, Llewellyn Leigh
Watts, Adrian Joseph Beachleigh

CHAPTER 3

WORLD WAR I AND POST WAR NAVY 1917-1923

Eric had just turned 18 when he boarded the passenger ship RMS *Omrah* in Brisbane in early January 1917. He was the first of the midshipmen to begin the journey to Plymouth. The next to board were the eight from New South Wales, together with the Reverend Andrew Hardie, who was accompanying the Pioneer Class, and 36 were picked up in Melbourne and Fremantle.

George Armitage had an eye injury so could not join in Adelaide and would have to follow a month later. The ship he travelled on, the *Ballarat*, was torpedoed on the way over but he survived to join his comrades as planned.

There were few actual passengers. Most on board were troops from various units. The midshipmen were treated as passengers and were given cabins to share. Eric shared a cabin with John Collins. While the ship was taking on coal in Fremantle, the Army decided not to grant the troops leave. This was incomprehensible to the Pioneer Class who were used to the Navy giving leave whenever possible. Some of the soldiers sought help from the coal-loaders. The union rep of the coalies told the Captain of the *Omrah*, 'Well, no leave, no coal.' This had the desired effect and Eric thought it was a kind action by the coal-loaders union.

It was on the *Omrah* that Eric started to smoke. This was a habit he was never able to break, and he wished he had never started. Also during the voyage he read, for the first time, a book on the Stoic philosophy. The ideas it contained appealed to him and continued to do so for the rest of his life. Although more complex than this, one explanation given of Stoicism is that in an unpredictable world we don't control and cannot rely on external events, but we can (to a certain extent) control our mind and choose our behaviour. Another description says: Stoic ethics can perhaps be crudely chopped down to a few basic tenets: 1.) applying self-discipline and logic to become free from emotion in decision making and judgment, 2.) happiness is a choice of free will and one shouldn't let the world's rigidity make that choice for you, and 3.) actions and behaviour speak louder than words.

Eventually the ship reached the shores of Africa, the continent that had claimed Eric's only brother's life and where Paul Kruger, the probable inspiration for his childhood nickname, had lived. The young men went ashore in Durban, where they did some sightseeing, and then the ship went on to Cape Town. Here they joined a convoy escorted by an armed merchant cruiser for the passage north.

They landed at Plymouth and went by train to Portsmouth. The weather was bitterly cold and for most of them it was their first experience of snow. Eric was to later say he felt 'actually, that I wasn't warm again for another four years.' Their first destination was Whale Island in Portsmouth Harbour, which is the RN gunnery training school, where they spent two weeks. Eric believed

> ... we were sent there to make us realise what discipline really was. As it happened, we found Whale Island fairly easy. It wasn't as tough as Jervis Bay was as far as discipline was concerned.

While there, they were grouped and assigned to various battleships and battlecruisers:

HMS *Canada*: Collins, Feldt, Gilling, Newman, Armitage and Kimlin.

HMAS *Australia*: Burnett, Conder, Esdaile, Long, Reilly and Sadlier.

HMS *Royal Sovereign*: Calder, Farncomb, Hirst, Larkin, Thompson and Watkins.

HMS *Glorious*: Cunningham, Getting, Mackenzie, Nurse and Showers.

Canada and *Royal Sovereign* were part of the Grand Fleet based in Scapa Flow in the Orkney Islands off the north coast of Scotland. *Australia* and *Glorious* were part of the Battle Cruiser Force based at Rosyth on the Firth of Forth in Scotland.

On 5 April the midshipmen caught the train from Portsmouth to London. While stopped at Waterloo Station, Eric made a lucky buy of a pair of sheepskin gloves. The wool lining was to save his hands from being frozen in the days ahead.

The two groups headed for the Grand Fleet took the *Jellicoe Express* to Thurso, and the two bound for Rosyth boarded the *Caledonian*. While waiting to change trains, Eric, Leigh Watkins and Norman Calder had the good fortune to run into Captain Chambers, their original captain from Geelong. They were pleased to be able to tell him of their posting to the Grand Fleet.

After arriving in Thurso, they travelled across to Scapa Flow in a small tender, and on the way saw the *Canada* exercising in Pentland Firth. They were taken to a depot ship and then by trawler to their respective ships. Eric's group arrived on the *Canada* about 11pm feeling cold and hungry. They were given a cup of tea and then shown to their hammocks. 'It wasn't a very warm welcome in any way.'

The gunroom was about 30ft by 15ft and accommodated about 30 midshipmen and the three sub-lieutenants in charge of them. There was a table and a few chairs and a locker for each person. A messman placed the meals on the table for two stewards to serve. The food was navy rations, which could be added to by the midshipmen paying a mess bill. This they did for the first time in their lives. Their pay was 5 shillings a day, and their mess bill was 2 shillings a day, making it about 3 pounds a month. 'We were allowed to drink beer or wine, but not spirits, to the value of 10 shillings a month, which didn't allow much latitude for any wild parties.' The quality of the food was probably below standard. Many of the group developed boils. They had a small but adequate bathroom for their numbers. The ship had a laundry, which was an innovation in those days. One duty fell to the marine bandsmen: a tradition which required them to sling and trice up the hammocks for the midshipmen.

When stationed in harbour, the young Australians rose at 6am and did half-an-hour physical drill on deck, usually in snow. They were each assigned a part of the ship and an action station. When not on duty in those positions they had lessons in navigation, gunnery, torpedoing, seamanship and engineering.

The first action station Eric was given was in B turret, though he was moved to the spotting top at the head of the tripod mast about 120ft above sea level soon after. There he worked the rate instrument, called the Dumaresq, after its inventor, Captain (later Rear Admiral) John Dumaresq. This was a calculating instrument by which the rate of movement of enemy warships could be determined within seconds; this range-finder, named the Dumaresq by a grateful Admiralty, gave naval gunnery an unprecedented accuracy.

Eric remained in the spotting top for the rest of his time in the *Canada* and found it cold, windy, dreary and with very little shelter. It was a hard climb to get to the top of the mast and Eric got plenty of exercise climbing up every morning for instrument testing and at other times when cruising at sea, at action stations or when they went up for exercises. The cold weather meant having to rug up in many layers of clothing, which decreased mobility and made the climb very uncomfortable. The only advantage was that being high up meant being able to see more of what was going on.

The ship's company were divided into three watches and the ship was kept ready to defend itself. If an immediate threat was perceived the whole ship went into action stations. As a matter of course it went into action stations before dawn every day as that was the most dangerous time. At night, visibility was low, but as the day broke a ship might loom out of the gloom and sight your ship before you saw it. Everybody stood at the ready until daylight showed that the coast was clear. They never sighted an enemy ship. Lack of sleep was their greatest trial, particularly in summer, when in the far northern regions the sun rose at 3am.

The *Canada* was a coal burning ship and the crew envied their oil burning counterparts. The oiler would come alongside and start pumping. Most of the crew could go to sleep. On a coal burner everyone had to join in loading coal. Coal in the hold of the collier was shovelled into bags. About a dozen bags would be attached to a hook at the end of a wire on a derrick, the bags were lifted up and pulled over to the ship and dumped on the deck. They were then wheeled to chutes and poured down into the bunker.

One day they had to load 1,200 tons, which took the whole day and left them exhausted by the time it was finished.

Eric had a slight accident while he was coaling. He was hit on the head by the iron fitting of a coal bag and required three stitches. It was his only injury in World War I.

Coaling was dirty work and, afterwards, the ship had to be cleaned whether it was day or night. 'You had to get the ship clean before you could live in it.' Then they had to clean themselves. The hardest part to clean were eyelids, where coal dust adhered and made eyes look black. Butter was used to remove the dust, but it tended to sting the eyes. Clothes used for coaling were kept in a special bag and never washed. Once they wore out, they were thrown away.

Rank was all important in the Royal Navy. This did not sit well with Eric:

> On board ship there was a completer pecking than any fowls ever evolved. The captain was on top and he was next to God. He could give orders to anyone under him. Theoretically, he could only give a lawful order, but I never heard of anybody arguing whether an order was lawful or not. I wouldn't have dared myself. There was a saying that a midshipman was junior to the captain's dog.

The captain of the *Canada* was Jimmy Ley, an anxious character who was regarded as being a bit mad. The previous captain, William 'Maddo' Nicholson, also had a reputation for being a bit unbalanced. One day Jimmy Ley rushed up to the midshipman of the watch and said, 'Tell him, tell him, 20 minutes, 20 minutes', and hurried away. The midshipman, when asked what he did, said, 'Oh, I just went and hid for 25 minutes, knowing whatever happened would have happened by that time.'

The commander, Robin Dalgleish, on the other hand, was a thoroughly well-liked and respected officer. He was Australian, born to parents who could afford to send him to the Royal Naval College in England before the existence of the Australian College. Dalglish was a huge man, an athlete. When he walked round the ship, he had a tread like a cat, which 'was amazing for such a large man. He was always cheerful and never bothered by anything untoward. Dalglish treated everyone like human beings, including the lowly midshipmen'.

Amongst the lower ranking officers, a system of fagging existed. The juniors were expected to serve those who were more senior and if they refused they could receive a beating. On the *Glorious* the juniors went along with this at first, but when Dick Cunningham was beaten for a minor incident, the lads of the Pioneer Class staged a revolt lead by Frank Getting. The Australian midshipmen were bigger and stronger than their British counterparts and though outnumbered four to one the result was an end to the fagging.

Members of the Pioneer Class also refused to bow to fagging on the *Canada*. They were successful, but it didn't endear them. As Australians they were expected to misbehave and 'the hand of authority was quite ready to descend' on them. Further, they often couldn't understand some of the British accents and that was also viewed as opposition and got them into even more trouble.

Eric remembered the first three months as being absolute misery. 'There was the cold, the hard life, the strangeness of being at sea and the environment was largely foreign'. Although they did not like the pecking order, they eventually became used to it. 'The next seniors were more tolerant and friendly and life became much more bearable for us.' Three Canadians arrived during the year and the Australians became friendly with them. By the end of six months, the group from the Pioneer Class had settled in on the *Canada* and felt they were not much different from the others. However, they were not quite fully accepted, being very rarely referred to as 'the Australians' but generally as 'the bloody Australians'.

There was not much opportunity for sport on board ship, though they had the occasional game of football at Scapa Flow. They also had boat pulling (rowing a small boat). The boat was known as a gig, a six-oared boat, single banked and the fastest of the ship's boats. The gunroom gig's crew was quite good and Collins was their stroke.

Eric took up boxing as it was the only sporting option on board. A retired professional boxer visited the ships and gave lessons. Eric practised hard and was eventually boxing quite regularly on the ship. His prowess may have drawn attention to him and gained him the spotting top position, which should have gone to Collins on seniority. Collins had a position in the gun control tower, where he did the same job as Eric.

Letters and parcels from family and friends back in Australia and writing home in return helped to lighten the dreariness of the young men's existence. Eric wrote not only to his family but also to his girlfriend Gwen in Nowra, and she sent him letters and parcels.

On 9 July 1917 the Grand Fleet was anchored in the harbour at Scapa Flow. About 11pm there was an enormous explosion as the battleship HMS *Vanguard* blew up. All ships immediately went into action stations, fearing a submarine attack. Eric had the dubious distinction of not being woken from sleep by the actual explosion even though it was less than half a mile away. The blast was so strong that there was very little debris, although the sea was covered in oil. Only two survivors were found and picked up. No cause for the explosion was found, however it was thought that heat from a bunker fire may have set off cordite in an adjacent magazine or that cordite may have deteriorated abnormally.

Not knowing the actual cause was unnerving for those onboard ships in Scapa Flow; perhaps the same thing could happen to them at any time.

> 'Jimmy Ley put extra sentries on the magazines and told them to shoot anybody that went there out of hours, but the only one who ever went there after hours was old Jimmy himself, who used to go round seeing the sentry was there. But they didn't shoot him fortunately.'

Shortly after, the *Canada* was sent to Rosyth and was based there for a while. This was a welcome break for Eric because he could see green fields and trees on shore. He had been underwhelmed by the Orkneys landscape.

> 'At Scapa, you could just see the Orkneys covered in heather, and with all due respect to the Scots, heather is a dirty, grey bush and it's not inspiring. About on a level with mallee or she oak or something like that. If any Scotsman starts getting lyrical about heather, I feel that I ought to throw a haggis at him and be done with it.'

At Rosyth, Eric and his midshipmen mates were given leave to go ashore occasionally and could go to Dunfermline and even

Edinburgh once. A regatta was to be held in the First Battle Squadron to which they belonged. Their gig's crew entered. Eric had also entered for the midshipman's boxing tournament in the lightweight division. He had not inherited his father's height, but was short like his mother, having grown to 5ft 8 ½ inches (174cm). The tournament was to be held two days before the regatta. The commander sent for Eric and said that if he was injured boxing it would ruin the gig's crew's chance, so Eric withdrew from the boxing. With their crew of six, which included Collins as stroke and three other Australians, the gunroom team fancied their chances. The race was over a mile and a half in a choppy sea. Despite their fitness and putting up an epic battle with the crew from the *Resolution*, the crew from the *Canada* were pipped at the post.

The Grand Fleet was positioned defensively ready for big fleet action, but this never occurred. Only the Australian midshipmen on *Glorious* saw action. The nearest those on the *Canada* came to action was a sortie that left from Rosyth on 16 November 1917. The following day there was an inconclusive battle between British and German squadrons, which became known as the Second Battle of Heligoland Bight. On the *Canada*, the gunfire could be heard in the distance, and then a very thick fog descended on the North Sea making it impossible to see the ship ahead except by use of a search light.

It was later heard that the Admiral leading the column in which the *Canada* was sailing had gathered his officers around him and said, 'I don't know where we are. I don't know where the enemy is. If I see anything, I'm going to ram. More steam, engineer, commander, more steam'. Luckily nothing was seen.

Eric left to do his destroyer training at HMS *Prince* not long after this incident. The sub-lieutenant was Charles Simons, who was to come into Eric's life later on. Eric grew a beard while aboard. When he returned to the *Canada*, they had a new captain, who allowed Eric to keep his beard. Eric was the only bearded midshipman in the

Grand Fleet, which he credited as his sole distinction during World War I.

The new captain was Adolphus Williamson, who had his beard trimmed to look like a bird's beak, earning him the nickname of 'Partridge', which pleased him. He had a reputation for being different and, at times, decidedly odd. 'Partridge' owned a folding chair, a treasured possession with which he would not part, and had his coxswain carry it about after him wherever he went on the upper deck.

Williamson bewildered the midshipmen one day by appearing in the gunroom and announcing, 'Dundee is the greatest root-producing area per acre in the United Kingdom and its marmalade is made chiefly from carrots, turnips and the lowest form of swede. You now understand why Dundee elected Winston Spencer Churchill as its member of Parliament.'

One evening in February 1918 during an operation when the Grand Fleet was acting as a support force for a convoy going to Norway, John Collins came on watch on the bridge. He was surprised to find both Captain Williamson and Commander Dalglish there. He soon discovered the reason for Dalglish's presence when he became the recipient of a series of strange orders and statements from the 'Partridge.' Williamson sat on his folding chair with a rug around him and ordered John to stand next to him and put a cough drop in his mouth whenever he coughed. Before John went off watch he was ordered to bring some hot cocoa. When John brought a jug of the steaming beverage, the 'Partridge' downed it all in one gulp.

Shortly after, the new Officer-of-the-Watch altered course to 25 degrees port, in accordance with the navigation plan for the entire formation of ships. This having been done, Williamson ordered 'Starboard 25'. Dalglish immediately told him he had ordered the wrong course. The 'Partridge' sought to exonerate the young Officer-of-the-Watch and ordered the Yeoman of Signals to send a 10-inch flashing light to the Flagship to the effect that it was his (Williamson's) fault.

> To send such a signal, particularly in a fully darkened formation in an operational sortie, was demonstrably aberrant behaviour that would be observed by the Flagship. It was what Dalglish had been waiting for. As the signal started to be sent he ordered it to be stopped and then sent a smaller red flashing light, a personal message to the Flagship to inform the Admiral that he was taking over command and placing the Captain under restraint below. Captain Williamson left the ship when she returned to Scapa Flow.[1]

Eric concluded that based on the *Canada*'s three captains and fortified by later experience 'you might think insanity was an occupational hazard for senior naval officers.' The next captain, Hugh Watson, did his bit to reverse that opinion, for he was 'probably the sanest man you could ever find anywhere.'

The ship became due for a refit and much to their astonishment the midshipmen found themselves on leave. Being of Swedish descent, Eric had no relatives or friends in England and didn't really know what to do with himself. He had about 32 pounds, which to him was an enormous amount of money. He booked into a hotel in London for 5 shillings a day for bed and breakfast. By having a late breakfast at 11 o'clock, Eric could skip lunch and manage to afford a few shows at night. However, his calculations of his finances did not match reality and his money was running low when he got a telegraph from Gilling saying he was coming to London. Eric met him at the station, which Gilling thought was a very nice thing to have done. Little did he know that Eric's ulterior motive was to borrow some money, but all was soon revealed.

On the evening of 31 January 1918 a disastrous series of accidents occurred among Royal Navy ships on their way from Rosyth to fleet exercises in the North Sea. There were five collisions between eight vessels. Two submarines were lost and three other submarines and a light cruiser were damaged. More than one hundred men died. Dick Cunningham, who had been doing his submarine training in one of the K class submarines, was one of the casualties. When they heard the news, his classmates were filled with shock and disbelief. World War I had claimed the life of one of the Pioneer Class. That it was by accident and not in battle seemed to make it even more tragic. Eric lamented the loss of a promising officer who had attained top 6 in his final college exams and who might have been headed for a very successful career in the Navy.

The midshipmen sat for their exams not long after Cunningham's death. Seamanship was considered to be the most important subject as it was recorded as a permanent result on a naval officer's record. Eric put every effort into it but did not try as hard with other subjects, including engineering. Later changes made engineering a permanent record as well. All the Pioneer Class passed, and on 1 September they proudly became Acting Sub-Lieutenants and sported a single gold stripe on their sleeves.

They were entitled to a transfer to other ships. On doing so, they received an S-206 Officers Report from their Commanding Officers. These reports were vitally important for careers but were held in confidence, so an officer rarely saw the contents. Instead, the officer received a small certificate called a 'flimsy', which was meant to be a summary of the S-206 report.

Eric requested a transfer to a destroyer in Harwich. Dalglish had left the *Canada* and was the captain in charge of appointments at the Admiralty, which may have helped his cause. The request was granted. Eric found himself on HMS *Sybille*, a Yarrow M-class destroyer. John Collins went to the flotilla leader HMS *Spencer*, which did a few sorties towards the Dutch coast but saw no action.

The sudden end to the war came as a surprise. The official end to the conflict was declared on Armistice Day 11 November 1918. The feelings of relief and joy were phenomenal. Eric confessed, 'I got tight twice that day - once before lunch, slept it off in the afternoon, then got tight again that night.'

The end of the War was met with equal joy back in Brisbane. Eric's parents had felt the tragedy of war, reading in the papers of so many being killed and injured. They had seen the plight of the sick and wounded men arriving home and had felt anxiety for the safety of their son and the sons of friends who were overseas in battle. Eric's sister Ada, working as a nurse at the Brisbane General Hospital, had seen the full extent of the suffering that the war had inflicted on Australia's young men. Her fiancée, Dr 'Jim' Albert James Reye, had enlisted and was working as a medical officer on the Western Front in France. Eric's brother-in-law, Archibald Crichton, husband of Mabel, had also joined up and was serving overseas.

It was a Saturday evening when Peter, Gussie and Lucy heard the news. They boarded a tram and went into the city. They sang and cheered, surprising those who had not yet heard the great tidings. People walked up and down, singing and cheering for joy, banging on kerosene tins and blowing whistles. They marched on until nearly midnight. The Feldts met some friends who went home with them. 'We celebrated by singing the National Anthem, they having a son at the front. And then the emotion carried right away and we cried with joy.'

For Eric, in England, the weeks following Armistice were spent escorting surrendering German submarines into Harwich. Their crews were taken back to Germany. Christmas was spent at Harwich, and then Eric, with the rest of the crew, went on the *Sybille* down to Sheerness for her refit. They were paid off and had to wait for another appointment. Eric got one to HMAS *Swordsman*, one of five S-Class destroyers gifted to the Australian Navy by the Admiralty. Eric joined the *Swordsman* in Greenwich, where she had just been built. Her captain was Hugh White. Eric formed a very high opinion of White and felt a great deal of affection for him. They sailed the newly completed *Swordsman* to Portsmouth.

The Australian Navy had six obsolete River-Class destroyers which were to be replaced by the Admiralty's gift of five S-Class destroyers, plus *Anzac* as the destroyer leader. The RAN was also gifted six J-Class submarines. The plan was that after the obsolete destroyers had been returned to Australia, their crews would be returned to England to man the new destroyers on their voyage to Australia. Unfortunately, when the RAN got back to Australia in the old vessels, so many men signed off that that there weren't enough crews to send to England.

Some of the Pioneer Class were able to return home early. On 6 March 1919, George Armitage, Rupert Long and Eddy Nurse were on board the six old destroyers bound for Australia. On 9 April 1919, others joined the J-Class Submarines. They were Frank Getting in *J1*, Frank Larkins in *J2*, Harry Showers in *J3*, Leigh Watkins in *J4*, Jack Newman in *J5* and Norman Calder in *J7*. The J-boats were accompanied by the *Sydney* and the depot ship *Platypus*. Alfred Conder and Cyril Sadleir were aboard the latter. The submarine flotilla made slow progress towards Australia.

Inside the J-boats the heat was so intense that many of the crew set up their bedding on the upper deck and slept under the awning. At 6.30 on the morning of 20 June one of the sailors on *J2* noticed Frank Larkins was missing. A thorough search of the boat found no sign of him and it was sadly concluded that he had been washed overboard. He had last been seen asleep in his bedding on the deck at about 3am. A small wave had washed over the submarine around 3.30am. A signal was sent to the rest of the flotilla and all the submarines began searching, but there was no sight of Larkins. The search was called off at dusk.

Of all the members of the Pioneer Class, Frank Larkins' death was the most unexpected and incomprehensible to the group. He had been their undeniable leader, starting as their first Cadet-Captain and going on to become Chief Cadet-Captain. He was an excellent athlete and the captain of several of their sporting teams.

Added to this was his cheerfulness and friendliness which made him popular not only with his classmates but also with the shipmates with whom he had served.

Others of the Pioneer Class found their way home in the *Australia* and the *Brisbane* and arrived at Fremantle on 28 May. Remaining in England were the seven who had joined the new destroyer squadron. They were Collins, Esdaile, Farncomb, Feldt, Hirst, Mackenzie and Thompson. The *Anzac* was also at Portsmouth, but the other four ships were at Chatham. The sub-lieutenants had very little to do but wait as the months of 1919 ticked by, and towards the end of the year, Farncomb, who was on the *Anzac*, suggested to Eric that they apply for an Intelligence Officer's course being held in Greenwich, just for something to do. They were accepted and spent a couple of months there. According to Eric, they didn't learn a lot, but it gave them some insight into what was involved in Intelligence.

While Eric was on the *Swordsman* in Portsmouth he entered the RN Officers' Boxing Tournament and, although not in training, was runner-up in the lightweight division. Living on the destroyer did not give him much chance for exercise. He was leading on points for two rounds but got tired and then was knocked out.

The months spent on the *Anzac* with nothing much to do got to Hugh Mackenzie. It 'was enough to drive anybody up the wall'. He decided that life in the Navy was too dull.

Mackenzie had an eye condition he had managed to conceal in his medical examination to get into the Navy. He sought attention from one of the Navy's doctors, saying it had been caused by gazing through a telescope looking for submarines. He was believed and invalided out of the Navy and sent back to Australia.

At the end of 1919 the rest of the Pioneer Class returned from Australia to attend the required lieutenants' courses at Greenwich Naval College. 1920 was to be the last time the full contingent of remaining classmates would be together. The Greenwich Naval boxing tournament came around, but Eric had flu so could not take part, however Leigh Watkins won the officer's middleweight competition.

The lieutenants course included mathematics, physics, mechanics and navigation, with examination in those subjects at the conclusion. One of the Pioneer Class, Peyton Kimlin, scored results below the average of his class and, after consideration, was discharged from the Navy. The others all passed and were promoted to lieutenants, so gaining their second stripe.

After six months at Greenwich they were sent on leave. Eric, having nowhere to go, as usual, applied for service at sea in manoeuvres with the Reserve Fleet. The ship he went to was *Nimrod*, where he served under Roger Reid, a captain for whom Eric had a lot of admiration. Eric enjoyed his time on the *Nimrod* but on the final day, as they were packing up, he fell down a darkened hatch and cut his shin very badly. He had to spend three weeks in hospital. That stopped him having more leave so he joined others of the Pioneer Class who were doing a course at the navigation school. Then they went to the gunnery school to do the course there, and then on to the torpedo school.

In 1920, Peter and Gussie decided to embark on a trip to Europe to see their native land. When Gussie had arrived in Australia, Peter had promised that they would make a return visit in 20 years or sooner. For Peter it was more than 40 years since he had left Sweden. They thought it better late than never as they planned their trip. Lucy went with them. They stayed in a first-class hotel in Sydney for four days and Gussie, who had spent most of her life looking after others, found it was a great novelty to be able 'to press a button to summon our slightest wish.'

In March they boarded the *Mégantic* to New York via the Panama Canal. There they visited Gussie's brother, August, and his wife, Sophie, and stayed with them for three months, having a marvellous time.

When the Feldts tried to book a passage to Europe they found it impossible because many others were trying to do the same. Those wanting to visit Europe and the United Kingdom previously had had their plans curtailed by the war. Now there was a backlog. Eventually a single berth was booked for Lucy to go to London so she could meet up with Eric while he was on leave. Peter and Gussie were able to secure a passage to Gothenburg on a Swedish steamer, the *Drotningholm*. Their visit to Sweden was wonderful but marred by news of the death of Gussie's mother, Bothilda, a few weeks before they arrived.

After six weeks in Sweden, Peter and Gussie travelled to Denmark and boarded a boat bound for Harwich. From there they caught a train to London and were very happy to find Lucy waiting for them on the station platform. Eric came from Portsmouth to join them. Gussie was very excited to see him again after nearly four years apart. She felt moved and proud that he had become a lieutenant. Peter, in his usual quiet way, said little, but Gussie could see pleasure and pride in his blue eyes.

Lucy and Eric, as the two youngest of the family, were close. The parents and their adult children made a happy foursome as they set off on a sight-seeing tour of London. Eventually, though the trip came to an end and Lucy booked berths on the *Nestor* for the return to Australia, leaving from Glasgow on 16 October.

Eric really wanted to go home after being away for so long. In a letter written to his sister Ada (Pat) on 13 November 1920 he apologised for not writing sooner but said it was because he had lots of work to do. He went on to say that he was fed up with being E.A. Feldt, Lieut. RAN. Eric finished the letter with "Lots of Love, Pat, old thing. Chin chin to Eric James and Jim, Yours Kruge." Eric James was his 6-month-old nephew, Ada and Jim Reye's first child.

Eric and John Collins left shortly after his letter to Pat and travelled together on the *Orsova*. They arrived in Fremantle on 18th December. He had plenty of leave due to him and he went home. By this time, Gwen, the girlfriend from Nowra days, was no longer in the picture. What happened is unknown, but she may well have become tired of waiting for Eric to return.

After a well-earned rest, Eric was appointed to HMAS *Melbourne*. John Collins, after an exchange with Farncomb, was also appointed there. The friends were pleased to be together again, but as they were the only watch keepers, they did not see much of each other. When one was on watch, the other was off. They did, however, get to meet in the mess.

The *Melbourne* was the flagship, and the Commodore was John S Dumaresq, the man who had invented the rate instrument that Eric had worked with on the *Canada*. Eric described him as 'a most intellectual type of officer with a great knowledge of every technical thing that went on board ship. He was also a man of great energy, inclined, rather, to do too much himself and not leave enough to staff.'

The ship's first cruise was along the Queensland coast, calling at Brisbane and Gladstone and then on to the Solomons. They called at two or three outlying places then went on to Tulagi, Tikopia, Utapua and Vanikoro. On leaving Vanikoro they sailed into an area which was marked blank on the chart, only to find it was all reef. Fortunately, Eric had been made lookout up in the crow's nest and they narrowly averted disaster. Eric continued to be stationed in the crow's nest whenever they were in known or suspected coral areas and uncharted waters.

The next port of call was Vila, in Vanuatu, known as the New Hebrides then. Eric felt like going for a swim but wanted to find out if there were any sharks. He decided to ask a Frenchman and Melanesian man he saw together. He tried to talk to the Frenchman, but couldn't remember the word for shark so instead said 'large fish that could eat men'. This drew a blank look so Eric tried in English, but that did not work either. Then he turned to the Melanesian man and said "Sharky stop?" and the Melanesian answered, "Yes, too much." The Pidgin that Eric had learnt when talking to the South Sea Islanders on his parent's cane farm came in handy for that part of the trip.

Next stops were Noumea and then Norfolk Island. Eric was one of the few who went ashore on Norfolk and he loved it so much that he vowed to return when he had more time.

The *Melbourne* headed back to Sydney and then onto Melbourne. At that time the squadron was short of a physical training officer and Eric did the duties. That meant arranging football matches, cricket matches, boxing shows, swimming tournaments amongst other sporting activities. After Melbourne they went to Jervis Bay to do exercises. While there, the torpedo lieutenant became sick and Eric had to do his duties as well as his own, making for a busy time. He managed to fire and recover torpedoes successfully, but he felt worn out and developed eye strain. He had to ask to be relieved of specialist duties. This showed a character trait that was to reappear during his working life. Eric was willing to shoulder responsibility but had a tendency to take on more than he could handle, to the detriment of his health.

Eric went on leave and then returned to easier duties. He was becoming increasingly aware that he would rather not spend the rest of his life in the Navy. However, when they had signed on as cadets it had been on the condition that they would serve in the Navy until they were 30. There seemed to be nothing for it but to stay.

The next cruise of the *Melbourne* was to New Zealand, where Eric was able to visit all the main towns. Then they sailed on to Hobart, where a regatta was being held. Following that the *Melbourne* cruised to Brisbane, Gladstone, Samarai and Rabaul. They were prevented from landing in Samarai because one of the crew had measles. While in Rabaul, Eric met and made friends with Reg Halligan, who was employed as a senior accountant of the Territories Department. Madang was the last port of call before they travelled back to Australia.

With more leave owing, Eric headed for Norfolk Island and stayed with the Nobbs family. It had the effect of further increasing his desire to leave the Navy.

> It broke me. The freedom of life ashore and being able to do what you felt like doing, not having to think of what a senior officer would think of something all the time, just put the cap on it with me, and I decided to leave the navy if I possibly could.

Fate was again about to lend a hand. The J-Class submarines needed repair and it was proving costly and difficult as the makers and suppliers of parts were in England. The Government cut its funding to the Navy. The Navy, in turn, decided to scrap all the submarines. Then four of the destroyers were also decommissioned, leaving two cruisers, two destroyers and a mine sweeper. There were too many officers for the remaining ships and the Navy needed to reduce the number. In 1922 they introduced a retirement scheme. Although his prospects looked good for a career in the Navy, Eric tendered his resignation. His family were very disappointed, but he felt he could not face a life in the service. His resignation was accepted. Two others from the Pioneer Class, Winn Reilly and Leigh Watkins, did likewise.

For his last couple of weeks in the Navy, Eric was sent to Jervis Bay as an officer of the term. He often wondered why the authorities did that, as it seemed a waste of time to him.

> However I packed up, travelled back to Sydney and the sun was still shining, the breeze was blowing, the trees were green and the world was just the same, although I wasn't any longer in the Navy.

Eric was not quite ready to sever his ties with the sea. His first idea was to buy a ship for trading between Norfolk Island and New Zealand. With the 700 pounds he had from severance pay and his war gratuity, he went to Hobart and bought a small ketch. When advised that the Norfolk Island plan was not likely to work, he had her converted to a cray fishing boat. Cray fishing was profitable, but only if pots were used. While this was illegal in Tasmania, it was allowed in Victorian waters.

Not having any experience, Eric sought advice. He made the acquaintance of an older man called Dick, who professed to know a lot about cray fishing. Unfortunately, Dick knew as little as Eric and their first two trips were a loss. When Dick became ill, Eric found another man called Tim as a replacement. Tim had been an able seaman on the river class destroyers and the two got on well together. They caught a large number of crayfish and had fun. Eric would call out 'Clear lower deck' and Tim would come up in good navy style.

They set off for Western Port and handed over their crayfish to an agent there. They had both grown beards and caused the comment that the Kelly Gang had arrived. A local told them that there was good anchorage at the eastern entrance of Western Port so they went there to anchor. A few days later Eric got an unexpected telegram from Charles Simons, his sub-lieutenant when on the *Prince*. Charles had migrated to Australia.

He joined them on the cray fishing boat. He had not been with them for long when disaster struck. One night while at anchor there was a sudden bump as the weather turned nasty. The three men jumped to their feet and Eric went to start the engine. In the afternoon it had begun with one go but that evening it refused to start. They hoisted the sail and seemed to be making headway when they were hit by an extra-large wave and the ketch was cast onto the shore.

Eric and his two mates pushed and pulled, struggled and strained, but they could not shift the ship. They were totally exhausted when they at last gave in. There was no alternative for Eric but to sell the wreck where it lay, stuck fast in the sand, and for very little money.

They caught the train to Melbourne where Eric decided to call on Mrs Collins, John's mother. He found her ill with malaria after a recent visit to Papua. Eric took her to her daughter-in-law to care for her. Mrs Collins suggested Eric apply for work in New Guinea. Having no idea what he was going to do and being financially bereft, Eric decided to put in an application.

He did so on 1 August 1923, by writing to Senator Sir George Pearce, the Minister of Home Affairs and Territories, applying for 'any subordinate position offering'. In his letter, Eric included excerpts from his flimsies and also mentioned that on his father's cane farm he had spoken Pidgin with the Melanesian workers before he spoke English. He was unaware that Mrs Collins had also written to Sir George Pearce recommending him. Senator Pearce forwarded the application to Brigadier General Evan Wisdom, the Administrator of New Guinea.

Eric returned to Brisbane to stay with Peter and Gussie for a while to 'lick his wounds' and recover from his exhaustion. Charles Simons had travelled up from Victoria with him and had then packed a swag and set off. When he was feeling stronger, Eric joined Charles in Childers. The cane cutting season was due to begin and Eric was about to sign on with a gang of cane cutters when he received a telegram offering him a position in New Guinea. He returned to Brisbane.

The Administrator had confirmed that Eric could have a position as the last of ten vacancies for clerks in Rabaul. When Reg Halligan received Eric's application he was pleased to process it. He said in his brief to the Administrator that Eric was 'a good type of man whose credentials to be a clerk were not strong but in time may have the makings for a patrol officer.'[2]

Eight days later, on 9 November 1923, Eric set off in the old Burns Philp islander trader *Marcena* as a passenger to begin a new life in New Guinea.

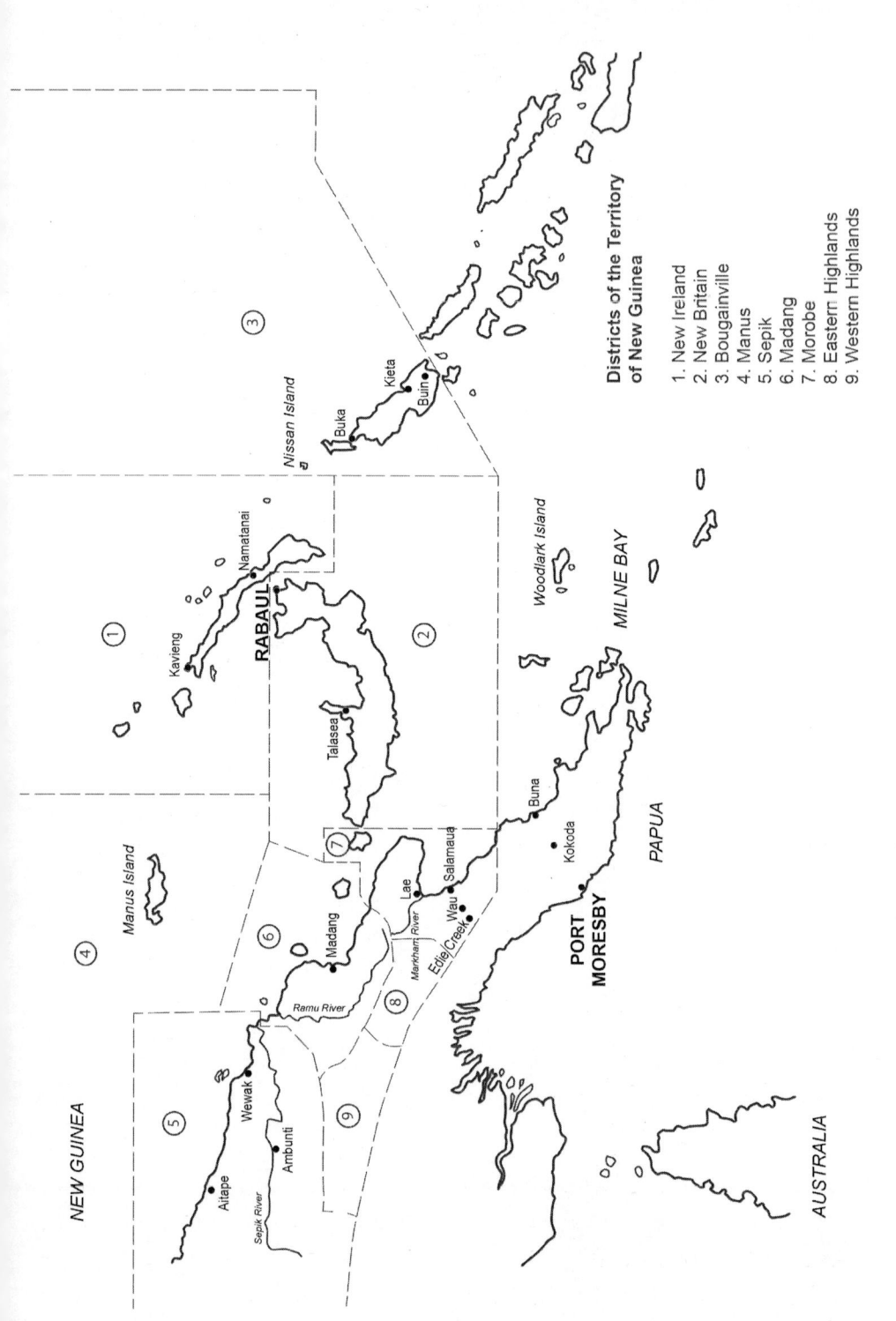

Districts of the Mandated Territory of New Guinea

1. New Ireland
2. New Britain
3. Bougainville
4. Manus
5. Sepik
6. Madang
7. Morobe
8. Eastern Highlands
9. Western Highlands

CHAPTER 4

NEW GUINEA PRE WORLD WAR II: 1923-1927

The history and naming of Papua New Guinea may benefit from some clarification. New Guinea is the second largest island in the world. The situation prior to 1914 was that the western half of New Guinea was part of the Dutch colony of the Netherlands Indies. The eastern half was claimed by Germany in the north and Britain in the south.

In 1883 the Colony of Queensland sought to annex the southern half of eastern New Guinea, but the British Government was not in favour. Germany began settling the north-east, and Britain changed its mind. In 1884 it proclaimed a protectorate over south-eastern New Guinea and its adjacent islands. The protectorate, called British New Guinea, was annexed outright on 4 September 1888. In 1902 it was placed under the authority of the Commonwealth of Australia. In 1905 British New Guinea became known as the Territory of Papua and formal Australian administration began in 1906. Sir Hubert Murray was appointed Acting Administrator of the Territory of Papua in 1907 and Lieutenant-Governor in 1908, a position he held until his death at Samarai in 1940. The headquarters of the Papuan Administration was in Port Moresby.

In 1884 the German Empire formally took possession of the north-east quarter of the island plus the Bismarck Archipelago

(New Britain and New Ireland), the Marshall Islands and the northern Solomon Islands (Buka, Bougainville and other islands) and it became known as German New Guinea in 1899.

With the outbreak of World War I Australia occupied German New Guinea. After the war, the League of Nations granted a mandate to Australia to govern in 1920 and it became known as the Territory of New Guinea. Its headquarters were in Rabaul.

Brigadier General Evan Wisdom became the Administrator of New Guinea and the Government Secretary was Harold Page. There were heads of departments for Treasury, Customs and Police. The Public Health Department was headed by Raphael Cilento.

The Territory was divided into nine districts: New Ireland, New Britain, Bougainville, Manus, Sepik, Madang, Morobe, Eastern Highlands and Western Highlands. They were run by the Government Secretary and ruled by district officers who were followed in rank by assistant district officers and then patrol officers. Each district officer was the representative of each department, except Public Health. However, if an officer was alone at a station he was naturally also the doctor.

The New Guinea Territory was responsible for its own finance and did not receive any subsidy from Australia. General administration and health services consumed most of the available revenue.

On board the *Marcena* Eric made acquaintances with other passengers, who included fellow new timers Duncan and Harry Bennett; McAdam, who was a district officer from Bougainville; Melrose, who was about to be a DO in New Ireland; and Woodward, who was from the Papuan service and was later lent to the NG service.

The *Marcena* was a very slow old ship and she called at every possible port on the way, so it was three weeks before they arrived in Rabaul.

Eric was taken to the Treasury and given his job as the lowest grade clerk. He had never been inside an office before and did not know what to do, but he soon gathered that nobody else did either. After a few days he was sent over to the district office to be trained to relieve the chief clerk, who was due to go on leave in a couple of months. This turned out to be good training and got Eric in on the bottom rung of the Administration. He served under Colonel John Walstab, for whom he had the greatest admiration and with whom he was later to become great friends.

Brigadier General Wisdom, as Administrator, was trying to sort out the situation in the wake of the war. The Germans had all been expropriated and sent home. Their property was being administered by the Expropriation Board, with returned soldiers being given various duties.

> Most of the properties were coconut plantations, and young ex-soldiers were brought up and generally just dumped on one of these plantations and told to take charge and make as much copra as they could and look after the place. It was surprising how well it worked.[1]

One of the difficulties was that they couldn't speak to the local labourers in their own particular version of Pidgin. It was not an easy language to learn, but over time the young newcomers adapted to the conditions and the language.

Rabaul was a town with a reasonable number of facilities. There was electric light, motor cars, a picture show and a couple of clubs. Cricket and tennis were played and there was beer to drink. Most drank more than they should, because there was not enough else to do. Women were in short supply and social life was practically non-existent.

Eric was not enamoured with Rabaul and did not envisage staying there for long. He wanted to venture out into the Territory. The Administration had recently brought in a new policy of enlisting patrol officers at the lowest rung of the district service. Eric applied to the selection committee and was accepted.

Some severe tribal fighting had broken out on the Sepik River and an expedition was arranged to try to settle matters. Walstab was placed in charge; George W.L. 'Kassa' Townsend, who was an acting assistant DO in Manus, was second in command; Stan Christian was the medical assistant; and Eric was the patrol officer. Never having gone bush before, he sought help from others as to what provisions to take.

They set off in the *Montoro* and Eric was dropped at Aitape, from where he was to take a little schooner, the *Aloha*, up the river. It had a Chinese engineer and a crew of four natives. After picking up supplies at Aitape, they went to Wewak and collected six native police before going up river to join the main expedition, which was travelling on the mission steamer the *Gabriel*.

The Sepik is the longest river in New Guinea and has flat mangrove and sago country at its mouth. Eric borrowed a pilot from the mission at Marienburg and he showed him how to skim alongside the banks and dodge the current, otherwise they could not have kept up with the *Gabriel's* 10 knots to *Aloho's* 6 knots. By getting up at 5am and steaming until fairly late at night Eric managed to keep up for the first two days. After that, though, she got well ahead of them.

Eric had taken quinine from the day he arrived in Rabual to contend with mosquitos. It was April when the expedition set out and that was when they were at their worst. On the Sepik the only thing to do was to get under a mosquito net as soon as the sun went down. At night the natives crawled into baskets made from woven rushes. The baskets were long, some as long as 10ft, and were held up by half hoops of cane. The whole family would crawl into it together, the father being the last in. He pulled a string or rolled in a log to shut the entrance, keeping the mosquitos down but increasing the heat. Eric did not think that anyone not brought up with it could have stood it. Some of the coastal native police tried it but could not bear it and preferred nets. The expedition had nets for everyone and long pants for the police to wear at night. These sorts of things weren't usually issued in kits.

The expedition travelled 100 miles up the river to the Middle Sepik, which was the most populated region. It took five days. Once they'd reached the trouble area, however, they were uncertain of how to deal with the natives. Those living near the mouth of the river were moderately civilised, those further up became less and less so. Headhunting was still an accepted way of life.

Walstab chose to make camp at a place called Ambunti. It was situated on a ridge running down to the river above Malu and below Yambon, which were two of the three villages they had to discipline. The other village was Awatip.

The patrol team built themselves some rough huts and unloaded the stores. The *Gabriel* then departed, leaving the *Aloha* as the only means of transport. They received a visit from a sorcerer from Malu, who came up the creek in a canoe and made charms against them. They tolerated him for a while until Walstab had had enough and fired a shot into the water near him. He got the message and left.

The killings that the team had come to investigate had involved 50 members of a village called Japandai. The account of the incident obtained from that village resorted to fingers and toes of several people to indicate that about 50 had been massacred by natives from the three villages of Yambon, Malu and Awatip. The story was that Japandai had become overcrowded and an agreement was made with Yambon for a group of their people to go to live in the Yambon village. They did so, building houses and settling in. One night, members of the three villages descended on them and slaughtered them all as they lay in their sleeping baskets.

Walstab decided to visit Yambon first, and Eric took him there in the *Aloha*. This far inland very few of the natives spoke Pidgin. Walstab had an interpreter with him and through him found out that the Yambon thought the white men had come to kill them. They were unable to explain that they wanted to apprehend those

65

responsible for the Japandai slaughter, so they left and returned to Ambunti.

Eric pondered the dichotomy between the indigenous peoples' way of living and the more civilised way of life the Administration was seeking to teach them. He questioned the right of the Australian Government to impose laws that the New Guineans did not know or understand.

> They had their own little life in their own village and didn't know anything beyond that. The answer to this basic question was that if we didn't come there, somebody else, the Japanese, in those days, first guess, would.

Walstab decided to attack the Yambon village at dawn. They travelled by canoe, which was quieter than the *Aloha*. Townsend and a team landed just below the village and Walstab and Eric went in from the front. Eric had his team of police. He asked them to spread out and keep in line with him, but he found that they formed a line ahead of him and had one police boy stay next to him as a bodyguard.

> The police would have died of shame if their officer had been killed.

When they arrived at the village it was deserted. The Yambons had moved off to a swamp. Walstab took a team to the lagoon where they had hidden but only one scout was captured. They took this prisoner back with them to the Ambunti station and talked to him about the crime of making agreements and then killing defenceless people, then they returned him to the village. The patrol team were not at all sure if they had made any impact, but it seemed villagers were now too scared to do any more killing. The Malu had gone bush for a while but when they returned peace was made with them. There was no punishment of the murderers and the question hung in the air as to whether or not they were murderers in their own culture. The present situation had existed for years and most villages were at war with neighbouring ones. As a result, there was an alliance of sorts between villages who were at war with the same neighbour. If someone had been killed or a death attributed to sorcery by a neighbouring villager, then retribution had to be made by taking the life of someone from that village, not necessarily that of the killer.

Some villages had also become headhunters, preserving the heads of their victims. They boiled the head, removed the flesh and replaced it with clay. Then they decorated it by painting the clay, sticking the hair back on top and placing two cowrie shells for eyes. Heads were viewed as trophies and a certain amount of pride and status was attached to ownership. A headhunter had badges to show how many he had. Some had sticks with danglers indicating his number of kills. Others had little danglers on their ears or arms. Headhunters had the privilege of wearing the skin from a flying fox as a pubic covering instead of grass or bark or going naked. Eric saw so many of them that, at first, he thought it was the customary dress. The biggest number of badges he saw a man displaying was eight.

The taking of heads was not heroic or honourable. The usual practice was a dawn raid when people were just coming out of their sleeping baskets. All heads counted. It didn't matter if it was man, woman or child. Eric even heard of one man capturing a small girl, taking her back to his village and letting his son, aged about ten, spear her to death. This made him a headhunter and gave him a start in life.

A message arrived that a recruiter further down the river had been threatened. After taking Townsend to Madang, Eric returned to ferry Walstab to the village where the trouble was brewing.

On the way there they saw a floating island of grass. It was Eric's first encounter with one of these unusual natural phenomena. Floating grass islands, sometimes with trees and birds on them, arise when the Sepik floods. The force of the rising waters tears off parts of riverbanks. The island continues downstream even after the flood has subsided until it eventually comes to rest. It is possible for a man to walk steadily across an island, but if he pauses or stands still his feet go through the grass and earth.

This island just drifted past them as they continued to the village.

They were met at the river bank by the villagers, who were lined up and armed ready to resist any attempt by the patrol team to go ashore. Walstab ordered shots to be fired at them, which they later heard had killed one man.

The team decided there was no more that could be done and left. There was plenty to do elsewhere.

Eric made a quick trip to Madang to pick up Woodward, who was on loan from Papua because he had a lot of experience in swamp country.

Woodward and Walstab made their way up the river to Karawari. 'Walstab told them to stop fighting and they told him to just go and boil his head'. He and half a dozen police got into canoes and headed towards the village. A shower of spears descended on them. Walstab opened fire but the villagers resisted for some time, showing great fortitude. Only when six of their number had been killed did they retreat into the bush. Usually when a patrol had to shoot, killing one or two men was enough to deter them.

The team stayed in the village trying to find out where the natives had fled. All the chasing had worried the villagers so much that they sent Walstab a young woman to buy him off. He sent her back with a message that all would be forgiven if they returned and lived in peace. Eventually, though, Walstab caught one scout, who was taken back to the station. By this time, Eric had also returned to the station as he had developed a tropical ulcer from a scratch on his hand.

The scout, although kept in handcuffs and leg irons, was well fed and well cared for. After a few days he was let out of the cuffs and irons. When he was returned to his village he was full of praise for the way he had been treated and became a good friend to the patrol officers. He was very grateful not to have been killed, which was what the neighbouring villages would have done. This also impressed the villages and helped to improve relationships between the white and indigenous men.

Woodward took over the station and Walstab left, taking Eric's admiration and loyalty with him.

The Sepik natives were adept at handling canoes, which they used for distance travel, there being no roads at all in the interior. Their canoes were long dugouts without outriggers, though some were very small, and they paddled them standing or with men standing and women sitting. Falling overboard was to be avoided at all costs, as crocodiles were numerous. All the canoes on the Sepik had their prows carved in the shape of a crocodile head.

Soon after Walstab had left, Eric and Stan Christian went on patrol down the river by canoe. For their trip they had decided to travel in comfort. They used two very large 30ft canoes they lashed together with a framework about 6ft apart and built a small house on it for shelter.

This was Eric's first patrol in command. In later years someone with as little experience would not have been sent out, however at that time there were not many who knew much more than he did. The big canoe could not go upstream, only down, or from side to side. Their modus operandi was the carrot and stick approach. The stick was the rifles with which they shot anyone who did not obey. The carrot was giving medical treatment, buying food from them, and distributing money owed to natives who had been away at work and had died. The first villages they came to were friendly. Christian offered to treat them for yaws. Just about everyone had it, some more severely than others. Because the injections were intramuscular and painful, Christian cunningly gave them to the babies first. When they cried, he said that's what babies do. He then gave injections to two young males both of whom writhed in pain. After that, everyone else refused.

When they went to the next village Christian decided to give intravenous injections. Everyone lined up for the treatment and there were no complications. Intravenous became the accepted way of giving the injections.

Yaws is an infectious disease caused by the spirochete bacteria *Treponema pertenue*. It is spread by skin contact with infected individuals and is most common in children, as they play together. The disease occurs in three stages. In the first stage, small, painless lumps appear on the skin. The lesions may group together and they may ulcerate. The second stage starts weeks or months after the first. In this stage, a crusty rash forms, which can involve the face, arms, legs and buttocks. Painful, thick sores can develop on the soles of the feet making walking excruciating and difficult, resulting in a crablike gait called 'crab yaws'. Although the bones and joints can be affected, second stage yaws usually does not cause destruction in these areas. Stage three begins at least five years after early yaws and can cause severe damage to the skin, bones and joints, especially in the legs. Late yaws also can cause facial disfiguration. In the 1920s, and continuing in the pre-antibiotic era, treatment was with a series of injections of bismuth and arsenical preparations such as NAB (Neo-arsphenamine).

At every village Eric visited he told them that they must stop fighting with their neighbours. The first three villages said they would, but Eric did not really believe them. When they came to a larger village about a mile from the river, Eric and Christian took four police with them and left two police to guard the canoes. Eric found an interpreter and told him to tell the villagers to stop fighting or they would be punished. The interpreter looked at Eric and said, 'No, I'm not going to tell them that.' After taking a look at the villagers and seeing the expressions on their faces, Eric had to agree with him, so they retreated to the river, followed by the natives brandishing spears. Feeling lucky not to have been massacred, they continued on their way.

After about 100 miles they reached a more civilised part where the villagers were not headhunters, unlike in the tributaries of the Sepik where the practice persisted. They were investigating another reported incident. As Eric's patrol approached the village the garamut drums began beating a warning. The raid was a failure; when they arrived the prewarned village was deserted.

A garamut is a slit gong drum made from a hollowed-out log and played by striking it with a stick. They were a remarkable signal system used for long-distance communication. A drum used a special code of rhythms and notes for signalling anybody's comings or goings, for sending warnings and to call people together for meetings. Eric found that each man had a call sound. Once when Eric was in a village and wanted to see a man who was out gathering sago, a message was sent on the garamut and he arrived in less than an hour.

The next port of call was Marienburg. There was a mission station which Father Kerschbaum had begun in 1912. He had been doing his best to civilise the New Guineans but confessed it had been a fruitless task and had come to the conclusion that force was needed as well as Christianity. He said, 'If they won't stop headhunting, shoot them. That will save lives in the long run. You may kill a few, but that will save the lives of many more who will be killed in the headhunting.' With his experience so far, Eric could appreciate Kerschbaum's point of view.

They waited at Marienburg for the *Aloha* to arrive because they could not go upstream without power. As they had travelled down the Sepik the water level had fallen and the locals were busy planting yams on the uncovered mud flats.

The arrival of the *Aloha* from Itebi brought a letter ordering Eric to meet the *Montoro* at Potsdam Haven and take over the pinnace for them to use on the river. They discovered that the Administrator, General Wisdom, and Governor-General Lord Forster, who was visiting the Territory, were onboard the *Montoro*.

Eric and Christian had to borrow coats for the official meeting. Also on board was Mrs Woodward, who had come for a visit, and Lambert, who was replacing Christian. The two craft headed up the river. The water level had dropped so much that the small wharf they had built at Ambunti stood about 30 ft above the water.

Not long after their return to Ambunti, Eric, who had suffered from a few mild episodes of malaria previously, was taken ill with a very severe attack.

> It started with a headache, then came a feeling of freezing cold and shivering inspite of three blankets and the outside temperature of 90, all the machinery clattering around in one's head, then a bit of sleep, then you felt a bit better, then it started all over again. During the attack, apart from when you felt freezing cold, you were sweating very profusely, couldn't eat much, taking 30 grains of quinine a day... it was very miserable. With a really bad attack you have the feeling you are going to die, but you are afraid you won't.

Eric was ill for a fortnight and was left feeling weak and needing to convalesce. Despite taking quinine very regularly, Eric was to suffer from malaria fairly frequently. Fortunately, none of the other times were as severe.

Once he had recovered, Eric carried out more patrols up and down the Sepik. During that time the fighting between the river villages ceased, but the patrol team suspected they were still raiding villages further back from the river.

On one trip, the village of Awatip complained that people from a village up in the hills had been killing their people. Eric had no doubt that they had been killing each other for many years. He took a patrol into the hills but made the mistake of allowing a large number of Awatip warriors to accompany him. He made them stand back so the patrol team could go in first. The Awatip agreed but Eric wasn't aware of a further agenda.

They ran into the village, with the police again getting ahead of Eric, except for the bodyguard. The village was practically deserted, however they found one woman in a hut. She had twins, about 2 years old, hiding in a sleeping basket. They got the woman out of the hut. While they were getting the twins out of the basket the Awatip arrived and started threatening the woman. One police boy was holding them off. Eric grabbed the twins and placing one on each hip, walked out of the hut and stood beside the woman. The police gathered round to keep the Awatip away. If not for the patrol team's presence, she and her twins undoubtedly would have been killed.

Eric made the Awatip make peacemaking signs, such as breaking spears and branches off trees. The team made the Awatip leave before them, then they left the village and camped in the bush that night.

It looked to Eric as if the venture had been a complete failure, but he later heard that peace was kept for more than 12 months. 'We were finding then that we sometimes built better than we knew.'

As murders were reported, a patrol would go out to try and catch the culprits, but with little success. Being in garamut country, whenever they set out, the drums would start pounding and signalling a warning that they were on their way.

Another tradition for the people of the Sepik was carving the skin of the young boys to create large scars. It was an initiation ceremony from which the women were excluded. Eric was once allowed to watch part of one of them. The boys, aged about 10 to 12 years old, were taken to a hut, where they lived by themselves. Cuts were made on the upper body, sometimes shaped like flowers or crocodiles. Ash was rubbed into the cuts and an oil from the trees rubbed over the top. Very few of the cuts seemed to become infected and very few of the boys died from the initiation.

Eric got to know his police boys and appreciated their individual abilities. He became fluent in Pidgin by spending time with the police and other natives. He tried learning the Middle Sepik language but did not become very proficient. Learning all the native languages in New Guinea was impossible because there were over 500.

When he had spare time, Eric read as much law as he could, including two volumes of Blake Odgers' *Common Law of England*, and he studied local ordinances. He harboured hopes of becoming a district officer and to sit on the Bench. He was starting to feel stressed by living near the Sepik. 'I think we all went a bit mad on the Sepik in those early days.'

After Christmas 1924, Eric went to Madang to meet the *Franklin* and pilot her up the river. She was the same old *Franklin* of his Naval College days. The Administrator was onboard and was visiting places that he usually did not visit. Eric's health was not good when he got to Madang, and on seeing him General Wisdom offered him sick leave. Eric replied that he would be all right for a bit longer if he could have a transfer to another station, where he could recover.

Eric acted as pilot in the river and kept a watch for the rest of the trip. He discovered that the Administrator had a trick that Eric fortunately woke up to. General Wisdom would ask a stupid question to see how someone would answer it. One day he said something to Eric which was completely wrong and Eric said, 'No, Sir.' After that Wisdom treated Eric as somebody he could talk to and rely on.

Onboard the *Franklin*, Eric found that none of the senior officers, except Walstab, could speak Tok Pisin, the Papua New Guinean form of Pidgin, properly.

> Well that became my hobbyhorse and I preached the need to have Pidgin studied as a language, which it is, and I think I was the first in the administration to do so.

After leaving the Sepik, they called at Aitape, Matty (Wuvulu) Island and Talasea and then back to Rabaul. This was an interesting trip for Eric because he could observe the Administrator's visits and gain better knowledge of the Territory.

Soon after, Eric was transferred to Buka Passage, between Bougainville and Buka. He went to Kieta first to get instructions from DO McAdam and then sailed up in a little schooner called *Wanderer*. Going with him was Eric Robinson, known as 'Wobbie' because 'Ewic Wobinson' could not pronounce his Rs.

At Buka Passage, Eric replaced an officer who had resigned to go planting. Eric described Buka Passage as a beauty spot:

> There is the deep water in the Passage itself tailing off to green where it gets shallower, then the coral reefs looking brown, the white sand of the beaches themselves and the luxuriant green of the trees of those tropical islands. It's a lovely spot and at night, particularly with the moonlight on it, when you've got a canoe coming up with all the natives chanting in time to the paddling, it really did have some of the romance of the tropical islands.

While there, Eric and Wobbie carried out patrols around Small Buka and on the Bougainville side of the passage. The natives were under control so there was no danger from them. They collected tax and met ships that came into Nissan. Eric was the customs officer.

Every six weeks a ship came into Soraken, which Eric met as customs officer, and as the local postmaster he collected the mail, sorted it and handed it to people, as most had come over to meet the ship. He took back what was undistributed.

They always had a very good meal on board, and this was the only time that they did. They bought some fresh meat to take with them as they normally lived out of tins. They'd buy steak or sausages to cook and eat straight away, and also a roast or corned beef to cook and eat during the next couple of days before it went off due to the lack of refrigeration.

The lighting was poor. They had hurricane lamps or miller lamps. To get enough light to read by they had to get close to the lamp, and that was too hot and also attracted insects and beetles that fluttered all around and onto them.

Eric found that he got to know men well from being on patrol with them. It was always a pleasure to be on patrol with Wobbie.

Because his health was still not good and he was due for leave, Eric requested a break. He went down through the Solomons to Sydney. There he 'did what everyone else did, lived gaily' (It was the Roaring Twenties). This he did until he was just about broke and ready to return. He also spent some time with his family in Brisbane, which was from where he caught a ship to go back to New Guinea.

When he returned to Rabaul, he found he had been promoted to Assistant District Officer and had a salary of 500 pounds a year. Eric thought this was not bad for someone aged 26. His posting was to Aitape, but before going he was sent on a short tax collecting patrol in the Duke of York Islands. Eric heard some minor court cases for the first time.

When the Germans left New Guinea it was about one third under complete control. The main focus of the Australian Administration was to maintain peace in these areas and extend them as far as possible. They also had to supervise labour by inspections. Labour was under a contract system. Copra, which was almost the only export from the Territory, was bringing a good price and the country was fairly prosperous. It differed in this from the Territory of Papua which was poorer and relied on a subsidy from Australia. The New Guinea natives participated in the production of copra. There was actually a shortage of labour.

The conditions of employment were that each labourer was issued with a box, blanket, bowl, plate, spoon and lap-lap, which was a yard and three quarters of calico to put round his waist. His rations were a pound and a half of rice a day and a tin of meat every week. He was also given a cake of soap, two sticks of tobacco and a box of matches every week. His pay was only 6 shillings a month, which was very poor, but the Administration had to compete with all the other lowly paid tropical countries.

Labour was obtained by professional recruiters who went around the villages persuading men to work. Presents were used as

NEW GUINEA PRE WORLD WAR II: 1923-1927

inducements and the family usually kept those. The recruiter would take the new recruits to one of the stations to be signed on.

The mandate had laid down that the Administration was to be for the moral and material welfare of the New Guineans. Eric could see that those who went to work appeared to be better off than those who stayed in the village. They were in improved physical condition, having gained some weight and their skin was shiny. They were more alert and owned more goods.

Recruiting was not always as above board as it might have been. There was a certain amount of forced work for natives, which of course was illegal. If a recruiter was found doing this he would be punished and could lose his licence.

As Eric set out for Aitape to take up his new position, he sought to continue to work as he had been doing, with the wellbeing of the New Guineans in mind and without fear or favour, as he saw it.

On the way there he saw Melrose, who was going on leave from Manus, and bought his gramophone. It was the beginning of an addiction for gramophone records.

The ship called at Seleo, a small island about 10 miles from Aitape, and Eric disembarked. He went over in the same old *Aloha* he'd had on the Sepik. The district officer Eric was to serve under had 'the good old English name of Bastard'. Eric secretly admired him for not having changed it. A clerk and a storeman completed the staff. They had a wireless station and so were in touch with the outside world. Patrol officers were at Vanimo and Wewak.

At Aitape there was a strip along the coast, approximately 20 miles wide, which was completely under control. Then there was an area where some natives had had contact with Europeans, and further inland there were those who had had little or no contact at all.

Eric's first job was to conduct a census and tax patrol, walking from village to village. A white man in authority was known to the villagers as a Kiap. In each village there was the Luluai, a government appointed chief, and the Tultul, a second-in-command who was usually a younger man who could speak Pidgin. There was also a Medical Tultul who had been given some basic first aid training and a few simple drugs.

On arriving at a village, an officer was met by the Luluai and Tultul. He then went to the House Kiap, a rest house built by the villagers for whites passing through. He would put his gear down and make a cup of tea. Then he requested the natives to line up in their families. The officer got out his census book, checked off the names and made any changes. Then he did a similar entry in the village book which was a small book kept by the Luluai. Finally, he made a summary of the numbers to be taken back to the station for the census.

Next they collected tax. The tax was 10 shillings a year, only paid by the able-bodied men who were fit to go away to work if they felt like it. Able-bodied men who had a family of one wife and four or more children were exempt from tax. Paying tax was not a hardship for coastal natives as they could earn it very easily.

At night the patrol officer cooked on an open fire using utensils he carried with him, usually a billycan, frying pan and saucepan. Eric slept in the House Kiap in a bed that was a tube of canvas strung on two poles supported by a tripod at each end. The essential mosquito net was always with him. The police accompanying him slept in the police house next to the House Kiap. When in uncertain country, the officer posted sentries for the night. In these areas there would not be a House Kiap and Eric would sleep in a tent.

The taxation money was collected in shillings. The New Guinea men did not trust bank notes. They had been given jam tin labels in the past, so coins it was. These became very heavy by the time the patrol had collected 500 pounds or more. To carry the shillings a .303 ammunition case was used and the coins were made up into rolls of 5 pounds. A stamp of the office was placed on each of the rolls. There were a few rare incidents of people using rolled up bars of iron to mimic the rolled up coins and handing them into trading stores.

A tax disc was given to each man when he paid his tax and an entry was made in the tax book. There was no real check, apart from the integrity of the officers concerned. Eric believed that there were no incidents of officers defrauding the villagers.

> It became a religion with us that anything a native was due for, they were paid. We had a very strong feeling on that and I think the whole commercial world, the planters and I know the miner later on felt the same way about it.

Having taken the census and collected tax from one village, they walked on to the next. Near the Aitape coast the ground was soft sand, a little way inland there were some swamps to be negotiated, and further on there were mountains. The upkeep of the tracks through the mountains was the responsibility of the locals, but they were not very conscientious about it. They only cleared the tracks if they heard that a patrol was coming.

After collecting the Aitape coast tax, Eric went to the Wewak area, where he visited the outlying islands of Kairiru and Muschu first and then travelled back to the mainland and collected there. Judd was the patrol officer at Wewak, and he had completed the census. The patrol officers tried to keep the census and tax collecting separate if they could, although often they had to do them together. If a man was trying to avoid tax he would hide but not if it was only the census. Once on record they could get him on tax later. It was a bit devious but fair in the long run.

The nearest plantation was Warum, owned by a planter with red hair whose surname was Draper. Naturally he was called Blue. Eric and Blue Draper became great friends and visited each other about once a fortnight.

Not long after, Judd went on leave and did not return. Eric was then stationed at Wewak on his own. All that was there was the house for the DOs or ADOs, as he was, a barracks for the police and a little storeroom. However, it was an attractive place on a flat hill that jutted out into the sea. There was a beautiful all-round view and a pleasant breeze most of the time. As with most places it was popular with the mosquitos.

Eric had a personal servant whose duties included cooking and laundry. 'As a cook he could generally boil water, boil potatoes and sweet potatoes and open a tin.' Eric was not a fussy eater but later thought he should have tried harder to have more variety in his food. He did try the local sago but found it totally unpalatable and that all it did was spoil the other food eaten with it. However, there were plenty of pigeons and they sent out a shoot boy with a shotgun, enabling them to supplement their diet with fresh meat, keeping them healthier than they might have otherwise been.

While stationed in Wewak, Eric patrolled all the surrounding area. There were steep mountains, but the worst area was along the coast where ridge after ridge of hard country ran down to the sea between the soft sand. Alternating climbing a steep hill and down the other side and then trudging along the soft sand made it the most tiring country Eric ever had to patrol.

Two cadet patrol officers were sent for training. Vertigan went on patrol from Wewak with Eric, and Roberts went to Aitape. Both stayed in the service for many years.

At that time, the Expropriation Board decided to sell its plantations to private individuals. Eric and many others did not take it seriously. A few people did bid and were able to buy at low prices. Then news came that gold had been found at Edie Creek. 'Kassa' Townsend, who was passing through, and Eric discussed the possibility of going there but it was a long way from where they were and they dismissed the idea.

In early 1927 Eric was given the job to pilot the *Franklin* up the Sepik again. He went to Potsdam Haven and piloted her. This time Commander Webb RANR was in command. Eric had known Webby in the Navy and a good friend became an even better one.

Soon after, Eric got notice that he was to be transferred to Namatanai. He left Wewak with regret. He had hoped to try to have roads built through or over the mountains to the grass plains inland and the villages there.

Namatanai was an old German station with good European houses. Eric was provided with a very large house all to himself. There were proper barracks and a fine office. The climate was comparatively better and the natives all lived on the coast, so there was no need for patrols into the mountains.

Eric had a horse to ride down the coast and stop at the plantations to inspect the labour.

He went to the trading stores, which were kept by the Chinese. At every store, Eric found a welcome of two bottles of beer and a glass waiting for him on the veranda. The hospitality was too much for Eric to consume as the stores were only 2 miles apart. However, he did appreciate having an occasional beer and a horse to ride instead of sweating in the hot sun as he had done when walking in Aitape and Wewak.

While Eric was at Namatanai, the Expropriation Board put the second group of plantations up for sale. They were in Namatanai and Eric put in a bid with Jack Melville, who was on one of the plantations, but their bid was not high enough to secure a property.

The time he spent at Namatanai was enjoyable for Eric. Chickens left by his predecessor meant he could have an egg for breakfast each day. A schooner came regularly from Rabaul with supplies. His staff included a medical assistant, a clerk and a storeman/jailer. The men on the plantations were 'good fellows' and they all got on very well together.

Towards the end of 1927, leave came around again for Eric. He was relieved by Mantle and headed to Brisbane, where he spent most of his time. Socialising was on the agenda as usual. Unlike in Namatanai, or perhaps because of his time there, he did manage to imbibe to excess and was pulled over by the police for driving under the influence of alcohol in the Brisbane suburb of Wooloowin. Eric was taken to the watchhouse before being released on bail and paying a fine. He did not end up as broke as previously but spent rather a lot on gramophone records, especially those by Caruso, his favourite singer.

CHAPTER 5

NEW GUINEA PRE-WORLD WAR II: 1928-1939

Eric returned to New Guinea early in 1928. The Public Service Ordinance provided six months leave plus three months recreational leave after six years of service. All the senior officers who had signed on at the beginning of the Administration were entitled to nine months' leave. Many of the senior district officers were taking leave at this time and it created a lot of vacancies that were being temporarily filled by junior staff such as Eric. Consequently, he found he had been assigned as Acting District Office at Madang, one of the senior stations. Before long, though, he was transferred to Salamaua, a lower rated district. Eric was rather perturbed by this and wondered what he had done to incur such an apparent demotion.

He soon discovered why. The town and station at Salamaua were a shambles. He had been sent on a mission to overhaul and restructure the station.

It was beautifully situated on a flat isthmus of land, all sand, just a few feet above high-water level. Coconut palms fringed the shores. A few basic European style houses, some native material houses, which included the District Office, and some very small huts used by the miners when they came down from the goldfield made up the habitation.

Eric was met on the beach by the officer he was about to relieve.

He said, 'There's a vacant house, but there's no furniture in it. That's all I can do for you,' and walked off, which wasn't much of a welcome. Well, I set myself in and went to the office and found there the staff very badly overworked and very badly directed.

The goldfield at Edie Creek had been in existence for a few years before the rush had begun in earnest in 1926. The Administration at Salamaua had been unable to handle the variety of challenges this had posed. Eric's predecessors had difficulty in getting stores up to the Warden and his staff on the goldfield and had put excessive pressure on the native carriers. The miners had also overworked and overloaded the carriers.

Overloading did not happen at the Salamaua end. A checkpoint had been established on the road as it left the isthmus and every pack was weighed before the carrier was allowed to proceed. A native carried 50 pounds as he walked, and it took him at least seven days to go from Salamaua to Edie Creek. He had a day's rest and then spent four to five days on the return trek. Before long, they set off again on the round trip of nearly a fortnight. 'The real heroes of the early days of Edie Creek were the native carriers'. Mostly they had the strength to do it, but dysentery broke out on the treks and many died from it. The overall effect of pressure and illness was that 'the natives were in a sullen mood with no respect or confidence in the administration.'

> We had to start from tors to get their confidence back. For instance, I wanted a small hut built for the Malay storeman. His was falling to pieces. And I asked a couple of villages to send labour in and they said 'How long will it take?' I said a month and they said no. I had a brainwave and said, 'All right, look come in by the week and I'll pay you by the week.' And they said 'Yes we'll do that. That's not long enough to send us up to Edie Creek.' That's what they were afraid of.

Confidence was gradually restored over time. Eric was very fortunate to have an excellent staff. Penglase, Downing and Kyle were patrol officers, and Magle and Farlow were clerks. Gregory was an ADO who had been sent to look after a road construction gang that was building a road from Lae up the Markham Valley to the goldfields. This was the third attempt to make a road, each from different starting points, none of which was successful in Eric's time at Salamaua.

A young doctor joined the station, but he left after three months as he found the challenge too great. He was replaced by Dr B.A. Sinclair who, over the next 12 months, organised the public health part of the Administration and restored confidence in that department. Sinclair was a very competent doctor who performed some remarkable surgical operations with only crude instruments and no skilled assistants.

Fortunately, flying was becoming more viable. Junkers aeroplanes had arrived on the scene and an airstrip had been built at Wau. As Gregory's roadwork was progressing, he also made some emergency airstrips so a pilot could bring down his plane more safely if it suffered engine failure. The pilots, such as Harry D.L. McGilvery, Alan Cross and Jerry Pentland, were more confident making the trip, having less fear of crashing into the jungle. They were remarkable pioneers in their own right and their daring played an important part in the development of PNG.

With most provisions being flown to Wau and just a day's walk carrying to Edie Creek, the strain on the native carriers was considerably lightened.

Not long after his arrival in Salamaua, Eric flew to Wau and walked up to Edie Creek. He met the Warden, J.D. Maclaine, who was a skilled warden but had little experience where native labour was concerned. He had used common sense as much as possible and the miners had made sure the labourers were fed well. Eric inspected them and found them to be in surprisingly good condition. He was also impressed by the miners, who were of varying occupations and 'were a very fine lot.' He formed the opinion that crooks didn't go to the goldfields in the early days as it was too hard for them. Most of the miners did well, with an average man earning about 5,000 pounds after two years, and some made much more.

However, Edie Creek was a dismal place. Situated 7000ft above sea level it was in cloud most of the time and extremely cold at night. The tree roots and the ground were covered in moss, sometimes feet deep. The accommodation for the natives was fairly crude and small but being tiny was beneficial because crowding in at night meant they kept each other warm. Coldness of such a degree had never been experienced by the coastal New Guineans before.

The Native Labour Ordinance was designed for agricultural labour on coconut plantations, but the same law applied to mining labour and didn't allow for working at night, though it happened anyway. 'Water shortage made people share water and use night labour on alluvial workings too.'

Eric hatched a plan with the Warden. He prohibited night mining and told all the miners to put in a big protest. At the same time, he and the Warden sent in proposals to cover mining labour and night mining. They received a wire back saying they could use their ideas in the interim in anticipation of future legislation. The problem was solved. If Eric had simply turned a blind eye to the practise and it had been discovered, he would have been the one in trouble.

In contrast to Edie Creek, Wau was a beautiful place.

> It was on the Bulolo Valley, high up the Bulolo. There were beautiful pine trees all around with Spanish moss hanging off them, clear areas of kunai and at 3,500 feet the climate was ideal. It was absolutely perfect and when you got there, coming from the coast, you sort of took a deep breath of air and your eyes lit up and you felt a different man altogether.

Back at Salamaua, Eric received a report that a white man had been killed in the Markham Valley. He set out to investigate and received assurances about the murder along the way. Eventually he found he had travelled more than 25 miles on a false rumour. Such rumours were not an isolated occurrence, but investigation was always required.

As well as rumours there were requests and demands. One request came from the Zenag Gap area where a tribal fight was brewing between the Parteps and the Mumengs. The Parteps demanded that Eric take a patrol out and shoot the Mumengs. Eric found out 'it was only a payback and the thing to do was make peace'.

He went with the Parteps and stopped in a dry creek bed just short of the Mumengs' village. The Mumengs were lined up on a ridge above the creek with all their spears ready and with one native in particular taking aim at Eric.

Eric sent the Parteps back to their village and walked out in front of his patrol and beckoned to the Mumengs to be peaceful. He had taken the precaution of having strapped a revolver on his back where it could not be seen. Suddenly one of his unarmed police boys came up and stood beside him, a brave move given the circumstances.

With friendly talk and gestures, Eric managed to persuade the Mumengs to make peace. Needing some of the Parteps as carriers for the trip back, the patrol went to their village to find them. The Luluai and Tultul met them and were friendly, but the rest of the village was practically deserted. Eric sent two police boys to tell the rest to come back, but they were attacked. The police boys fired a couple of shots over the heads of the Partep villagers and, together with Eric and the rest of the patrol, made a quick exit back to Salamaua.

Eric let matters cool off for a couple of days to give him the chance to have more ammunition flown in. Then the patrol set out again, but this time there was no one there; they had all gone bush. However, the intervention had the desired effect and peace was restored between the tribes.

Patrols were the way Eric and the patrol officers gradually gained the confidence of the natives. By spending time in a village, talking with the people, buying food from the village gardens and showing that they meant them no harm, they built rapport and gained respect. The villagers could see the good relationship that existed between the white men and the native police. That also helped instil confidence that the Kiaps' intentions were for their wellbeing and for peace.

Salamaua was the headquarters of the Morobe District, in which both the Edie Creek and the Bulolo goldfields were situated. The district areas Eric took over were the Waria River, except for its tributary; the Bubu River; and the whole area from the coast to the Bulolo, except for a part near the lower Watut River and a flat part of the Markham Valley. Most of the Huon Peninsula was under the control of the Lutheran Mission.

Harry Downing had a reputation for being a good negotiator. When he took a patrol to the Bubu River he had the added good fortune to arrive in the main village while most of the men were harvesting pandanus nuts up in the trees. They were in no position to fight and they made peace quite gladly.

The villages near the lower Watut were accessed by Gregory while he was looking after the road survey party, and peace pacts were agreed.

Kyle was the patrol officer on the Huon Peninsula. He had a rather difficult time dealing with the Lutheran Missionaries who regarded the area as theirs and thought the Administration was intruding. The Lutherans were mainly German, with a few Americans. A rift formed between them and the Americans left to set up in the Madang end of the area. Many of the German Missionaries would later become Nazis.

While in Salamaua, Eric organised the building of more native material houses for the Administration staff. He decided on the 'one man, one house' principle as he had found that two men together invariably led to quarrelling. He also arranged for the houses to have sawn timber floors, which was a definite plus. 'The roof was quite watertight, there were shutters instead of windows, but they were cool and reasonably comfortable.'

Salamaua had two stores — Burns Philp and Carpenters — so they were never short of life's necessities. However, there was no refrigeration so they lived on tinned food.

The majority of inhabitants were young, single, white men. There were only five white women. Drinking at the pub was the main social activity and the miners readily joined in when they came into town for a break. These were fun times for the youthful participants and the presence of very social and witty barman called Bill Cameron enhanced their enjoyment.

Fun was also generated by hard fought matches on the tennis courts. Kyle was an ex-A-Grade player and Penglase was also a good player. Many from other occupations in the town also took part in the friendly competitions.

One handsome, single, white man to arrive at Salamaua was later to become a Hollywood movie star famous for his swashbuckling roles. His name was Errol Flynn.

Not long after Flynn's arrival, Alan Cross, who had become the manager of Guinea Airways, told Eric he needed someone to manage their branch in Wau. The job involved receiving and distributing cargo brought in by the planes. Did Eric know of anyone? Eric replied that a new arrival by the name of Flynn might be interested. Flynn was given the job and flown into Wau. He did not shine in the position and was soon fired. Shortly after his employment was terminated, Flynn left the district.

The original district office, which had been made from native materials, was large but very rickety. Towards the end of 1929 it was replaced by one built from European materials, which was much more pleasant to work in. Overall, it was hard work but Eric and his team enjoyed it.

There was, however, a disturbing downside to living in Salamaua, and that was the number of deaths. Blackwater fever was the main cause. Blackwater fever is a severe complication of mainly the Falciparum type of malaria. Rupture of the red blood cells releases haemoglobin into the blood stream. The haemoglobin is excreted in the urine turning it dark red or black and at the same time damages the kidneys, leading to renal failure. Bilirubin, which is a breakdown product of haemoglobin, also accumulates in the blood, causing jaundice. The most probable explanation of the cause of blackwater fever is an autoimmune reaction resulting from an interaction between quinine and the Plasmodium Falciparum malarial parasite.

On one occasion, when Eric was visiting Lae in a little schooner, a man drove up in a car and asked if Eric would take a sick man to hospital. Eric said he would but not if the man had blackwater fever. If it was blackwater the best thing to do was not to move him but to keep him absolutely still. The man said he would find out and drove back to the aerodrome where the sick man was resting. When he returned, the patient was sitting beside him. Eric sent the dinghy to collect him. When the man came on board he was 'as yellow as a lemon'. Eric dashed ashore in the dinghy and exclaimed 'That man has blackwater, hasn't he?'. 'No, he hasn't passed urine for 24 hours,' was the reply. Eric decided there was no chance of saving the sick man but thought that, rather than move him off the schooner, it would be better to take him to the hospital. This Eric did and the unfortunate man died there a few days later.

Finding the death rate in the coastal population rather appalling, Eric did some calculations at the time and found the percentage matched that of the soldiers in the Great War.

As the nearest pastor was a German missionary about nine miles away, Eric conducted all the funeral services himself. All the young men of the town came to the funerals. After a while, a routine developed with men having regular tasks. 'There were people who manned their oaks. Others took away the planks from under the coffin... We put it through with perhaps more precision than we should have.'

When the funeral was over, they all adjourned to the pub to drink beer and forget about it. 'It was the only thing to do with the casualties being as high as they were. If we'd taken them really seriously, they would have got us down.'

Another of Eric's roles was hearing court cases. In Salamaua he tried more white men than was usual. There was some difficulty in this as the whites resented being convicted on the evidence of a native. Eric hoped he succeeded in being impartial, judging white and black evidence on its merits and not on who was giving it.

Only one appeal was lodged against Eric's rulings:

> That was a funny old Swede who didn't believe in injections. He said his blood was pure. Well we didn't allow anyone to go into the goldfields unless they had an anti-typhoid injection. The old chap wouldn't be reasoned with so the only thing to do was fine him, which I did. He thereupon went to Rabaul and lodged an appeal, but the judge listened carefully and just refused leave to appeal. So I think I was fairly successful in that case at least.

Eric tried several interesting cases in Salamaua. One case involved a man called Nash, a recruiter. The Luluai of a village where he was camped lost his temper and threatened him with a spear. Nash grabbed his shotgun and threatened to shoot. Just as he fired over the Luluai's head the Luluai lost his nerve, turned and ran up the hill. A pellet struck him in the back of the neck and killed him. Nash handed himself in to Eric and told the whole story frankly. Eric heard the case and committed him for trial. 'Our wise old chief judge Col Wanliss found him not guilty.' Then the Administration cancelled his recruiting licence, which made it impossible for him to live in the country and he had to leave. This seemed to Eric to be a satisfactory outcome.

Another strange case involved the shooting of a native. The only shotgun in the vicinity belonged to another native, who was a very fine labourer and of very good character. The suspect, however, refused to say anything. Eric was puzzled because although the evidence was clearly against him, it just didn't seem to fit. Eric thought that if he had been able to talk with the man in his role as a patrol officer he would have been able to find out what had really happened. However, his roles of ex-officio police officer and being the magistrate for his lower court trial prohibited that. Eric had to commit the suspect to trial and he was sent to Rabaul. The chief judge tried the case and sentenced him to three years. When Eric met the old chief judge later, he mentioned the case. The judge just said, "Well, what are you to do, Eric?"

Eric concluded that though the law might not be humane, at least some judges were.

It was a court case that brought Eric and his old friend from naval days, Hugh Mackenzie, together again. Hugh owned a small schooner, *Lady Betty*, that was bringing native recruits to Salamaua. He had overloaded and was spotted. A report was sent to Eric, who found that the natives were all in good condition. He calculated that it would have cost Hugh 30 pounds to have made another trip to Salamaua and fined him that amount. Then the magistrate and the trader went to the pub for a drink together.

One other case involved a murder in a native village, where the patrol officer had obtained a complete confession from the murderer, dug up the body and found that the murderer's axe fitted perfectly into the cut in the skull. Eric was trying the case for committal when he thought he needed proof that the blow would have caused death. He scrawled a quick note to the doctor, who by this time was Holland, and said, "Dear Doc, would you come to the court and tell us if a blow on the head with a tomahawk would be sufficient to cause death?" The police messenger came back with the note and scribbled on the bottom of it was, "If the head's as thick as yours, no." The Doc arrived at the court looking a bit anxious. He had begun to wonder if Eric might have him for contempt of court. Eric had other plans. Instead he 'fined' him a bottle of beer in the pub when the court session was over.

In July 1929 the Governor General and his wife, Lord and Lady Stonehaven, visited New Guinea, including Salamaua and Wau. They travelled in the HMAS *Albatross*. Eric was unsure how he should entertain the important visitors. He gathered all the Luluais, Tultuls and Medical Tultuls from the surrounding villages and lined them up for the Governor General to inspect. Then all the local whites congregated at Eric's basic bungalow for drinks and a meet and greet.

The following day they went to Wau, where one of the miners gave a demonstration of boxing alluvial gold. He asked Lady Stonehaven to wash the box and retrieve the gold. She was delighted to recover about 20 ounces, which the miner had placed there beforehand.

As his nine months' leave was drawing close, Eric requested a visit from the district inspector, who at that time happened to be Walstab. He arrived and completed a thorough inspection. Having a reasonable knowledge of the way things were before Eric's time, Walstab gave him a good report. Eric felt very proud both of his achievements in Salamaua and of the staff he had worked with.

At the end of 1929 a friend of Eric's, Lea Ashton, who was a miner who had just finished up his claim, accompanied him to Sydney. Lea was also from Brisbane so they bought a car in Sydney and drove up to Brisbane. In Australia they found signs of the Depression everywhere.

After spending time with his family and friends, Eric went on a trip to South East Asia. He visited Angkor Wat, Saigon, Manila, Hong Kong, Singapore and Java. Apart from seeing that part of the world, Eric was interested to see what life and labour was like compared with New Guinea. He found that unskilled labour was in much the same economic situation. He found that while there was skilled labour, such as carpenters, in the SE Asian countries, there was none in PNG. Chinese and Australian tradesmen had to be brought in, which was costly, as was paying their wages.

Eric was broke again after his nine months leave. On his return to Salamaua, where Townsend had been relieving him, Eric found the district in very good order and he was soon back in the swing of things.

Another of Eric's many jobs included marrying people. One of the first marriages he conducted on his return was between McGilvery, the pilot, and Jean Mitchell, the daughter of the manager of the BP store. Eric also had a part to play in the arrival of newborn babies.

> On one occasion he had to make a crib for the newborn son of the Guinea Airways local manager. He constructed it from a piece of tarpaulin made into a navy-like hammock and secures inside a wooden VB beer case. The quickly finished crib was escorted up the main street by a proud crowd to the anxious mother.[1]

Gold mining was progressing rapidly. Much of the gold from Edie Creek had been extracted and Bulolo became the main centre of activity, with dredging replacing alluvial means. Mining companies were formed, such as New Guinea Goldfields (NGG) and Bulolo Gold Dredging (BGD).

New aerodromes were built at Salamaua and Bulolo. BDG were requesting a near perfect drome for their three-engine Junkers. One day Eric had a conversation with Vessy Brown, who was working on the Bulolo Drome. Vessy had the reputation of being the court jester of the goldfields. Interested in the progress that work on the airfield was making, Eric casually asked how things were going. Vessy replied, "We've only got to varnish each blade of grass then McGilvery will crack a Moth across its bow and then we'll be finished."

Once the airfields were completed, BGD began flying in dredges and NNG flew in mining machinery. Much of the development of the New Guinea goldfields was the brain child of Cecil John Levein. He had been a district officer in the early days of the Administration but had resigned to pursue his gold mining interests. One success had led to another for Levein, and with shares in NGG, BGD and Guinea Airways Limited he had become a wealthy man.

Various sporting activities were developing in the area. A cricket pitch had been put down on the Salamaua drome. Cricket fields had also sprung up at Wau, Lae and Bulolo and inter-settlement sport competition had started. Tennis, billiards and snooker were also played. At one gathering the players suggested perhaps they should have a trophy. C.J. Levein stood up and said he would give one.

It was Eric's bright idea that the trophy take the form of a native carrier carrying a pack. Levein agreed.

> We had this silver statuette of a native carrier with a tin of biscuits on his back mounted on a plinth which was a very handsome little trophy known as the *Levein Trophy*, and was played for by the various little settlements there.

BGD began production with two dredges. In the 1930s, inflation was high and the price of gold escalated, so the number of dredges eventually ballooned to eight. The organisation was very efficient and large quantities of gold were mined, ensuring a good profit for the company. The 5% royalty was welcome revenue for the Administration.

All the activity led to Lae becoming one of the busiest airports in the world for a time. In order to load the sections of the dredges and other heavy equipment, the top of the Junkers would be cut off and a crane used to lower the large item into the plane.

Although Levein was a major shareholder in the three companies, he did not take any part in their management. When in Salamaua he lived very simply in an iron hut, and when stores for Bulolo or Guinea Airways were needed, he would load them. This was followed by having a bottle of beer at the pub, then dinner and bed.

Sadly, he did not live to see the first dredge commence operations. He died suddenly of pneumococcal septicaemia on 20 January 1932 while on a visit to Melbourne. His death came as a shock to the communities in Salamaua and the gold towns. 'It cast quite a gloom over the place because Levein was the leading citizen there of the private citizens.'

In March 1931 Eric received news that a German prospector, Helmuth Baum, and eight of his native carriers had been killed by the Kukukuku people. Of all the tribes in PNG, the Kukukuku were the most vicious, hostile headhunters, and the most feared. They lived in the high mountains in the south western area of Morobe. The warriors had the septum of their nose pierced and through it wore a short piece of bone or bamboo. Their heads were shaven except for a top-knot on the crown from which a cloak of beaten bark hung down to the back of their knees. When they wrapped the cloak — the *mal* — around them it served both as a protection from the biting winds and rain in the mountains and as camouflage. Even at close range it could be hard to distinguish them from a tree stump. The *mal* had a third purpose, to conceal the stone club attached on the back of the wearer's waist band. They were able to draw out this lethal weapon as quick as a flash.

The Kukukuku also carried bows, arrows and wooden shields in full view. Their expressions were almost always fierce and menacing, and their way of speaking seemed to convey a state of constant anger.

A permit was required for a prospector to venture into the Kukukuku territory past the Upper Watut Valley, which is beyond the Bulolo Valley. Permits were only granted to experienced men of good character. Such a man was Baum, who had an excellent reputation over many years with his native workers for being kind, generous and peaceful. 'Treat a savage with kindness and you have nothing to fear' was Helmuth's philosophy.'[2]

His contact with the Kukukuku had been friendly and they often came to trade sweet potatoes and sugar cane for salt, axes and knives. They arrived one morning when Baum was sick with a fever and his native workers were unarmed. Seeing him defenceless, any semblance of friendliness vanished. They grabbed their clubs from under their cloaks and clubbed him to death as he lay in his bed. His native workers fled, but eight were caught and also killed.

On hearing of the massacre, Eric chartered three Junkers to take himself, Sampson, twelve native police and three weeks provisions to Surprise Creek near where the attack had happened. After hearing the story from some of the natives who had escaped, Eric set off with his patrol. They walked for eight days to reach the village nearest the site of the attack.

> Natives fled on our approach, going up and down the slopes at speed we couldn't hope to equal, their bark cloaks flowing out behind them. They slapped their sterns at us in the age-old gesture that is the New Guinea version of the 'raspberry'.

Accounts of the attack on Baum indicated that several different villages had been involved. The chance of apprehending the actual killers was small, and then escorting them back through the jungle to face trial would be fraught with danger. Overriding this was the ever-present risk that Eric's small team would be attacked. However, to Eric, his duty was clear.

> A District Officer has a further duty than the punishment of a single crime, however serious that crime may be. The country has to be brought under a rule of law, so that men may go about peacefully in the future. To walk away and do nothing would not bring that condition nearer.

Aware that the villagers could wait in the bush until the patrol left, Eric ordered the patrol to eat from the village gardens as well as from their own provisions. After ten days of their gardens being decimated, the Kukukuku could stand it no longer and seven of their people walked into the village. They were arrested and placed in handcuffs.

The next morning, they were taken to Baum's campsite and the murder was re-enacted. Although denying it through sign language, 'there was guilt in their eyes'.

The group set off on the return journey, but one of the prisoners escaped. He had a concealed knife and during the night had filed away at his handcuffs, which he finally managed to snap on the walk. The knife was discovered and removed from one of the other prisoners and left sticking in a tree. The long walk back and the shared night watches took a toll on all of them and all became thin. The carriers were let go at the Upper Watut and the rest of the party went on to Bulolo. Here a slimmer Eric, now sporting a beard, was not recognised.

Eric and the six prisoners flew to Salamaua the next day. One prisoner died from mouth cancer while in gaol and the other five escaped. Four were eventually recaptured, including one who had been caught by the Buang natives. He was tightly tied up and several injuries had been inflicted upon him. This had been done in revenge, as some of Baum's carriers who had been slaughtered were Buang people.

Unable to discover this man's name, Eric called him Joe. While in captivity, Joe learnt to speak some Pidgin. Eventually all the miscreants were taken back to their area and released. Some months later the unexpected happened:

> One day at Wau, a line of black capes came out of the bush, there was the sound of clucking speech and a crowd of Kukukuku's arrived at the District Office, peacefully, to trade sweet potatoes for knives and beads and salt. Their leader was Joe, come good at last.

The patrol had been a long and arduous one, taking six weeks in total. Eric was left fatigued and unwell. He developed severe recurrent cystitis and had to decrease his workload. There were no antibiotics in those days and he eventually went to Rabaul and 'had a serum made'. He was told to give up all alcohol and to drink barley water. He was not enamoured with barley water but did as he was told. Not one to forgo socialising, Eric would take his bottle of barley water down to the pub and drink it at the bar while his mates were having a beer. These measures took effect and Eric recovered.

After the patrol, other events became the concern of the District Office. A pilot called Les Trist went missing in a single-engine Junkers, and the Leahy brothers had been attacked on the headwaters of the Langemar by more Kukukukus.

Kyle led a patrol out to try to find Trist but was unsuccessful. Four months later a native stumbled across the wreck of the plane and reported it. Eric and Alan Cross went in to where Trist's plane had hit a mountain on the west side of the Wampet River. It appeared likely that Trist had been killed instantly in the crash, judging by the state of his skeleton and because the plane had been torn to pieces. They collected Trist's bones to send south for burial.

Mick and Pat Leahy were experienced and able bushmen who had crossed the Watut only to meet up with hostile Kukukuku. In a dawn attack, the Leahys were both wounded and were fortunate to escape with their lives. Patrols were sent out, but they made little impact.

In an attempt to improve the situation in the Kukukuku lands, the Administration established a post at Otibandi, a few miles to the west of the Watut. Mark Pitt was placed in charge and he built an airstrip that was just usable by Moth planes. The next objective was to find a site for a post and airstrip further inland. Keith McCarthy was chosen to lead the patrol into the heart of the unexplored Kukukuku territory. He took Lance-Corporal Anis as his second in command. In a vicious arrow attack by the cloaked natives, McCarthy, Anis and several police were wounded. Anis later died in Salamaua hospital. McCarthy was also taken to the hospital and operated on for the arrow wound in his abdomen. Lucky to have survived, he later joked about how it had ruined the beautiful symmetry of his navel.

During the year, Eric and other members of the Administration received visits from a member of the Commonwealth Public Service in order to reclassify the New Guinea Service, which had grown somewhat unwieldy. Eric was asked his age and replied that he was

32. He was told he was far too young for the job. Eric knew this was true but came up with the only answer he could. He said if they had anyone else who could do the job better, then appoint him and Eric would serve under him. Eric retained his position unassailed.

1932 brought with it the commencement of operations by the first dredge, which for Eric was a sad thing. A grand opening was held in March, attended by the Administrator and two directors, Banks and Griffin, from America. Mrs Banks broke a bottle of champagne across its bow, pressed a button and started the bucket line moving. It was just two months after the death of Cecil John Levein.

Economically, the dredge was a welcome advancement. The bottom had fallen out of the copra market and the country's revenue had dropped with it. Gold production remedied this considerably. By the end of the year, Bulolo opened its second dredge, although with not such a big fanfare but with a nice little party all the same.

Eric's competitive streak came to the fore again one day in the pub. He was back on the beer, which may have been a contributing factor, as might drinking with Jimmy Dykes, who had been a professional boxer. Eric judged that Jimmy had the hallmarks of an unsuccessful boxer — cauliflower ears and a squashed nose. Perhaps it was the beer talking, or just rashness, but remembering his fighting days in the Navy, Eric suggested a spar and Jimmy said yes.

All the drinkers in the bar trouped back to Eric's place where he had a couple of sets of gloves. The contest was set at three rounds and held on a flat grassy area outside the house. Eric knew he had to keep out of the way of Jimmy's punches, which he found wasn't difficult because Jimmy was not a very good boxer. Still if one of Jimmy's punches hit Eric he could really be hurt. Eric did his best to box and try to score points. He started to tire in the third round. The lace of one of his gloves came undone and he had to stop to have it laced up. Fortunately, standing nearby was Bill Kyle, the time keeper. Eric said, 'Call time, Bill.' Bill said, 'No, there is another minute to go.' Eric replied, 'Be blowed to that, you call time. I'm done.' Bill restarted the match and let it continue uneventfully for a few seconds before calling time. The referee, who was from Bulolo, scored the match as a draw, which was a welcome outcome from Eric's point of view.

Another gold discovery was made on the headwaters of the Ramu River. Eric went with Alan Ross, who was posted on the Markham River, on a patrol to Kainantu, where the gold had been found by Ned Rowlands. In Eric's eyes, Ned had the best ability in dealing with New Guineans he had ever seen. Rowlands had a natural calmness and manner that the natives responded to in a peaceful way. The trip was an interesting one for Eric, and while there he and the team built a very small drome.

It was while on that patrol that Eric felt he had lost some of the fitness of his youth. At 33 years of age he noticed that the spring had gone out of his step and he couldn't go up and down hills like he used to.

Eric went on leave at the end of 1932. His memories of his time in Salamaua were to remain among the most pleasant of his life. He was very proud of the accomplishment he and his staff had achieved in bringing the district back from a woeful state of mismanagement into a well run and efficiently functioning service. He reflected that they had had to deal with some of the most difficult natives in the Territory, but their paramount concern had been the welfare of all the New Guinea natives in the district.

Being on leave brought a certain amount of relief to Eric.

> As number one Kiap in a district I was under observation of natives all the time. They watched everything I did, saw who I talked to. Anything I said to any native was repeated and you felt you had eyes on you all your life. It was a great relief, for instance, to get on a tram where you're a fare to the conductor and nothing to anybody else.

This leave was the most personally important one to Eric. In Brisbane, on 10 January 1933, he married Nancy Lynette Echlin. Nancy had been born on 11 July 1897 to parents Captain Richard Boyd Echlin and Maude Letitia White, and was the niece of General Sir Cyril Brudenell White. The bride was a well-known social journalist with the *Brisbane Courier*.

Eric divulged little about his personal and family life in his oral history. We can speculate that he met Nancy during his leave in Brisbane at the end of 1929. As a social journalist, Nancy would have attended many functions and may have met Eric at one of them. Another possibility is that they met through a family connection. Eric's sister, Ada, had been a nurse at the General Hospital in Brisbane, and Nancy's sister, Gladys, was also a nurse.

It would appear that romance blossomed by correspondence from 1930–1932. It is not known whether Eric took a leaf out of his father's book and proposed by mail or whether he waited until he returned to Brisbane to propose in person.

Staff at the *Brisbane Courier* knew about the engagement prior to 9 December 1932. An article in the paper the following day reported how she had been presented with a canteen of silver cutlery and silver sandwich dish, suitably inscribed on behalf of Brisbane Courier Pty Ltd and staff. The article said that Nancy had endeared herself to all with whom she had worked for seven years and would be greatly missed.

After the wedding, friends and relatives were entertained at a small cocktail party. The couple honeymooned briefly on the Gold Coast before they boarded the *Montoro* bound for New Guinea on 14 January.

Eric had been promoted to District Officer permanently just before going on leave. Although shouldering the responsibilities of a DO in his five years at Salamaua, his rank had remained Acting DO. His new posting was Madang. The *Montoro* called at Salamaua so Eric and Nancy were able to collect his belongings on the way to their new home at Madang.

For many years Eric had one native servant called Bonnicky. 'Well, it was well known there that any bachelor's boy didn't take kindly to a missus'. Bonnicky had worked for George Whittaker while Eric was away on leave and Eric arranged for Bonnicky to continue to do so.

The newlyweds arrived at Madang without a servant, but with the help of borrowed home help they managed to unpack and settle in. Eventually they found a servant of their own.

Nancy, or Nan as she was known to Eric, had initial difficulty in adjusting. She didn't speak Pidgin and was unfamiliar with the local customs. 'And it was very difficult to get on just pointing at something and hoping the boy would rub it with a cloth instead of hitting it with an axe, but she got by.' Although the natives could understand some English, Eric thought that learning Pidgin was mandatory. The only way to do so was by talking to the locals until she had mastered it. 'She thought I was pretty hard that way as she had me to interpret.'

The Administrator, General Wisdom, retired in June 1933 and was replaced by General Griffiths. A new Department of District Services had been created and Eric and many others hoped and expected that Walstab would be made the head. Due to Commonwealth seniority another officer was appointed and Walstab became the Superintendent of Police.

In Madang, members of Eric's staff were: as ADO, Woodman, then Gerry MacDonald; and as patrol officers, Jock McKay and Jack Read. Eric was impressed by Jack's determination right from their first meeting. Jack had come from the Sepik, where he had suffered severe dysentery and really should have been on sick leave. Going on sick leave actually cost quite a lot of money at that time. Eric surmised that, as a married man, Jack did not have sufficient money to go on leave and was determined to stay and continue working while he recovered, which he did.

Eric's system of running a district was to allocate an area to one man and leave him in charge of it. Jack Read was given Bogia, Jock McKay was posted in the northern centre region, and the ADO would do the area around Madang, the shelf and Karkar Island. Eric needed someone for the Rai Coast and he was the only one left for the job.

After about a month at Madang, Eric had to go out with Jack Read to establish a patrol post at Bogia. That meant leaving Nan on her own, which she thought was very unfair and rather heartless. Eric claimed he was only being cruel to be kind and that she would learn more about the natives and the running of the house, if he was away for a while. Apparently 'it worked out all right' but was a time that was never totally forgiven by Nan.

The Rai coast was a very arduous area to patrol, although not densely populated. The mountains came right down to the coast. The easiest way to go from one inland village to another was to go back down to the coast, rather than cross the steep ridges and deep gorges.

Eric caught up with an old friend, Blue Draper, who was now living in the district. Blue had left his dog with Eric when he had departed from Wewak to go to the goldfields. Eric offered Blue his dog back, but Draper said the dog was now Eric's to keep.

Not long after his arrival in Madang, Eric experienced his first hanging. The native had been tried by Eric's predecessor and sentenced to death. It was a job that Eric hated, but told himself the punishment would act as a deterrent to others. He felt that as DO and an ex-sailor used to tying knots, the best he could do was to see the offender was at least despatched quickly.

The Depression was still having an adverse effect on the price of copra. Those who had bought plantations from the Expropriation Board were allowed to struggle through without having to make any

NEW GUINEA PRE-WORLD WAR II: 1928-1939

payments on their properties. This allowed copra to continue to be produced and the owners to remain on their plantations.

Madang's lovely harbour and beautiful surrounding islands gave the ex-sailor the desire to build a boat. Eric had a log towed from the Rai coast. He employed two native pit-saw men to saw it into planks. However, dressing the timber proved to be too big a job so Eric did a deal with the Catholic Mission, which owned a sawmill. They dressed one half of the timber in exchange for the other half of the timber. Finding time to work on the boat was difficult and not much progress was made so Eric engaged a Chinese boat builder, who was very good, if a little slow.

General McNicoll took over as Administrator and travelled round more than any previous Administrator had done. He visited Madang and spent a couple of days with Eric and Nan.

There were changes in the staff as various people went on leave. Keith McCarthy temporarily came as relieving ADO. The District Office kept up steady patrols to the peaceful villages and sent out extra ones when there was trouble. There was no set plan to open up the country. They simply did not have enough staff.

Having seen the advantages of flying in the Morobe District, Eric decided Madang would benefit from having an airfield. He presented his idea to the Administrator and in due course was granted authority to proceed.

Late in 1934 Nan suddenly became ill with severe abdominal pain. One doctor suspected appendicitis but another was not convinced. The diagnosis was later found to be diverticulitis. Nan went back to Australia, where she stayed until Eric had leave and joined her. While in Brisbane, Eric purchased parts for his boat. When the couple returned to Madang, he was able to oversee its completion.

Work started in earnest on the aerodrome. They had begun with very little in the way of tools, just a few picks and shovels. 'We gave a great cheer, we really felt mechanised, when we got a dozen wheelbarrows to help with it.' The ground was upraised coral and the tops of the ridges needed to be chopped off and the hollows filled in. Eventually a professional builder was sent to finish the construction.

Eric took a patrol to the Ramu River and on the way back he fell ill. He didn't know what it was but it didn't feel like malaria. He became so sick that he had his carriers stretcher him to the coast where he was met by a small motor boat and taken to Madang.

In all probability Eric was suffering from scrub typhus, although the illness was not known in New Guinea at that time. Its existence had been first recognised in Japan in 1931, but more cases occurred in Wau shortly after Eric's episode, which led to diagnoses being made in the Territory.

Scrub typhus was a result of a bite from a mite related to the tick family. It looked like, and was thought of as, a tiny tick, although it was known by the patrol as a bush mokka. The tiny creatures lived in the grass and attached themselves to the skin of humans, under their clothing, particularly round the ankles. A little red lump developed, which itched intensely, especially in the warmth of a bed at night. Eric had lots of mokka bites on this patrol and did not think much about it. He remembered that one had looked black, but it didn't feel any different from the others.

Scrub typhus is a mite-borne disease caused by *Orientia tsutsugamushi* and is transmitted by trombiculid mite larvae. After an incubation period of 6 to 21 days, fever, headache, muscle aches and enlarged lymph nodes suddenly develop. At the onset of fever, a black oval-shaped scab, called an eschar, often forms at the site of the bite. A rash can appear on the trunk and spread to the limbs. In severe cases of scrub typhus, pneumonia, acute renal failure, encephalitis, and multiple organ failure can occur and result in fatalities.

Eric was extremely ill and almost at death's door. One morning he heard dynamite being exploded and he knew what it was for. The cemetery at Madang consisted of upraised coral and was extremely hard to dig. A few sticks of dynamite were used to shatter the coral before digging the graves. Eric knew the hole was being prepared for him. 'I rather set my teeth and said you won't get me in there.' As we know they didn't, but he still had a very hard battle to fight in order to cheat death. Luckily for Australia, his determination to live won through, or perhaps Fate was once more playing a part to ensure his survival so Eric could take on his vital role in the future.

As one of the consequences of having malaria is its likely recurrence when a person's resistance has been decreased due to another illness, accident or stress, Eric was soon suffering from malaria as well. Having both scrub typhus and malaria made his survival even more miraculous.

A miner, named Normie Neil, called in to see a weak Eric and told him there was a vacancy for the position of Warden of Wau and suggested Eric should apply for it. This was a huge decision for Eric to make. There were several factors to consider. It would mean leaving the District Services, which gave the best chance of career advancement, but Eric was starting to feel that he had lost his ambition for promotion. The highest position was Administrator and most likely a politician would be chosen, so the chances of reaching that level were remote. Even if it was possible, Eric did not fancy the life it would entail and he thought Nan wouldn't have liked it either. It would involve a lot of entertaining officials with whom they had little in common and there would be too little privacy.

A life in Wau was more appealing. It had a wonderful climate and seemed like an ideal place to recover from his recent serious illness. In some circles, the Warden's job was touted as being very important and demanding, but Eric thought it probably was not as arduous as it was claimed to be. With the balance in favour of Wau, Eric put in an application.

Sick leave was essential and, with Nan, he headed to Queensland in August 1935. On the ship going down was Sir George Pearce, Minister for the Territory. He had completed a visit around PNG and was returning home. With him was Reg Halligan. Eric confided to Reg his decision to apply for the job of Warden.

During the three months on leave, the couple spent time, in September, with Nancy's uncle and cousin, the Warren-Whites, and their families at Mt. Tamborine, and then with her parents in Clayfield, Brisbane. They returned to Madang at the end of October on the *Macdhui* to find that his application had been accepted and he was the new Warden of Wau.

The climate at Wau was nearly perfect, with warm days and pleasantly cool nights. If anything, it was almost too perfect. Some people of European descent found they missed the marked change in seasons from summer to winter.

Eric was still fairly weak despite his sick leave. In fact the illness was to have a permanent effect on his health. 'I was never really robust after that attack of scrub typhus.'

Fortunately, Eric found the job of Warden interesting. In the first couple of months he had to deal with a strike of the engine drivers at the Edie Creek mine, and there was a new find on the Wampet. It turned out to be a small find, but initially there was a big rush, with lots of pegging out going on, so Eric was kept very busy. After this burst of activity, the pace settled down and life became more like the way Eric had envisaged it would be.

The inspector of mines was Mr. Fry, who was a sort of offsider to Eric. They saw eye to eye on administration with both having a policy of not interfering with the mining unless there was criminal activity or a life was being endangered. Any complaints could be heard at the court over which Eric presided. It was his first experience with solicitors, who he felt made things a little easier but not significantly different.

There was a little more social life in Wau than at a district office post. Finding work was not very busy, Eric turned his attention to making a golf course. He gathered nine others, and together the ten foundation members each put in a fiver to provide the slender 50 pounds that started the Wau Golf Club.

Eric found a satisfactory means to provide builders for the course. The miners sent their labourers to Wau to be paid off and returned home. They had to be sent down a few days early as it was not known beforehand when an aircraft would be available to transport them to the ship that would take them home. The labourers would receive their pay and usually have to sit around waiting in Wau for two or three days. Eric suggested they fill in the time making the golf course. They would be fed, paid at casual rates and it gave them something to do. All agreed, and it didn't take long to get six holes finished. Once they got six holes, a lot of people started playing. After that it was easy, and they got nine holes.

> They were short, but they were holes and later Billy Hughes, when he was on a visit, played a round on it just to say he had played on a golf course at Wau. Because he had been very instrumental in Australia getting the Mandate, he was very proud to see any development that went on.

One interesting water rights case came before Eric. After a lot of argument and expert evidence he eventually gave a decision. When both sides immediately appealed he thought it must have been the correct one. After thinking it over, they both withdrew their appeals, further convincing Eric that in at least one court case he had got it right.

Another role that Eric took on was president of the Returned Sailors & Soldiers Imperial League of Australia (Later to become the Returned and Services League of Australia). The RSSILA held quite large functions. A sports day was held every Anzac Day, 25 April, and returned servicemen came from all over the goldfields to attend the big commemorative and fun-filled gathering.

Eric was optimistic that war was unlikely, but with a lot of speculation and emotion being generated around him, he decided to write to the Naval Board in April 1939 and ask to have his name removed from the retired list and placed on the emergency list.

He and Nan went on leave in 1939. Towards the end of their holiday, Eric was in a shop buying shoes in readiness for their return. His attention was caught by a newspaper placard announcing Hitler and Stalin had signed a non-aggression pact on 23 August. He swore. He knew he would not be returning to Wau.

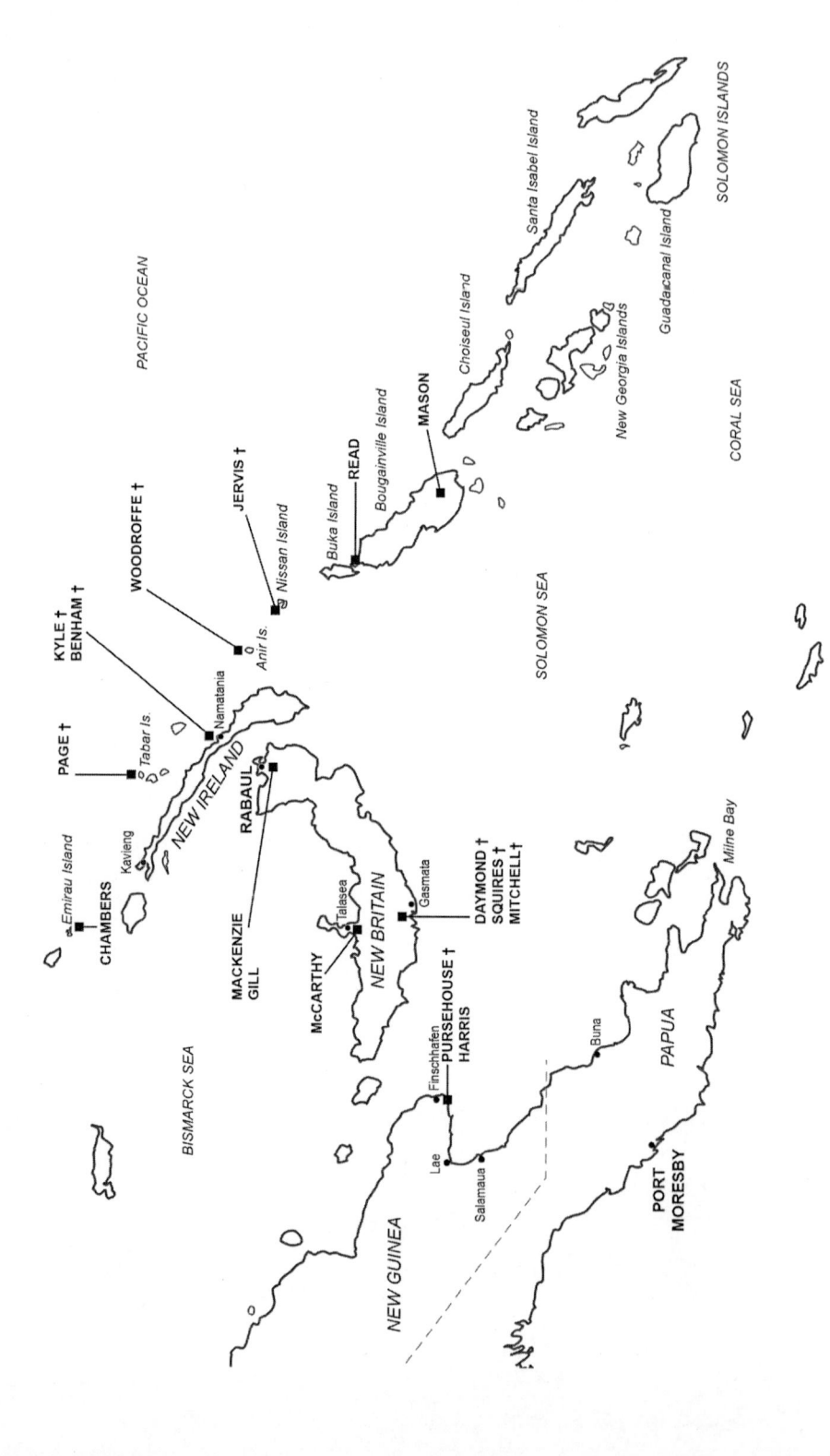

Positions of some of the Coastwatchers at the Beginning of the Japanese Invasion, 1942

CHAPTER 6

THE WWII COASTWATCHERS: THE BEGINNING

Many decades have passed since the Coastwatchers of the South Pacific sent their crucial messages, saved countless lives and helped to change the course of history. Yet in Australia, the land that benefitted most from their courageous sacrifices, they are little known.

Why is this so? Is it because the name The Coastwatchers conveys a totally inadequate picture of the impressive array of feats these men of valour performed? Perhaps names like Super Spies, Splendid Security Agents and Spectacular Saviours would provide a more accurate depiction of their amazing activities.

As Eric Feldt threw his hat into the arena of another war he was aware of the importance of having a surveillance network operating in the lands bordering the north-east of Australia. He could not have known how vital it would be to have a team of tough and trustworthy individuals in place, but as their leader he would have suspected that when the chips were down they would have rolled with the punches and come through as victorious heroes.

At the end of World War I the Australian Naval Board established a Coastwatching Organisation around the coast of Australia and in the adjacent island territories so that in the event of war suspicious sightings could be reported. It relied mainly on Customs Officers supplied with a code for reporting. However, much of the coastline was not covered due to lack of population and the distance between ports.

Fortunately for future developments, in 1934 Rupert 'Cocky' Long, Eric's friend from naval days, was appointed to Naval Intelligence as District Intelligence Officer in Sydney. He found the Naval Intelligence Centre poorly organised and underfunded and set about restructuring it. Rupert perceived the need to enlarge the existing coastwatching system. In 1936 he was promoted to Assistant Director of Naval Intelligence (ADNI) in Melbourne. Here, more good fortune appeared in the shape of Walter Brooksbank, a public servant who had worked in naval intelligence since 1922. Both men were passionate about intelligence work and also about the importance of establishing an effective coastwatching organisation. One area of vital importance was the chain of islands to the north-east of Australia. They were like a gateway should an enemy approach from that direction.

Rupert Long, while concerned at the increasing threat of Germany, thought that the greatest danger was Japan, whose 'Southwards Advance' policy appeared to focus attention on New Guinea and other island territories.

Eric described Rupert as being:

> A leader rather than a driver, and, if anything, over indulgent of the faults of his juniors. Years of secretive work had developed in him an indirect, oblique approach to problems... Experience had given him a wide knowledge and he combined a capacity for working long hours with an unfailing good humour. Above all other virtues, he could leave anything alone if it functioned properly.[1]

Meanwhile, Eric's old friend, John Collins, had joined the Navy Office in 1938 as Assistant Chief of Naval Staff and Director of Naval Intelligence. On joining, John was briefed by Rupert on the state of naval intelligence.

In 1939 Rupert gave John his opinion that a new Naval Intelligence Centre was needed in Port Moresby. From there the coastwatching could be expanded throughout the islands. John Collins fully concurred. Naturally they both had Eric in mind for

THE WWII COASTWATCHERS: THE BEGINNING

the job. 'Eric was the logical but nonetheless inspired choice for this pressing task.'[2]

A report came from New Guinea in March 1939 that the new 'Nazi pilot' of the Junkers aircraft at the Lutheran Mission at Lae had said that Germany would occupy New Guinea in September. He was suspected of taking aerial photographs and sending them to Germany for forwarding to Japan.[3]

In May 1939, Rupert Long and John Collins reported to the Chief of Naval Staff (CNS) Admiral Sir Ragnar Colvin about the need for naval intelligence in Port Moresby. Colvin strongly agreed with the proposal. Finance for the venture had to be approved by the minister. For various reasons this took months, but at the end of August things began to move fast.

After the German-Russian pact of 23 August, Emergency List Officers were ordered to stand by. On 24th August, Cabinet and the Naval Board began to view the prospect of war seriously and finally approved finance for the intelligence centre in Port Moresby. On 25 August, John Collins divested himself of the role of Director of Naval Intelligence, making way for Rupert with his greater experience in intelligence to be appointed DNI. On 26 August, Rupert sent Eric a telegram asking if he would take the job of Staff Officer Intelligence Port Moresby with rank of Lieutenant-Commander, to which Eric agreed. On 28 August, the Admiralty asked that RAN ships be put on a war footing. On 1 September, Germany invaded Poland. On 3 September, Britain declared war on Germany and Australia followed suit.

Eric may have 'known' he would not be returning to Wau but was given reason to be uncertain about that. He received a telegram from the Navy saying, 'Your services are not required for the present. You will be advised when needed.' On 4 September he asked Rupert what was happening.

Rupert needed Eric immediately and was determined to get him. On 5 September Rupert wrote to the Chief of Naval Staff and the Finance Minister explaining the need. The Naval Board had approved the appointment but the Minister for Defence, rather overloaded with work from the escalating situation, had not signed it. On 7 September an anxious Rupert requested a decision on Port Moresby be made urgently as the officer he had in mind for the position was due to return to his civilian job the next day and would be lost if a decision was not made immediately. Eric received his appointment on 8 September and flew to Melbourne shortly after to confer with Rupert and Brooksbank about the task ahead.

Walter Brooksbank became known as B1 to distinguish him from his younger brother Lieutenant Gilbert Brooksbank, B2, who also joined Rupert's team.

Rupert and B1 had worked tirelessly to revitalise and reconstitute the Coastwatchers in Australia. Brooksbank had written the *Coastwatching Guide*. Eric paid tribute to Rupert and B1, 'who had borne the long struggle to build up the coastwatching organization, [and] provided me with all the information — a considerable amount — which would be of use to me.'[4]

Although to Rupert's mind the one man with the experience, know-how and energy to provide the realisation of his vision of the vital surveillance set up was Eric, this was to be achieved with virtually no staff or equipment. Eric's new title of Staff Officer Intelligence at Port Moresby did little to signify the importance of the position. He was allocated 200 pounds to cover the costs incurred in travelling throughout the territories while seeking to enlist the services of civilian volunteers.

The islands were under the jurisdiction of four different governments — Papua, Mandated New Guinea, the British Solomon Islands Protectorate, and the Condominium Government with the French of the New Hebrides. These Territories, together with the northern part of Queensland, comprised what was known as the North East Area.

As the Coastwatching Organisation had developed in peace time Australia, its means of communication was by telegraph. There were no telegraph lines in the islands of the North East Area. Radio was the only means of communication. There were no railways and less than five hundred miles of trafficable road in the whole chain of islands. However, there was considerable air traffic in Mandated New Guinea and the existing radio communication was well developed.

In Papua and New Guinea all radio was managed by Amalgamated Wireless of Australia (AWA). The Australian government owned 51% of the shares so had control. In the Solomons, the Administration had its own radio.

Radio sets had been developed by AWA and the most recent model of teleradio in 1939 was a Type 3B. It consisted of a transmitter, a receiver and a loudspeaker housed in three metal boxes, each about two feet by one foot by one foot (60x30x30cm). Power was provided by a car battery charged by a small petrol engine that weighed about 70 pounds (32kg). In Eric's view 'It was a grand instrument which stood up to heat, wet and amateur handling.'[5] Its size and weight were disadvantages, as twelve to sixteen carriers were needed to transport it. However, at the time, it was the best and most compact set available. It had a range of up to 400 miles by voice and 600 miles when transmitting by Morse Code.

There were four transmission frequencies, which were controlled by crystals. To increase security the Naval Board had special crystals called "X" crystals produced. These gave the advantage of being able to operate on frequencies not normally used. Because they were small they could be sent by airmail and were easy to install. The receiver covered the middle frequencies that allowed the operator to hear news broadcasts.

After spending nearly a week in Melbourne with Rupert and Walter becoming *au fait* with existing knowledge and making further plans, Eric flew back to Brisbane on 15 September. He touched base with the Staff Officer Intelligence Brisbane and arranged payments.

While in Brisbane, Eric took the opportunity to spend time with Peter and Gussie. His father's health was failing, and when Eric said goodbye he was aware that it might be for the last time. This thought proved correct. Peter Feldt died on 15 October, aged 86. Eric was at this time on a mission too distant and too important for him to be able to return for his father's funeral. For Gussie it was a big wrench to lose her partner and 'best mate' of 56 years.

Eric flew into Port Moresby on 21 September. Lieutenant Commander R.B.A. Hunt RAN, the Naval Officer in Charge (NOIC), was building up a base. After an hour's talk informing Hunt of the plans, Eric flew onto Rabaul to begin work on the outer perimeter, which was obviously the most urgent sector.

In Rabaul, Eric met with the Administrator, Sir Walter McNicoll, whom he knew from his days as a District Officer. Once acquainted with the Navy's initiative, McNicoll promised every assistance, and from then on the New Guinea Administration gave the Coastwatchers the utmost help with personnel and materials.

Eric knew personal contact with potential Coastwatchers was of paramount importance. 'Taking a sheaf of printed coastwatching instructions with me, I set out to visit every man who had a teleradio, to teach him how to code in Playfair, to tell him what to report, and to impress on him that speed in reporting was the prime essential.'[6] The encounters worked both ways. Not only could they learn one-to-one and gain more confidence in their leader, but also he could assess their personalities as an aid to future evaluation of their reports.

On 25 September Eric boarded the Chinese schooner *Magai* and alighted at Ululpatur on the west coast of New Ireland. Then, partly on foot and partly by lorry, he made his way to Namatanai. The following day he travelled to a further station, 2 miles (3km) by lorry and another 25 miles (40km) by bicycle, carrying a haversack and a few personal belongings. The next day he journeyed another 20 miles (32 km). He then made the return trip to Namatanai the same way as he had come. On the round trip he had successfully achieved his mission of recruiting, distributing copies of the *Coastwatching Guide* and teaching the newly assigned Coastwatchers their duties.

Next it was on to Kavieng by car, stopping on the way at plantations to enlist more Coastwatchers. The Administrator placed MV *Leander* at his disposal for his trip from Kavieng to Manus and back to Rabaul. Eric signed up the captain of the *Leander* as a Coastwatcher. After sailing to Pak Island and Manus, he returned to Rabaul on 6 October. His previous work in the Territory meant that many of the men he asked to become Coastwatchers were friends or acquaintances. 'I saw nearly everybody and nearly everybody saw me. I already knew more than half of those I met, and all were helpful.' He reported to Rupert that he had travelled 600 miles by sea, 200 miles by car and about 90 miles on foot or bicycle.

As well as enlisting Coastwatchers, Eric was responsible for collecting information. He reported the suspicious behaviour of the Japanese captain of the schooner *Edith*, a trochus fisherman who had long periods of bringing in surprisingly small amounts of shell, and a Japanese resident who had been sending letters to a naval address in Japan.

On 7 October, Eric left on the *Malaita* for Tulagi in the Solomons. The Acting Resident Commissioner, Mr Johnson, lent him an auxiliary vessel, the *Tulagi*, and Eric set off for Vanikoro. He traversed most of the group of islands, including Maka, where he met the Reverend Thomas Wade; Ulawa Island, to contact Albert M.Andresen; then Numa Numa, Kieta and Buka.

They struck bad weather along the way and made hardly any headway for 28 hours. Ultimately, the port bulwarks were damaged by the sea and they had to run before the wind to shelter at San

Cristobal. They were unable to make it to Vanikoro due to lack of fuel. Eric changed to another schooner to visit other islands.

Eric's next step was to make a survey flight by flying boat from Rabaul to Tulagi via Kieta, Faisi and Gizo, taking course over Anir, Nissan and Buka Passage. This was to see the area from the air and to test Coastwatcher efficiency. He asked Coastwatchers to report any flying boat activity. Buka reported him before he arrived in Kieta.

It became obvious to Eric that the Coastwatcher line of defence could be likened to a fence extending across the North East Area. But the fence they had built had a significant flaw. 'The position will be that a fence has been put up but the gate not shut, the gate being the space between New Ireland and Buka'. On 17 October, Rupert replied, 'These arrangements are noted with considerable satisfaction, and it is pleasing to find you were able to cover so much territory in so short time.'[7]

To close the gate and secure the fence Coastwatchers needed to be in position on the islands of Anir and Nissan. With the Navy supplying a teleradio, a plantation manager, C.C. Jervis, on Nissan, agreed to watch from there. As planes were more likely to take a route over Anir, this island was considered the more important and a decision was made to install a naval rating on it as a Coastwatcher. Chief Yeoman of Signals, S.Lamont, was chosen. Lamont was Irish and an old sailor with no experience of life on an isolated island. He was flown in and a temporary camp was set up for him. Then he was left alone, where he managed to adjust to his surroundings and carried out his watch very ably.

On 30 November, Eric left Port Moresby for Salamaua by Carpenter Airlines. The following day he flew to Madang by Mandated Airlines to instruct DO Oakly, then he went on to Wewak to see Kassa Townsend, who was DO. On 3 December he chartered a Fox Moth from Parers Air Transport to But to meet K. Parer. At Aitape a crosswind prevented landing and the plane flew on to Tadji. Eric walked three hours back to Aitape to see

ADO H.R. Niall. The next day he walked back to Tadji, then flew back to Wewak and Nubia. He was picked up along the coast by the government schooner *Nubia* and taken to Boia to see his best friend, ADO Alan Fairlie 'Bill' Kyle. From there he went on to Madang and other outposts.

On a trip to Salamaua on a Mandated Airlines plane, the tip of the port propeller shattered. Although the pilot feared he would have to land on a beach, he managed to land on the airfield with only one engine.

Eric chartered a small ketch, *Siassi*, to go to Rooke Island to see Reverend A.P.H. 'Harold' Freund, an Australian born Lutheran Missionary whose parents were also Australian born. Freund had agreed to be a Coastwatcher. Unfortunately, his German surname became an issue for some of the civil officials. At the onset of war some of the Germans in New Guinea, including some Lutheran Missionaries, were members of the Nazi party. They had been quickly interned. When Eric proposed to make Freund a Coastwatcher, 'A high civil official said, horror in every syllable: "But he spells his name F_R_E_U_N_D". I could only reply, weakly, by spelling my own.'[8] Eric thought that Freund was a very sincere man and undoubtedly a loyal one and had no hesitation in handing him a copy of the *Coastwatching Guide*.

On the return from Rooke Island, Eric called at Finschhafen and took on native passengers for Salamaua, which helped to reduce the charter cost. Of his original 200 pound allowance, he had 43 pounds and 16 shillings remaining.

Eric returned to Port Moresby and stayed there for a few weeks. During this time he wrote reports and recovered from his exertions. A report sent on 19–20 December said:

> Should it be thought that I have overused aircraft, I would like to make it plain that I take no pleasure in flying over routes on which there are no emergency landing grounds, in single engine planes ... The Coast Watching Organisation in New Guinea, the Solomon

Islands and Papua is now sufficiently advanced to anticipate that movements of Foreign Warships or suspicious movements of Merchant Vessels will be reported.[9]

With the more important northern region having been completed, attention was turned to the New Hebrides, lying south east of the Solomons. Captain R.D. Blandy was the Admiralty Reporting Officer in the New Hebrides. He was asked to set up a network in co-operation with the RAN.

In Port Morseby conditions remained meagre but they were fortunate with the staff members. Writer Carden was appointed to keep office records. His reliable memory was an asset for the team. James Connal Howard 'Connal' Gill from Brisbane was a valuable addition. He had enlisted in the RANR in July1939 and had been sent as secretary to Hunt in September. He was a very tall young telegraphist who was also a recently qualified solicitor. Connal became interested in the Coastwatchers and assisted Eric when he was in Moresby, doing much of the office work when Eric was away visiting Coastwatchers.

Shortly before the war with Germany, the Army had established a small military force at Port Moresby, manning two six-inch guns, and at the outbreak of war, a squadron of R.A.A.F., with two Empire flying boats and two smaller aircraft, was moved there, so all three of the services were represented.

By the end of 1939 Eric had sent a comprehensive report to Rupert detailing the structure, location and names of all the enrolled civilian Coastwatchers. The network extended over half a million square miles.

So began a series of letters which flowed between the two classmates for over five years of the war. Eric's letters to Rupert always began with his old college nickname 'Dear Cocky…'

> Rupert was keenly aware of Eric's intense character and at times strong emotions. Eric had maintained his lack of patience for 'stool polishers' from his Rabaul days. This shortcoming was more than

offset by his peerless talents and knowledge for his most vital work. Tensions between the men did exist as Rupert tried to keep up with Eric's demands, but humour and goodwill were manifest.[10]

The importance of the Coastwatchers observations being received quickly was obvious. To prevent delay in reception of vital messages, loudspeakers were kept at all times switched on in Rabaul, Port Moresby and Thursday Island to receive any signal sent on 'X' frequency.

Eric assessed that in addition to the teleradios in existence, an extra eighteen radios were needed in New Guinea, the Solomons and the New Hebrides. These were requested and eventually supplied by the Royal Australian Navy. Assistance in distributing the teleradios was provided by the RAAF and the Administrators of the Territories. Despite the team working as fast as possible, it was August 1940 before all teleradios were in place.

Despite the need for a defensive line, the importance of the Coastwatchers did have some detractors:

> Many officers made fun of the DNI's scheme for civilians with little wireless sets and a schoolboy cipher, but Long had the loyalty of subordinates and generally the support of the CNS Colvin, and of his classmate, Captain Joseph Burnett, who had been ACNS since Collins left to take command of *Sydney* in October. While Feldt tracked around the islands, Long fought the battles in Melbourne for money and equipment. Some of these, say men from Navy Office, were long and bloody, and they made some highly placed personal enemies for Long.[11]

The essential elements in the field for coastwatching operations were the teleradio, the Coastwatchers themselves and the native scouts and carriers. The linchpin on which the success of the venture relied was the ability of a Coastwatcher to interact with both his native employees and the natives living in the many villages throughout the territory.

In 1939 the importance of these factors may not have been as apparent as they were to become in the future. Most of the

Coastwatchers thought the set up was a necessary precaution which may never be used, but they kept up regular transmission of the practice signals they had been given to make sure everything was in order. The native workers had little part to play except when teleradios needed to be moved or if they were asked to report any unusual sightings. The only enemy vessels the Coastwatcher might expect to see were German raiders.

'Of course, if Japan entered the war...'

Past experience during times of war had shown the need for co-operation between the Navy, Army and Air Force services. In Melbourne, an Area Combined Headquarters (ACH) was formed and an ACH followed in Port Moresby '... as it had authority to initiate operations against an enemy, it was arranged that all local intelligence should be passed to ACH Port Moresby as well as Melbourne.' This meant that an intelligence officer had to be at Moresby but maintaining the efficiency of the widespread Coastwatchers could not be done without travel. Rupert wrote to Eric suggesting an assistant and would Hugh Mackenzie do?

'Would Mackenzie do?' Eric was ecstatic. He could think of no one more suitable than his old friend from Naval College days. Since leaving the Navy in 1920, Hugh had spent most of his time in PNG. He was far beyond anyone Eric could have hoped for.

> He had spent most of the intervening years in New Guinea and Papua, at first a rolling stone in schooners and later as a planter at Meggi, on Cape Hoskins, near Talasea in New Britain, His experience of the North East Area qualified him ideally for intelligence work and his likeable personality was assurance that others would work with him, He was conscientious and thorough in an unsystematic way, and occasionally would do something quite illogical. He had none of the qualities of salesmanship or showmanship whatsoever. In appearance he was of medium height, fair and sturdily built, looking then, much younger than his forty years[12]

Eric quickly sent a request for his appointment and Hugh joined him in November 1940 with the rank of Acting Lieutenant, RAN.

In December, two German raiders that had sunk ships and taken the passengers and crew on board as prisoners landed at Emirau Island, north of Kavieng. More than 500 prisoners were offloaded and made their way by boat to Kavieng. The DO there, who was a Coastwatcher, signalled their arrival. Arrangements were promptly made to pick them up. Hugh was sent to Kavieng and he and Eric were soon very busy collecting information from the passengers and crew about the appearance of the raiders, their armaments and the routes they had followed.

A decision was made to move ACH from Port Moresby to Townsville, and this was done in May 1941. With the move, Eric's title was changed to Supervising Intelligence Officer (SIO). The title remained that of the officer in charge of the Coastwatchers in the North East Area for the rest of the war. In Townsville, Eric's office was a back room with a staff of one Civil Assistant, K L 'Paddy' Murray. Paddy 'enjoyed best using his encyclopedic knowledge of North Queensland to obtain the unorthodox supplies we required later on.'[13]

With the commencement of ACH Townsville, Eric found himself Acting Naval Officer in Charge for three months, until the position was taken over by Commander VC Eddy, who had been in Port Moresby.

> Eddy was a good friend to the Coastwatchers — a short, baldish, competent man who was plump when he arrived but slowly lost weight late on, under the strain, until he was positively sylph-like.[14]

The officer in charge of the RAAF was Air-Commodore FA Lukis, and Wing-Commander WC Garing was his Senior Staff Officer, who, along with other RAAF officers, later did much for the Coastwatchers.

A Combined Operational Intelligence Centre (COIC) was formed at ACH Townsville. It consisted of officers from the three services working together to evaluate and collate intelligence into a form that could readily be understood by the operational staff.

Eric was concerned about the military and legal standing of the Coastwatchers. On a visit to Melbourne he discussed this with Rupert. The result was that the civilian status of the Coastwatchers was to continue. However, it was decided that naval Staff Officers Intelligence be appointed to key positions. It was recognised that the civil officers of the Administration were often overloaded with their own affairs during times of emergency.

The postings were: Rabaul, Lt Mackenzie RAN; Thursday Island, Lt-Cdr Crawford RANR; Tulagi, Sub-Lt Macfarlan RANVR; Vila, Lt Bullock RANVR and Port Moresby Sub-Lt Gill RANVR.

Connal Gill had been uncommissioned when he had commenced working in Port Moresby. At that stage the Naval Board could not bear anyone being commissioned without having completed a required course. Eric recommended he be promoted, and Rupert fought for it. In October 1940 Gill passed an examination as an accountant and became Paymaster Sub-Lieutenant in 1941.

In July 1941 Sub-Lieutenant Donald S Macfarlan arrived in Townsville on his way to Tulagi.

> Here this dark, sturdy man with an upturned nose and confident voice first entered the picture. He had been an assistant purser in the merchant service in his youth and had later been a successful businessman. He had the directness of the business executive, a forthright extrovert in his early thirties, who knew nothing about the Solomons and little about what he was expected to do, but would learn.[15]

Expecting that if Japan were to enter the war it would be in August or thereabouts, Eric visited the bases to see if all was in readiness. Connal Gill had Port Moresby well organised, Hugh in Rabaul had been forced to take on other naval work in addition to his Coastwatcher responsibilities and needed more staff.

THE WWII COASTWATCHERS: THE BEGINNING

Eric lived with Don Macfarlan in Tulagi for about a fortnight, explaining what duties were expected of him. It was also a chance for Eric to become acquainted with the latest member of his team. Lack of staff at Tulagi meant that keeping a full-time watch was impossible. The RAAF had a base on Tanambogo Island in Tulagi Harbour. Already aware of the value of Coastwatchers reports, they arranged to keep an 'X' frequency watch.

It was in November 1941 that Lieutenant H W Bullock took up his appointment at Vila, but Eric was unable to see him then. Sub-Lieutenant G Lockhart arrived in Townsville for training to be Hugh's assistant, but developed dysentery and Connal was sent to Rabaul instead. Lieutenant J H Paterson RANR was appointed to Port Moresby. Eric's description of him was:

> He had demonstrated his remarkable memory for ships. Later, he was to show, that he had a sane, competent brain and considerable adaptability. In appearance he was a fat young man, and a beard which he grew was not a success except in length.[16]

By the end of November 1941, the Coastwatchers existed as a chain across the islands that could signal sightings of intruders both to local forces and to a distant high command. There was, however, still a grave weakness: Australia lacked sufficient military force to back up its intelligence screen.

The Army had little more than a battalion stationed at Rabaul and the same at Port Moresby. If the enemy did decide to invade, the coastwatching bases might be occupied and the chain broken. Some links in the chain might remain, some of which might be in enemy-occupied territory. From these, important reports might possibly get through.

The question of what should be done in the event of an invasion had been considered. Those Coastwatchers who were naval officers could be ordered to stay in their area, taking to the bush if necessary. No such orders could be given to the civilian members of the organisation. They had been told to bury their teleradios and escape.

However, Eric had privately discussed the question with many of them and told them their services might be of greater value if they remained. The decision whether they did or not was entirely up to them.

To 'go bush' was not a simple matter. All components of the teleradio and enough supplies for the Coastwatcher and his carriers had to be carried, often over rough tracks through the jungle. Local natives were needed as carriers, and extra food might be needed from local village gardens, so co-operation from the villages was necessary and experience in interacting with them was essential, as was being able to speak Pidgin. Living in the wild also carried the risk of accidents and diseases such as malaria, dysentery and scrub typhus.

When he was still stationed in Port Moresby in August 1940, Eric had made arrangements to continue reporting if the enemy invaded. He had three months supplies for himself and 10 native soldiers stashed away at a plantation 30 miles inland, and a teleradio was on standby for instant transportation. If the port were to fall, Eric had every intention of keeping watch from the mountains. Hugh Mackenzie and Donald Macfarlan were ordered to take similar preparations, with Hugh to head to the Toma area and Donald to Guadalcanal.

Despite all his careful organisation, Eric confessed that by December 1941 he had come to discount the likelihood of war. 'I privately concluded that Japan, having missed better opportunities, did not intend to enter the war. The news of Pearl Harbor came to me with just as much surprise as it did the best informed on the United Nations.'[17]

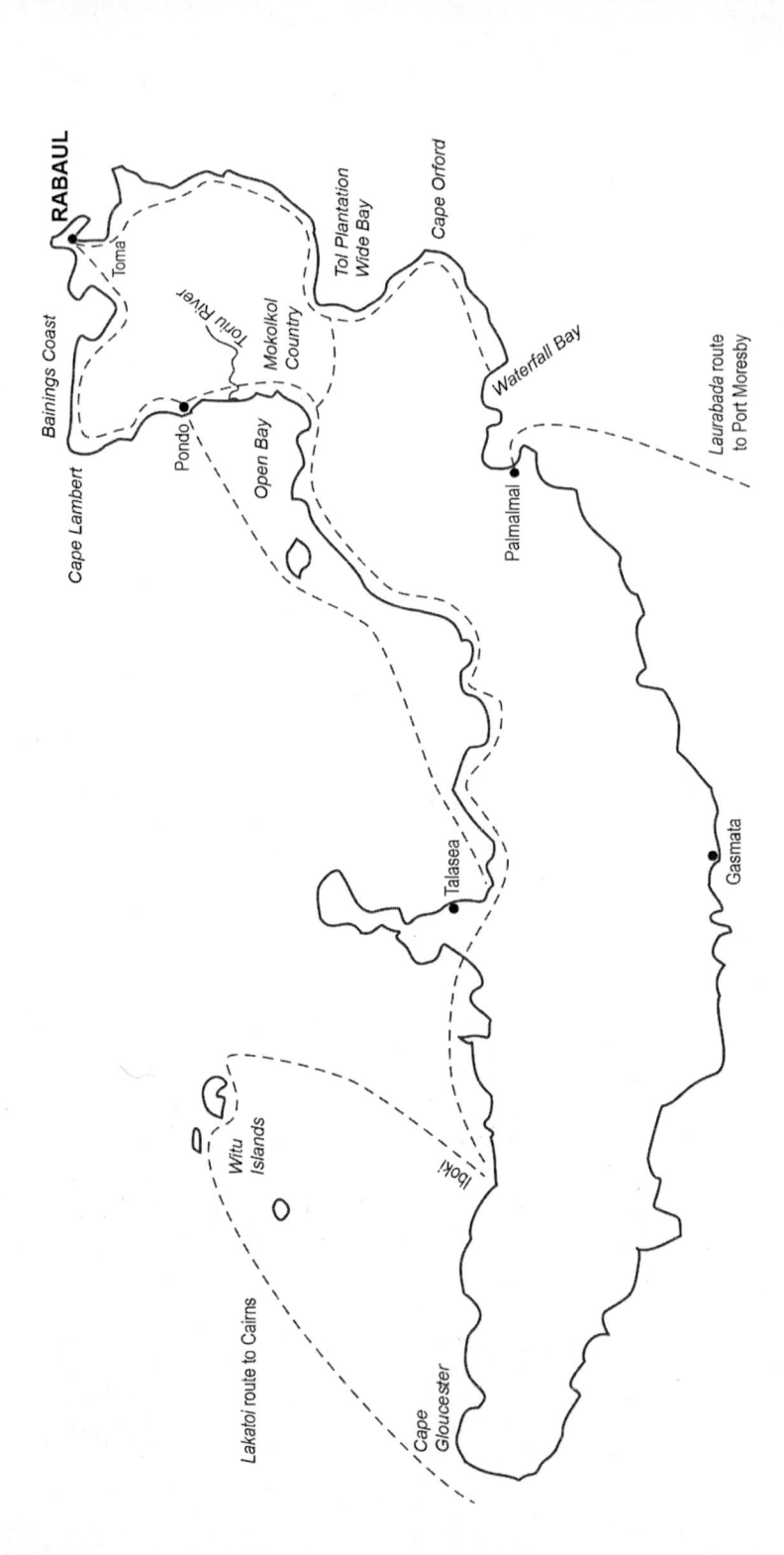

New Britain Army Evacuation

CHAPTER 7

THE FALL OF RABAUL AND THE AFTERMATH

Two days after the Japanese attack on Pearl Harbor on 7 December 1941, the first sighting of an enemy airplane by a Coastwatcher was made by Cornelius Lyons Page on 9 December from his base on Tabar. The plane was on its way to reconnoitre Rabaul. Women and children were evacuated by ship or plane as soon as possible from New Britain, with the exception of a few nurses. No further sightings were reported until the end of the month when large flying boats flew over Lae, Salamaua and Madang.

The Australian troops stationed at Rabaul from April 1941 were the 2/22nd battalion, with Lieutenant Colonel Howard Carr as its commanding officer. They numbered about 900 men. Also the New Guinea Volunteer Rifles (NGVR) had been formed early in the war with Germany from local white volunteers. In Rabaul there were about 80 members. Together with the 2/22nd and other small military and medical units, they comprised the Lark Force and numbered 1,400 under the command of Colonel John Scanlan. Several 6-inch guns were set up to guard the entrance to the harbour. This garrison army would be no match for a full-scale invasion. Since the majority of Australia's armed forces were far away fighting in the Middle East and North Africa available men and resources were scarce. The RAAF had established a base in Rabaul with a few Wirraways, some Catalina flying-boats and Hudsons. In all, the military protection was described as 'the line was so thin that it was stretched to invisibility'.

On 4 January 1942, Con Page reported two formations of bombers headed for Rabaul. The first bombing came before noon and the second late in the afternoon. Hugh Mackenzie passed the warnings on to everyone and so casualties were kept to a minimum. Bombing raids continued almost daily, but radio warnings were received of them all, coming from Page at Tabar, McDonald at Kavieng, Chambers at Emirau, and others.

Japanese aircraft flew widely across the North East Area over the next couple of weeks, going as far as Tulagi. On 20 January, Zero fighter planes accompanied the bombers for a heavy raid on Rabaul. Zeros meant aircraft carriers were near, and that meant the Japanese were on their way.

The following day a Hudson bomber reported four Japanese cruisers steaming toward Rabaul. On hearing this, Hugh decided his naval records, especially the confidential books and codes, had to be burnt. On the evening of the 21 January he and Connal Gill set about burning the papers in the trenches they had previously dug. It took them seven hours and a sleepless night to complete the task.

Hugh began to carry out his preconceived plan in the event of Japanese invasion. In the morning he sent Connal, Private Stone of the NGVR and two sailors to Toma to pick up the teleradio and supplies he had hidden in the jungle. In civilian life Stone had been an AWA professional radio operator. Connal was to make his way a village called Malabonga with the aim of eventually reaching Mt. Taungi, which overlooked the sea approaches to Rabaul on both sides. Hugh went to Military Headquarters to offer himself and his small naval unit's services to Scanlan for any fighting the latter might require of them.

Waves of bombers descended on Rabaul during the day on 22 January. The defenders responded by blowing up the airfield and anything else of potential use to the Japanese. It is not clear whether the destruction of Radio Rabaul VJZ was accidental or was intentionally destroyed by army intelligence. When Connal and

THE FALL OF RABAUL AND THE AFTERMATH

Stone set up the teleradio in the hills to try to raise VJZ and were unable to, their initial thought was that their teleradio might be defective. Whatever the reason for the demise of VJZ, the result was that Rabaul was cut off from local communication and from the rest of the world.

The Japanese did not land any forces until 2 am on 23 January. The Lark Force put up some resistance and some heavy fighting ensued. As day dawned it became clear they were no match for the eventual 5000 Japanese troops. With the hopelessness of the situation apparent, Scanlan said, "It's every man for himself." Men began streaming out of Rabaul in all directions. Some were captured and some surrendered.

Hugh gathered his small number of navy men into a truck and set off along the Toma road to join Connal. When he reached the camp, which was where the road ended, there were numerous abandoned trucks and cars, with more arriving. The soldiers were heading off in groups into the jungle totally unprepared for the hardships they were about to face. Most had left in haste and did not carry adequate provisions with them.

Perhaps the Army officers of Lark had expected substantial reinforcements would be sent from Australia in the event of an invasion by Japan for no consideration appears to have been given to the possibility of retreat. There was no evacuation plan. In their nine months in Rabaul the soldiers had not received any jungle training. They had not been taught guerrilla tactics or any phrases of Pidgin.

Keith McCarthy, as ADO at Talasea, had offered to give the troops jungle experience if they were sent in batches to Talasea, but his offer had not been accepted. This was to become an ironic twist of fate. Keith was well qualified to teach because he had in his possession a treasured copy of the Blue Book written by Colonel John Walstab when he had been Superintendent of Police. It was a plan of action Walstab had written if New Guinea were ever overrun by the enemy and included, amongst other strategies, the establishment of small supply dumps of food and ammunition in isolated spots in the jungle. Keith thought the Blue Book worked in perfectly with the RAN Coastwatching scheme.

In Toma, Connal's group picked up the stores and teleradio and headed to Malabonga, where there was a Mission, a police post with a native sergeant and prison compound. Connal arranged with the police sergeant for thirty prisoners and two police to carry the equipment to Taungi the next morning. He then set off to travel as far as possible by truck until the end of the road forced them to stop. As none of them had slept for over 30 hours he ordered a three-hour rest for them all. Then at 5pm they assembled the teleradio for the unsuccessful attempt to raise Rabaul. After that they turned in early.

The next morning, 23 January, Hugh and his group of naval ratings arrived at 5am. When the carriers failed to turn up at 6am, Hugh and Connal went back to look for them and found Malabonga almost deserted. The DO, Henry Gregory, had come through the previous night and told all the natives to go bush. However, with the help of Hugh's Pidgin, they were able to secure the help of two police boys and six prisoners. Transportation still remained a problem as their total numbers were less than half that required to carry the load. They decided the only feasible strategy was to relay the gear forward a mile at a time.

The group was just about to move the first batch of gear when an army staff car arrived. In the car were Lieutenant-Colonel Carr; his adjutant, Captain Ivan Smith; three other members of his staff; and W.B. Ball, Superintendent of Police New Guinea. Carr informed Hugh that the Japanese were barely twenty minutes away and that he thought the plan to relay all the gear into the bush had little chance of success.

Hugh was faced with a dilemma. If Carr was right then there was not enough time left to move the gear, if he was wrong they might still be able to manage it. As Hugh pondered this difficult decision, Japanese float planes flew over the area and started blazing at anything that appeared to be moving. Hugh had the lives of the men with him to consider. If they moved slowly with the teleradio, it might cost all their lives. Without it they might have a chance of survival. Regretfully he ordered the teleradio be destroyed.

Carr's group decided to join up with Hugh's. When the sad task of destroying the teleradio was completed, the six prisoners were loaded with 40 lbs of stores. The rest of the party took as much as they could carry of stores and ammunition and set off for the Kalas Mission. They arrived at the same time as a float plane. Fortunately, rain pelted down, hiding them from view as they scurried across the clearing to the Mission House. While there, Superintendent Ball advised the missionaries to move inland, but they declined, only to be later taken prisoner by the Japanese.

So began a lengthy trial which was to sorely test their endurance. They stayed in the area for a while as they waited for Captain Mcleod, Lieutenant Peter Figgis, the Military Intelligence Officer, and Private Harry, who Carr had said were following behind them. Hugh had left a message at the Kalas Mission to let them know the route his group had taken. They hadn't turned up and Hugh sent a couple of men to find them.

He also sent out patrols, each headed by two or three men, to try to find out what had happened to the troops who had fled Rabaul. It was ascertained that while many had headed out on a northern route, others had taken to the south. They also discovered that the Japanese were increasing their patrols inland and had been dropping surrender leaflets which read:

> To the Officers and Soldiers of this Island. Surrender at Once and we will guarantee your life, treating you as war prisoners. Those who Resist Us Will Be Killed One and All. Consider seriously, you can find neither food nor way of escape in this island and you will only die of hunger unless you surrender.
>
> January 23rd 1942
>
> JAPANESE COMMANDER IN CHIEF

While none of Hugh's party took this very seriously, they were amazed to discover later that the Japanese had achieved results and about 200 soldiers had gradually returned to Rabaul and given themselves up.

Taking stock of their supply situation, they found they had enough food for 10 days for the whole party, including natives. It was decided to buy food from villagers, to live off the land as much as possible, and to save tinned foods for absolute emergencies. Connal appreciated Hugh's forethought in providing for the monetary needs of their retreat:

> We were able to purchase native foods—Mackenzie, that long-headed Scot, had a special intelligence fund of £100 which we had brought with us all in New Guinea shillings—the sort with the hole in the middle. That money repaid many times over the labour of carrying it about with us. Our ability to pay for what we wanted invariably won goodwill as it was even then a very simple native who did not know the value of money. More important, it meant we could hire carriers, although many of these were too frightened to be reliable. They all knew about the natives who had got in the way of a fragmentation bomb during the first raid on Rabaul and the approach of an aircraft, even when we were in the thickest bush, caused eyes to roll and teeth to chatter with apprehension.[1]

A conference was held to decide which way held the best prospects of escape and rescue. A decision was made to proceed to the south coast via a Mission Station called Lamingi near the centre of the Gazelle Peninsula. It would mean following primitive native tracks in the jungle, up and down mountain ridges, but on reaching the coast there might be a chance of finding or being picked up by a boat and sailing to the Trobriands. On 31 January they set off. Ahead of them were hundreds of troops who had hurried away unprepared. The soldiers had taken the coastal route south which, while still challenging, was easier terrain. However, ominously, it held greater risk of being discovered by the Japanese.

The mountainous nature of the land the Coastwatcher-led party had to traverse meant that to go one mile often involved having to climb up and down four or five miles nearly vertically. Heat and sweat, rain and mud, made their clothes and boots wet and dirty. The nights were chilly and brought on attacks of malaria. Fortuitously, they had 1000 x 5 grain quinine tablets in their kits. Tropical ulcers developed on shins scratched as they dived for cover from searching float planes. The diet of native foods such as taro, kau kau (sweet potato) and tapioca was not always enjoyable to European tastes and some of the party found foods such as broiled breadfruit almost unpalatable. But they knew it was essential in helping to keep them alive and for that they were grateful.

On 2 February a plan was made for Hugh, with Figgis, Stone and Chessell, to proceed overland to Waterfall Bay, where there was a teleradio. Hugh thought if he moved quickly he might reach it while it was still intact. A party of 21 people with carriers would move too slowly, but a party of four could go directly south of Lamingi through an uninhabited area to Wide Bay, from where the coastal track would allow quicker access to Waterfall Bay.

The rest of party was to proceed to Marai, then north to SumSum and from there on to Wide Bay to meet up with Hugh.

After carriers were arranged and stores for the overland and coastal parties split, both groups set out on 7 February. Heavy cloud in the mountains had delayed their start for a few days.

The Kalas Missionaries had given Hugh a map of the tracks in the Gazelle Peninsula. It was more than ten years old but was surprisingly accurate. Hugh gave the map to Connal for him to make copies for Figgis, Smith, and himself. It was thought best for each party to have two copies in case one was lost or destroyed.

Connal's party arrived at Marai on 11 February. The next day Smith, McLeod, Harry and Able-Seaman Matthews went to SumSum, which was a plantation about two hours north of Marai. Smith and Mcleod brought back the news that it was occupied by some soldiers who were not planning on going south because of a rumour they had heard of a massacre of Australians at Tol Plantation.

The group left Marai on 14 February and proceeded south to Ili. They stopped on the way at Adler Bay and bought tobacco. About half an hour after leaving Adler Bay they met Colonel Scanlan, Major Mollard and a private, the last carrying a white flag, proceeding north. Connal recalled 'I never saw a more dejected trio in all my life. I said "Good morning, Sir" as we drew level and saluted. The Colonel returned the salute but kept going. I realised he was on his way in to surrender and probably did not feel like talking. When I got to Ili, Smith told me Scanlan had ignored Carr and the others except for McLeod who was a permanent soldier. However, whilst Scanlan spoke to McLeod, Mollard spoke to the others. The rumours of a massacre at Tol were confirmed and Scanlan was on his way back to Rabaul to give himself up, the Japanese having offered to spare the lives of any further Australian troops captured if he either suicided or gave himself up.'[2]

As Connal's group continued, they were slowed by some who were lagging behind. One was the elderly Chief Yeoman of Signals Lamont, who had been the Coastwatcher at Anir Island, and the other was a twenty-year-old signalman called Francis. Lamont was tough and if left to go at his own pace would get through. However, Francis was of concern as at times he seemed to be in a world of his own. He had no fever but appeared to be in a state of semi consciousness. If offered taro or other native food he vehemently refused to eat "the filthy stuff". It was just as though he was seeking to retreat from reality.' Nowadays his condition may have been diagnosed as severe Post Traumatic Stress Disorder (PTSD).

They decided that those who were able, must get through to Tol, where there were native gardens. The nearer they got to Tol the carriers became restive and talked about going home.

THE FALL OF RABAUL AND THE AFTERMATH

On 21 February Connal and Smith managed to help Francis on the way to Tol and were able to keep him going reasonably well. They left him by the track in the middle of Tol Plantation while they went to look for evidence of the massacre.

> Near the Plantation House we found steel helmets, webbing gear and paybooks in three separate heaps. Some of the pay books had been torn up, but we counted them all and the total came to 120. We then went looking for bodies at the back of the plantation but did not find any. We did find the remains of about six large and apparently fierce fires. I sifted through the ashes and found a few pieces of bone, but too badly calcined to identify as human or animal. The edges of the fires were sharply defined in the green cover crop and grass as though the fires had been fed with petrol or kerosene. Smith and I both felt that there had been dirty work of some sort but lacking positive evidence in the shape of bodies we felt some doubts about a wholesale massacre—both being lawyers.[3]

However, as it turned out they missed the part of the plantation which would have provided all the evidence they needed.

Francis's condition was deteriorating. He still had no fever but would not take any food at all. They opened some of their precious tin of food and force fed him. However, he was unresponsive to any attempts at conversation.

On the afternoon of 23 February W.O. Sexton of the New Guinea Police arrived with Private Alf Robinson N.G.V.R. to see Ball. Robinson had been found roaming round the bush half crazy, with his thumbs tied together behind his back. They then heard the full story of the Tol Plantation Massacre:

> At approximately 6 a.m. on 2 February a Japanese cruiser entered Henry Reid Bay at the head of Wide Bay and sent ashore five motor landing craft each carrying about 100 troops and a machine gun in the bows. Tol House was machine-gunned. The surrender of approximately 145 Australian troops was accepted, no action having taken place. There were 120 troops at Tol, nine at Waitavolo just west of Tol and sixteen at Karlai, They were all assembled at Tol.

The troops, twenty-two in number, who had been with white flags on the beach at Tol when the landing craft approached were kept separate from the others and sent aboard the cruiser. At approximately 7.30 a.m. on 4 February the balance of the troops, approximately 123 in number, had their thumbs bound behind their backs and were taken into the cover crop at the back of Tol and bayoneted or shot.

Robinson was in a line being marched off for execution when he rolled under a dense bush and his escape remained unnoticed by the Japanese. The cruiser left later in the day but Robinson, who had heard all the shrieks and yells of the victims, remained where he was overnight. Next day he wandered off and was found two days later by the European Police.

On 8 February the cruiser returned again to Tol. It is not known how many troops were captured or killed on this occasion as the Japanese went up the Mavolo River to the Police Post at Kasileia and are presumed to have wiped out a fairly large concentration of fugitives there. The cruiser departed on 11 February on the afternoon of which we saw it from Marai heading towards Rabaul. It returned to Tol again on 12 February, departing on the following day. This time four troops were picked up on the sandspit between the Wuluwut and the Mavolo and taken on board the cruiser, Waitavolo House was burnt over the heads of two wounded survivors of the massacre of 4 February who had been placed there by another survivor from whom the police also obtained the story, and who was still with them.[4]

Keith McCarthy's version of Alf Robinson's escape is as follows:

The Australians were divided into small groups, with Japanese at the head and rear of each party. There were ten men in Robinson's party as it was led, single file into the overgrown plantation. When Robinson saw that the man in the rear was carrying a pick and shovel, he realized finally that this was to be a murder party. So did others. One shouted, 'You murdering bastards! They'll get you one day for this, you yellow shit!' But he was silenced with a blow of the rifle butt... Suddenly the track veered and Robinson saw his chance, He threw himself into the bushes and lay still. The man following pretended to stagger, halting the line for a second and hissed into the bushes at Robinson "Lower down, sport. The bastards can see your feet."[5]

Francis, who had weakened further, died on 24 February. His death was not unexpected as he seemed to have lost all will to live. One of the natives asked if he had had a bone pointed at him. Father Johann Maierhofer, who they had previously met at Kalai Mission, agreed to bury Francis. Knight and Connal took his body to Kalai and there Connal sewed his body inside a blanket and Francis was laid to rest.

Saddened by the loss of Francis, the party continued their journey southward and found Hugh and his group at Iwi. It was here they heard confirmation of the gruesome events at Tol. Hugh told how he had found bodies at Tol, and the two bodies in the burnt house at Waitavolo.

He had also had a lucky escape. He arrived from the interior early in the afternoon of 13 February. He was taking aim at a large hornbill near the intersection of the interior and coastal trails when something startled the bird and it flew away. Scouting the trail towards Tol they found a Japanese ration box and so they lay low until they saw the cruiser sail away towards the north. The hornbill being disturbed by a Japanese patrol returning to Tol was indeed a stroke of luck for Hugh and the other three.

Since coming down from the mountains, Hugh's group, with the exception of Figgis, had developed malaria, which had delayed their progress. They had been able to buy a gig, complete with sails, from a native for £2. Hugh thought it best to keep the two parties separate as it decreased the demands for food placed on the villagers at any one time.

Connal's party headed for Misetiwai. Soon after their arrival on 28 February, a native brought a note to Ball from W.O. Feetham of the police. It said a European had arrived at Kalai with good information. Pte Harry volunteered to go back to investigate and left immediately. In the afternoon, Chessell was sent on to Sanpun to advise Mackenzie.

During the day, four of Connal's group, including himself and Smith, fell ill with malaria. However, they soon sweated it out with the aid of 10 grains of quinine each, with a further 5 grains that evening. Since arriving at Wide Bay, various members of the party had been laid low with malaria.

On Sunday 1 March, Chessell arrived back with word from Hugh that he had developed an infected leg and asked if Connal could please bring any news to him. Thankfully all the malaria patients were recovering.

The return of Harry brought the first ray of hope they had had since leaving Rabaul. A European named Holland had come from the north coast under instructions from Keith McCarthy, ADO at Talasea and Coastwatcher. McCarthy was endeavouring to evacuate all personnel from New Britain. Chessell and Connal left immediately for Sanpun, where they found Hugh, whose lower left leg was badly inflamed. However, he said he would return with them in the gig to Misetiwai in the morning, which he did.

The next morning's discussion decided that Hugh would proceed to Waterfall Bay with the hope of assembling any troops on the south coast of New Britain, east of Gasmata, at or near Palmalmal, ready for evacuation. If nothing had happened by the end of March, he would sail a small cutter he intended building at Waterfall Bay using components from the gig he already had to the Trobriand Islands. His aim was to reach somewhere that had a teleradio.

Connal was instructed to return to Kalai, contact Holland, proceed quickly to McCarthy on the north coast and send word to the navy of Hugh's intentions. Connal was then to continue with McCarthy giving him whatever assistance he could. Once Hugh reached Waterfall Bay, he would have a watch kept at Waterfall Bay Anchorage and Palmalmal each Wednesday and Saturday afternoon for aircraft to drop food, medical stores, instructions, and/or to evacuate personnel.

Connal asked Hugh about rejoining him after contacting McCarthy, but Hugh said it would take too long and, in any case, he considered Connal was not fit enough. Connal replied that it was a case of the pot calling the kettle black, but Hugh remained firm.

Hugh then addressed the whole party. He told them he had given Connal orders that must be carried out at all costs. If anybody in the party fell sick they would, regardless of rank, be left at some suitable place and to carry out any instructions left with them if they recovered. Hugh then announced he would keep Figgis, Stone, Chessell, Bonnitcha and Harry with him. The others were to return to Kalai.

With them went Alf Robinson and another survivor from Tol, ambulance driver Private Bill Collins, who had been shot twice, once in the shoulder and once in the wrists. Collins, despite the pain of his wounds, had lain still and quiet with his eyes shut until he felt that the Japanese had left. When he eventually opened his eyes, he found he was surrounded by dead bodies that had been partially buried. The shot that had struck his wrists had also cut his bonds, so his hands were free. He struggled to his feet and into the jungle where he was lucky to be found by the European police.

On 3 March the party left Misetiwai and arrived at Milim, where they spent the night. The next morning Knight and Douglas fell ill with dysentery.

Connal hoped against hope that he could persuade Fr Maierhofer to nurse the sick men at Kalai. However, from his earlier contacts with him, Connal knew that although Maierhofer was prepared to die for his faith, he feared and hated disease, especially cholera and dysentery. At Kalai, Connal put Knight and Douglas in the mission hospital. Then he went to see Fr Maierhofer, who gave him his only bottle of chlorodyne. Despite Connal's pleas, the Father wept and said he could not bring himself to nurse Knight and Douglas and he could not ask any of the mission natives to do what he himself was unable to do. Connal gave the sick men each a dose of chlorodyne.

Knight gallantly said, "Don't you worry about us. Mr. Mackenzie is depending on you and if you come near us too much you might get dysentery yourself." After leaving the patients, Connal washed himself and his clothes in the first stream he came to with his cake of carbolic soap.

He felt torn between not wanting to desert his sick comrades and wishing to obey orders in trying to get the rest of the party to safety. He discussed it with Ball and Lamont. The kindly Lamont volunteered to stay with the sick men, saying, "Christ, this would have to happen! Those two poor sods can't be left to die on their own, I'll stay with them if you like, and you get on with the job of getting Mackenzie and the swaddies rescued."

Connal recalled, 'We had always jokingly referred to Lamont as the "heart of oak". It was the old story of many a true word being spoken in jest. I gave Lamont £25 from the cash I had and also gave him a rifle and 200 rounds of ammunition and told him to use them if necessary to get anything he needed for the sick and himself. Ball and I went to Ril sick at heart.'[6]

Hugh reached Waterfall Bay on 11 March. As expected by that time, the teleradio was no longer there. When he reached Palmalmal, he found more than 100 men camped there. Major Bill Owen was the commander of 'A' company of 2/22nd. He had passed through Tol just before the Japanese arrived. Finding that food was scarce, he had moved on. Owen and about 25 of his men, including Major Edward Palmer, the Senior Medical Officer, arrived at Palmalmal Mission where they were helped by Father Ted Harris. As more men trickled in, bringing the numbers to about 150, Owen set up a well organised camp at two nearby plantations that had native gardens, and Dr. Palmer organised a makeshift casualty station. Palmer later reported that 100% of the men had malaria and had had at least one recurrence. Only 33% could do any sort of work. They were in such poor condition due to malaria, anaemia, privations of the journey and lack of food that he thought it would not be possible to keep them alive for more than a few weeks.

Connal's party were relieved to arrive at Frank Holland's camp on 5 March. That evening the group dined on a cassowary shot by one of Holland's police. It reminded Connal of very tough mutton.

The group then proceeded to walk across to the other side of the island in order to meet up with McCarthy. The trek was more of a climb than a walk as the three mountain ranges they traversed were nearly vertical. As well, that area between Wide Bay on the southern side of New Britain and Open Bay on the northern side was home to the Mokolkol, a very hostile, nomadic tribe. Fortunately, the party was not attacked. After reaching the northern side, and with a combination of travelling by launch, canoe and walking, they finally met up with Keith McCarthy at Valoka on the 14 March.

Connal told him about Mackenzie and Lamont. Keith said that he and his helpers had needed to use their teleradios more often than he had hoped. Air patrols had escalated around the Talasea area. He thought that it might be due to the Japanese having detected teleradio transmissions. Keith felt it would be safer not to send any long messages east of the Willaumez Peninsula. Within 48 hours they would reach Iboki in Rein Bay, from where they could transmit the messages.

When hell had rained down on Rabaul on 22 and 23 January, Keith McCarthy, at his post as ADO at Talasea, was feeling somewhat annoyed by the lack of instructions from District Office headquarters at Rabaul.

Keith McCarthy and Eric had worked together in Madang, Eric as DO and Keith as ADO. John Keith McCarthy had been born in St. Kilda, Victoria, Australia on 20 January 1905. It seemed that what most people noticed about him was his red/ginger hair and moustache. Eric was appreciative of Keith's character and characteristics.

> He was a tall, red-headed man of Irish descent, with the nature of a red-headed man of Irish descent. His was no cold, calculating brain; his affections and emotions often governed him, but when his fine free carelessness had landed him in trouble, he could extricate himself, cool logic guiding his Celtic fervour until the danger was past... he had a boisterous sense of humour, a habit of appropriating other people's matches, and a gift for caricature which he indulged at the expense of his friends.[7]

With no orders forthcoming, Keith decided to give himself some. He thought the most important task was to destroy the three small airstrips on the north coast of New Britain, at Talasea, Cape Gloucester and Ubili. More than 250 miles separated the airstrips. Keith and his planter friend, Rod Marsland, set out for Cape Gloucester to dig ditches across the runway while another planter friend, Ken Douglas, sailed for Ubili to do the same.

Keith reviewed the available transport. There was only the 36ft government launch *Lolobau*, which Keith controlled; Ken Douglas's 10ft *Dufaur*; and the 36ft *Aussi*, owned by Burns Philp, which was 70 miles away at Witu Island. A few days later he learnt that a new 300 ton BP vessel *Lakatoi* had moored out on the Willaumez Peninsula by a skipper new to New Guinea waters. Keith was annoyed because a big vessel such as that would have been a help in transporting the civilians who were arriving from all directions. He planned to get them to the western tip of the island at Cape Gloucester from where they could be ferried across to Salamaua or Lae. They set off down the coast, travelling only at night to avoid being spotted by Japanese air patrols.

In Townsville, Eric's concern for the fate of the troops and the Coastwatchers in Rabaul was growing. With nothing but silence from the town, it was a matter of urgency to find out what had happened. Two days after the fall, Eric sent a signal to Keith asking him to take his teleradio to the vicinity of Toma and investigate the state of the Australian forces, if such actions did not conflict with any other instructions he had. Eric rightfully suspected that Keith had no instructions of any sort. As Keith was a civilian, Eric had no right to give him orders. Eric knew it was a tall order. In an attempt to soften the request, he made reference to Keith's sketching skills and asked him to 'send out a caricature of the Japanese commander there'.

It was obviously time for a parting of the ways. Keith put Frank Henderson in charge of the heavily loaded *Lolobau* on its 400 mile trip to Salamaua with the civilians, while Keith took the smaller and quieter *Aussi* back to Talasea to prepare for the 200 mile trip to Rabaul. Henderson remarkably took the *Lolobau* and its human cargo all the way back to Australia.

Luckily for Eric, Keith McCarthy was just the man needed for the task. He was to become another example of the right man being in the right place at a very challenging time.

Days after Eric's communication with Keith, the Townsville office was besieged with signals and phone calls from Melbourne requesting someone be sent to Rabaul to discover what had happened.

Eric's conversation always went the same way:

'McCarthy is on his way.'

'How long will it take?'

'A fortnight to three weeks.'

'That's too long!'

'It's quicker than anyone else could be.'

'He may not get there.'

'If McCarthy can't get there, no one else can.'[8]

After signalling that he had set out, Keith kept silent for two weeks.

The little *Aussi* was rather overloaded for the trip north. Keith took with him Rod Marsland; 16 native police; Nelson Tokidoro, Keith's excellent 14-year-old native wireless operator; and Joseph Tokiplau, Keith's cook who was from Rabaul and who might be helpful; and the teleradio. Bad weather gave the *Aussi* good cover from the Japanese aircraft they often heard. They were three days into their journey and three quarters of the way up the coast when they heard from coastal natives that destroyers had landed Japanese at Pondo Plantation. They would have to pass by Pondo if they continued up the coast so they decided to take 'the back door route' to Rabaul. They went about a mile up the Toriu River, hid the *Aussi* and then set out on foot across the hills to Rabaul. The police who were already carrying arms and equipment, took on the extra burden of carrying the teleradio.

They were surprised to find that the back door track was busy, with many natives coming from the other direction as they streamed out of Rabaul. Among them were some native police in khaki uniforms but carrying no rifles. Reluctant to talk at first, they eventually disclosed that the Australian Government took their rifles and buried them before the Japanese landed. They were dismayed that they had been denied the ability to fight in the battle for their own country along with the Australian soldiers. Worse than this, they had been insulted by having been stripped of their arms. Keith told them that as many as he had arms for could serve with him. 'They joined me willingly and served to the end.'

With so many natives using the track there was no chance of a secret entry to Rabaul so Keith remained in the hills with the radio while Marsland went to investigate Pondo Plantation. He found the Japanese had left but had placed Albert Evenson, the manager, and his European staff on parole. They had blown up his schooner and some store buildings and said they would return. There were now quite a number of Australian troops camped at Pondo.

Marsland rejoined Keith, bringing with him Captain Alan Cameron and 11 of his men. Cameron told Keith the details of the Battle of Rabaul, which Keith coded and had transmitted to Port Moresby by Nelson Tokidoro. For the first time in its short history, Australia heard that an enemy had invaded an Australian governed territory.

Keith asked Cameron what had happened to the rest of the troops and what could be done to help them. Cameron replied that the troops had split in half, with some, like him and his men, going north and some going south. He thought it would be hopeless to try to do anything for them as it was now three weeks since the Japanese had landed and the soldiers were starving and ill with malaria. Keith disagreed and thought they might be able to do some good.

Cameron then requested a message be sent to Moresby for a Catalina to fly in and pick him up, and that Keith and Marsland could go with him. Keith did not like the idea. There was not enough room in a Catalina for the number of men at Pondo and, besides, Keith did not intend to leave New Britain yet.

Cameron wrote a message to the Army at Port Moresby asking for the Catalina and gave it to Keith, who refused to have it sent. Cameron became annoyed and ordered Keith to send it, which received another refusal. Separately, their groups went back to Pondo.

When Keith arrived, he saw there were white sheets flying from tall poles positioned on the beach. Pondo was a large plantation with a factory that manufactured desiccated coconut. About 800 natives worked for Albert Evenson and his white staff. The Japanese had not inflicted full-scale destruction so reasonable stocks of food and supplies had remained undamaged.

It was evident that Evenson and Cameron had been having a violent argument. It turned out to be a continuation of one from Cameron's previous time at Pondo that he had not bothered to tell Keith about. Everson was under considerable stress, trying to feed and care for sick soldiers as well as looking after his large number of native workers.

Cameron had demanded all the remaining plantation food for his troops. Evenson refused, needing to feed his workers and any other soldiers who might find their way to Pondo. An emotional Evenson told Keith that Cameron had threatened to shoot him as a traitor.

Keith's efforts to mediate backfired. Cameron turned on him, saying that Keith was under his command and, furthermore, was to hand over the teleradio. Keith responded that since the fall of Rabaul he was the Senior Administration Officer in the district and he didn't want any trouble from him. When Cameron retorted that he had 11 armed men with him, Keith lost his temper. "Why, you stupid ass!" he roared. "I've got 20 armed police! Are we going to have a private war or are you going to help out in the jam we're in!"

The situation settled down as more troops staggered into Pondo and Evenson and his staff fed and cared for them. At this time, the beginning of a rescue plan started to form in Keith's mind. That night he put his ideas on paper and by 4 am, with Rod Marsland, he wrote the plan out in detail.

With the limited information they had, they estimated there would be about 400 troops, many incapacitated, positioned along the coast between Pondo and Rabaul. 300 others had headed south trying to get to Gasmata.

The first part of the plan was for a patrol to travel north to Lassul Bay 50 miles away, collect the scattered men and march them to Pondo. The second stage of the plan was for the troops to walk down the coast to Cape Gloucester. In the third stage they would be rescued from there. How they would be picked up was as yet unknown.

Fourteen staging camps would be set up on the journey. The logistics of food supplies for Keith's evacuation plan were considered. Their Blue Book supply dumps would help keep the staging camps going but would not solve the supply to the troops. As the coastal villages could not cope with feeding hundreds of men, a ration was instigated of half a pound of rice plus one coconut per man per day.

The troops, in detachments under the command of an officer or NCO, would move off at regular intervals so that the staging camps could cope with the numbers arriving. The one glaring problem with the plan was that the distance was 350 miles. Even for fit men such a trek would be a challenge. For sick and malnourished men, it could be impossible, but no better plan was available. In fact, no other plan existed. No alternative was forthcoming for the troops abandoned by the Australian Government and the military.

When Keith signalled his plan to the military in Port Moresby a reply came giving approval and granting Keith 'full authority over all officers of rank'. One of his first moves was to assign Captain Cameron to the staging area west of the Willaumez Peninsula. He and his 11 soldiers went off in a small launch called *Dulcy*, which Cameron had acquired from a coastal plantation. Keith's planter friend, Bert Olander, went with them.

Other friendly faces arrived to offer their services. Among them were Ken Douglas, Leung Chu, Lincoln Bell and Frank Holland. Frank himself volunteered to lead the party through the rugged, trackless, Mokolkol country south towards Tol plantation to find troops to bring across the island to be included in the evacuation. Keith gave him six of his best police and a Webley revolver, the only weapon he carried with him as he went off whistling.

Fortunately, the Japanese had done a poor demolition job on the plantation schooner *Malahuka* and Rod Marsland and helpers set about repairing it. An extra vessel would be a valuable addition for transporting those sick and wounded who were unable to walk.

Keith and his cook and friend, Joseph Tokiplau, a patrol of two, paddled off at night in a small outrigger canoe to find as many troops as they could.

When Keith reached the Bainings coast, the findings were abysmal. Australian soldiers, shadows of their former selves, were dejected and starving, sometimes in the presence of food.

> Men lay in batches in the shade of the beach scrub, or in abandoned huts. Small groups were spread for miles, ill with malaria and dysentery, weakened by blistering sun and the lack of food, their uniforms already in remnants. They lay awaiting death or capture.

These were men who had been garrisoning in Rabaul for twelve months, but who had been given no proper training, who had been given no instructions on how to live off the country, or given even the geography of the island they were on. They had escaped from Rabaul, yet they were lost.

'Christ, have you brought anything to eat?' asked one man of a pitifully weak group I came across near Langiona. He could hardly stand as he spoke.

'There's your food,' I said, pointing at a patch of *manioc* ripe for the digging. The men were actually starving in a native food garden because nobody had taught them how to recognise tapioca. Tokiplau dug up a few roots and soon the men were eating, cursing the Army that had failed to train them.[9]

At one plantation Keith found 60 hungry men, their clothes in tatters, lying near a storeroom filled with rice and meat. They knew the food was there but the plantation manager refused to give it to them unless they paid for it. There was no need to save it for the plantations labourers for they had wisely deserted, but the manager had misplaced loyalty to the company who owned the plantation and was protective of their property. Keith was amazed that the soldiers hadn't broken into the supplies. When the manager still refused to hand the food over, Keith signed an impressment order and took charge of the food. They divided it into rations for the march to Pondo.

Over the next couple of weeks, Keith, with the help of other able men he met on the Bainings coast, gathered more than 200 men for the 50 mile walk to Pondo. Many, sick with malaria, exhausted or dispirited, did not feel like moving. While inwardly empathising with them, outwardly Keith encouraged, cajoled and bullied the men into rallying for the march. He knew they could not linger or the Japanese would add them to the already large list of those taken prisoner or killed. However, Keith himself did not head back to Pondo until the natives had assured him there were no more Australians between him and the Japanese.

Keith acknowledged with gratitude the role played by the fine men who helped in his quest to rescue the soldiers. Those men were planation men: Bill Mason, Frank Conroy and his young son Joe; Captain Pip Appel; Captain Fields and Lieutenants David O. 'Mick' Smith and Donaldson; Sergeants Kent, Jane, Crawford, Laws and Bert Smit; Corporals Mac Hamilton and Headlam; Signallers Aird and Hockings, three native constables from Rabaul and many others. Speaking of them, Keith said, 'Nothing is hopeless when there are men like these.'

Arriving back at Pondo, Keith was relieved to find all the soldiers had also arrived and the Japanese had not returned. The good news was that the *Malahuka* had been repaired, but Bert Olander had come back with the bad news that they had lost the *Dulcy*. Captain Cameron had dropped Bert at a spot down the coast and waited while Bert set up a staging camp, but then he took the *Dulcy* and his men and headed to the New Guinea mainland. Keith was furious. They needed that boat. Cameron made it to Salamaua just before the Japanese did. Later in the war he was awarded the DSO twice. It was not his courage that was in question in his action but his lack of consideration for his fellow soldiers in their time of need.

Most of the men gathered at Pondo were emaciated, but there was a new spirit in them as now there was a ray of hope. Movement of the troops away from Pondo began. Leaving in small groups as planned was even more essential as Japanese planes were ever present and large groups would be more easily spotted.

For Keith, insisting the troops keep moving was heart-wrenching:

> Many of them were almost naked, the sun had raised great blisters on their bodies and their lips were cracked with open sores. The mosquitoes and insects drove them mad at night, for we had no nets and the smudge fires affected their eyes. Boots had begun to give out so that some wore hessian and cloth wound around their feet to protect them from the coral and rocks. Each man carried 10lb of rice and a tin of meat — these were all the rations that could be

given, and in most cases all that a man could carry in his weakened condition.[10]

At Pondo were 74 wounded and severely incapacitated men who could not walk. They were embarked on the recently repaired *Malahuka*. Rod proudly showed Keith the spare parts for the engine he had fashioned out of scrap metal.

As they headed off, Keith tried to persuade Albert Evenson and his assistant to come with them, but all his arguments failed.

"I've got hundreds of natives to look after," explained Evenson. "Anyhow, you'll never get out of New Britain yourself — have you seen yourself lately? You must be due to crack!" Keith had been so busy that he had not considered his physical condition. He went over to the copra scales and discovered he had lost 50lbs during the past couple of months. He also realised that for weeks he had been dreaming of chocolate, cake and other sweet things that he did not normally eat.

Keith wrote out a letter demanding Evenson give the troops help in the hope that if the Japanese returned and accused him of breaking his parole, it would aid his defence. It was to be of no help. Evenson and his assistant were to join the ranks of those never heard from again.

The *Malahuka's* resurrection proved to be less than perfect. She began to leak and the engine to misfire. One night her engine stopped and she grounded on a reef. Most of the sick men who had been lying tightly packed on the deck had to disembark and in their weakened condition help push the *Malahuka* off the reef. Keith was full of admiration for their efforts that night, and eventually they reached the comparative safety of Talasea.

The rest of the troops were coming through to Talasea by virtue of the staging camps, the encouragement of their leaders of their groups, and their own strong will. The damage the Japanese had inflicted on the *Malahuka* was more than originally thought and despite her valiant role in the transportation of the invalid troops to Talasea, she had to be scuttled.

There was still a long way to go to the end of New Britain and Keith worried about how on earth they could ever reach it. He told himself to stop thinking as 'something would come'. And something did indeed come — in the form of a Mini-Dunkirk of New Britain.

With the fall of Rabaul, the civil Administration in Mandated New Guinea ceased to exist and the Administrator handed over his authority to the military commander at Lae. Older civilians were sent out of the country and younger men became part of the Australian New Guinea Administrative Unit (ANGAU). 'Kassa' Townsend was its first head.

Major Townsend was passing through Townsville when he learned from Eric at ACH the dire situation of the troops in New Britain. As soon as he arrived at the Coastwatchers' base in Port Moresby, he and Paterson sent out messages by teleradio for all available small craft in New Guinea to assemble at Finschhafen. The aim was to collect the troops and ferry them across the straits. Kassa appointed G.C. 'Blue' Harris to be in command of the operation.

> G.C. Harris was a Patrol officer at Lae when Rabaul fell — a big, fleshy young man with a bald head surrounded by a fringe of fiery red hair. He had a hard face and a soft, lisping voice, a truculent disposition and a courteous manner, little sense of humour but a generous good nature — in fact a contradiction of a man whose only quality not offset by another the opposite was his courage. Being red-haired, he was, following the Australian custom, called 'Blue'.[11]

The Harris Navy consisted of an assortment of vessels and volunteers. They were manned by 20 men, mainly planters and missionaries. The largest ship was *Bavaria*, a 45-ton schooner of the Lutheran Mission Finschhafen. Adolph Obst and Dave Rohrlach were the skippers. The 23-ton *Umboi*, the Australian Lutheran Mission vessel, was run by Vic Neumann and Jack Goad. Bill

Money, Gus Kuester and Snow Blakey were in charge of the 15-ton *Gnair*, the Guinea Airways launch from Lae. From the Lutheran Mission Madang came the 35-ton *Totol*, with Ted Radke as her skipper. Blue Harris decided to make *Umboi* his flagship.

The fact that many of the volunteers and their ships had German or German sounding names appealed to Bill Money's London-born sense of humour. When the Harris Navy flotilla met up with Keith at Walindi, near Talasea, Bill, speaking with a guttural German accent and giving a Nazi salute, proclaimed, 'Herr Townsend und Herr Erik Feldt send Obst, Neumann, Radke und Freund to New Pommern. Heil Hitler!' New Pommern was the name for New Britain when Germany had held the territory.[12]

Keith decided to make Iboki plantation, 100 miles south of Talasea, the destination from which the final evacuation was to take place. It was suitably far from Rabaul and there were cattle which would provide much needed meat. The flotilla began the task of ferrying the troops to Iboki.

The flotilla had been instructed to travel only at night and hide by day. Cover was provided along the New Britain coast by mangroves in water deep enough to take the Harris Navy vessels. They hid when they could but travelling only by night was impossible due to the numerous coral reefs in the area so the craft often had no alternative but to travel by day. Even then they could not always avoid the reefs. Every one of the ships was stuck on a reef at least once in broad daylight. One day the *Bavaria* was stuck for eight hours. Nine bombers flew over and later returned the same way but did not attack nor apparently report them.

At Iboki, Mrs Gladys Baker, who had managed her own plantation on Witu since the death of her husband some years before, took over the care of the sick and set up the plantation residence as a makeshift hospital where she devotedly tended the suffering soldiers, for which all were grateful.

Better food and knowing the Harris Navy was at hand improved the morale of many of the men, but many others had reached the limit of human endurance. 'They wanted to sleep and not be awakened again.'

Keith knew evacuation was essential. He signalled Port Moresby for directions as to where on the New Guinea mainland the Harris Navy was to take the men. The reply from the army was that they were to sail to south of Madang, from there the men were to be marched 75 miles over the ranges to Chimbu in the New Guinea Highlands — at least a month's trek over mountains thousands of feet high.

"Brainless lot of buggers!" Keith 'exploded to a skeletal-like Rod Marsland, who was bootless'. When he had cooled down, Keith reported that the troops were not fit to march to Chimbu and asked about the possibility of air evacuation by flying boats. Less than a year later Catalinas would have been sent, but at that time they were in short supply and Keith's request was declined. They signalled him to use his own discretion.

Before Keith and Connal met up, Keith had been signalling with the basic Playfair code the Coastwatchers initially used. Connal was able to explain Eric's self-invented variation of Playfair, the 'Feldt Method', which would give messages even greater security and enable longer use of keywords.

Fortuitously for Connal, whose footwear had finally disintegrated, Keith was able to find him a pair of sandshoes which fitted his size 10 feet.

Good news came to hand with the confirmation that the missing *Lakatoi* was moored in the Witu group 50 miles away, and Keith was granted permission to commandeer her. He planned to embark the whole contingent and head for Australia. The Harris Navy would ferry the men to Witu.

He sent Bell and Marsland to take charge of her. Connal suggested that her white colour might act as a beacon and so a mix of any available dark paint was slapped on her to act as camouflage.

On 20 March, before leaving Iboki for Witu, Keith received intelligence from Port Moresby that the enemy had occupied Salamaua, Lae, Hanisch Harbour, Finschhafen, the Markham River Valley and Gasmata.

Keith and his group arrived at the ship early on 21 March. They found 800 bags of copra in the hold of the vessel. Connal had seen a copra fire start from a spark on a ship in Port Moresby and he advised it all be thrown overboard. When the ship's captain objected and asked who would pay for it as it was worth 1000 pounds, Keith suggested, 'You could put it on my personal account.'

Connal thought the result might make the ship a little too light in the bows and suggested that 10 tons of sand in bags be placed in the forward part of the hold. Keith put the troops to work, and with the aid of *Lakatoi's* loading gear the copra was soon dumped overboard. Meanwhile, a detail was busy emptying 200 copra bags, which another detail filled with sand. Thus they made more room in the hold for personnel, removed a fire hazard and still maintained stability of the ship.

Ken Douglas, Lincoln Bell and Bert Olander opted to stay behind and continue coast watching, and Keith gave them his teleradio. Bell wished them good luck as they set sail as darkness fell on the evening of 21 March with over 200 on board. The cabins were filled with the sick, the rest slept in the hold or wherever they could find space on deck. Three days later they made the Trobriands Islands, where the *Laurabada* was anchored. She had been the Papuan Administrator's yacht and was now under the command of Lieutenant Ivan Champion RANVR. As Champion viewed the crowded decks of the *Lakatoi*, he jokingly commented that Keith ought to be arrested for overloading.

They took on supplies of food and medicine from the *Laurabada* and then continued on their way to Cairns, North Queensland, entering the harbour on 28 March, nine weeks after the fall of Rabaul. A launch, with a pilot to guide them to shore, came alongside. Also on board it were also a doctor and Eric Feldt.

Eric later wrote:

> As the ship touched the wharf, McCarthy who had carried the burden for so long, drooped and wilted in complete mental and nervous exhaustion. With never a quip or a joke he found nothing now of interest or value. Ashore, he sat at a table, a dead cigarette between his lips, an untasted glass of beer before him, and answered questions in grunts and monosyllables.[13]

Hugh Mackenzie and the soldiers with him would have to wait longer before landing safely. On 6 April Lieutenant Alan Timperley of ANGAU took a fast launch by night from the Trobriands to Palmalmal. He located Hugh and the troops and reported the area clear of the enemy. Then on 8 April Champion made a night run to Palmalmal in the *Laurabada*, Hugh and his party and 147 other troops were embarked on 9 April and made the run out that night. It was Champion's turn to be in charge of an overloaded vessel.

Laurabada arrived safely at Port Moresby on 12 April. The troops returned to Australia via MV *Macdhui* in late April. Many troops had died of starvation and disease in the Waterfall Bay area and there was even a death during *Laurabada's* voyage out.

Lamont, Knight and Douglas were never heard of again. Even inquiries after the war did not elicit their fate. Major Bill Owen after a period of recuperation in Australia was promoted to Lieutenant Colonel and died in the Kokoda campaign. He received the United States Distinguished Service Cross and was Mentioned in Despatches.

Rupert Long recommended Hugh for a Mentioned in Despatches, but this was not awarded. Keith was later awarded an

MBE and Harris was Mentioned in Despatches. Mrs Gladys Baker, Rod Marsland and Frank Holland were also awarded MBEs and Douglas, Bell and Olander were Mentioned in Despatches, the last two posthumously.

The outcome for the soldiers taken prisoner in Rabaul was to be a very sad one. The officers were separated from the other ranks and remained in Rabaul. The others of Lark Force, about 853, plus 209 civilians, including Deputy Administrator Harold Page and District Officer Henry A Gregory, were loaded into the *Montevideo Maru*. On 1 July she was torpedoed by American submarine USS *Sturgeon*. Her captain was unaware that the unmarked ship was a POW vessel. None of the POWs survived, making it Australia's largest maritime disaster of World War II. In the Battle of Rabaul, only one honour was bestowed on the 2/22nd Battalion.

Of the 214 evacuated on the *Lakatoi* only six were passed fit. All the rest were debilitated, mentally and physically exhausted, weakened by inadequate food and exposure to the elements, suffering from malaria, sores and tropical ulcers. They were stressed and shattered wrecks.

> They had been abandoned by their Government and the Top Brass — with a few notable exceptions, such as Feldt and his team. But thanks to the skill, courage and determination of the remarkable Keith McCarthy and his supporting team, their lives were saved and some — in fact, just a handful - would live to fight again.[14]

Peter Feldt aged about 28.
Photograph sent to Gussie
(Alison Early, Feldt family photo)

Norland Feldt Family home in Ingham (Brenda Tait, Feldt family photo)

Gotty Feldt aged 20.
(Brenda Tait, Feldt family photo)

Eric, Lucy and Ada on the steps of Norland, Peter in doorway.
(Brenda Tait, Feldt family photo)

Feldt Family about 1914
Back row: Emma Caroline, Eric Augustas, Ada Bothilda.
Front row: Mabel Christina, Peter, Augusta, Lucy Victoria
(James Mitchell, Feldt family photo)

The 1913 Entry to the Australian Naval College
Back Row: Jack Bolton Newman, Eric Augustus Feldt, Paul Hugil Hirst, Adrian Joseph Beachleigh Watts, Elmer Benjamin Howells, Frank Edmond Getting, Llewellyn Leigh Watkins, Otto Edmund Albert, Frank Lockwood Larkins, Edwin Scott Nurse
Middle Row: Harry Bertram Vallentine, Winn Locker Reilly, Harold Bruce Farncomb, James Claude Durie Esdaile, John Augustine Collins, Hugh Alexander Mackenzie, Peyton James Kimlin, Norman Keith Calder, Rupert Basil Michel Long
Front Row: Cyril Arthur Roy Sadleir, George William Thomas Armitage, Joseph Burnett, Lloyd Falconer Gilling, Earnest Semple 'Dick' Cunningham, Henry 'Harry' Arthur Showers, Horace John Harold Thompson, John Valentine Stuart 'Jack' Lecky, Alfred Denis Conder
(RAN College Magazine 1913)

RIGHT MAN, RIGHT PLACE, WORST TIME

The Pioneer Class at Otto Albert's Grave (Peter Jones from George Kimlin)

Eric Feldt in Navy (Feldt family photo)

Eric Feldt in Navy (Feldt family photo)

RIGHT MAN, RIGHT PLACE, WORST TIME

Eric Feldt and his crew of *Aloha* on the Sepik Expedition 1924
(Peter Jones from NAA)

Eric Feldt and Nancy Echlin Wedding in
The *Brisbane Courier* 11 Jan 1933 (SLQ)

Commander Rupert Long (*The Coast Watchers*, 1946)

Commander Eric Feldt
(*The Coast Watchers*, 1946)

Eric and Nancy Feldt with Pickles the dog and
Hector the cat Port Moresby 1940
(Alison Early, Feldt family photo)

Teleradio (AWM 015364)

Lieutenant-Commander Hugh Mackenzie   Lieutenant-Colonel Keith McCarthy
(*The Coast Watchers*, 1946)

Lieutenant Jack Read   Lieutenant Paul Mason
(*The Coast Watchers*, 1946)

Lieutenant Alan Fairlie 'Bill' Kyle
(AWM P03419.001)

A Group of Coastwatchers
Back Row: Wright, Skinner, Bridge, Cambridge, Walker, Robertson, Seton, Williams
Front Row: Ashton, Noakes, Rhoades, Feldt, Mackenzie, Marsland, Koch, Campbell
(*The Coast Watchers*, 1946)

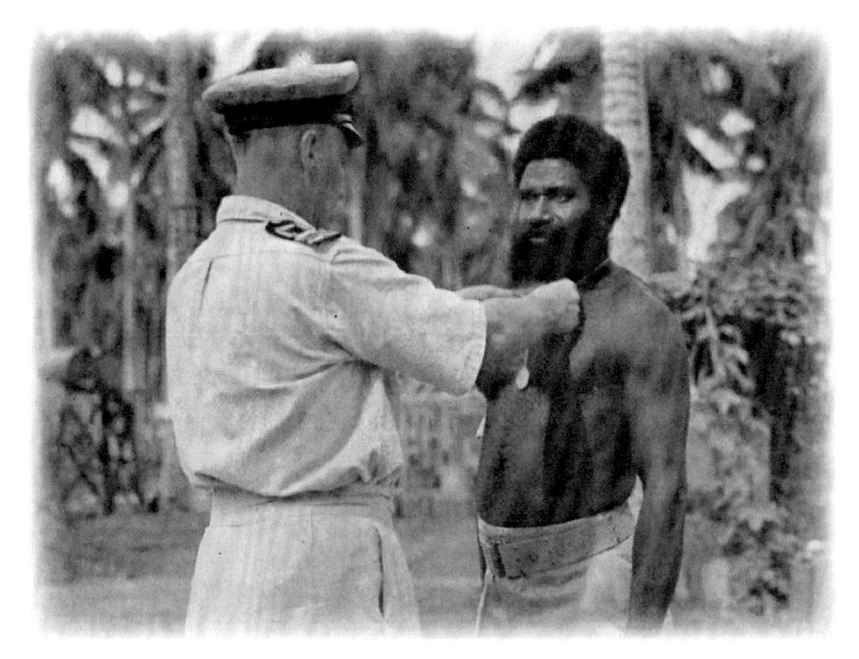

Sergeant Yauwika receiving the Loyal Services Medal (*The Coast Watchers*, 1946)

Major Donald Kennedy (*The Coast Watchers*, 1946)

Paluma being fitted out, Townsville, 1942 Castle Hill in background
(Image no. 115963 SLQ)

Paluma complete with a Gun deck at Nissan Island, 1944 (www.ozatwar.com)

COMMANDER ERIC FELDT HIS LIFE AND HIS COASTWATCHERS

Mr. W. H. Brooksbank
(*The Coast Watchers*, 1946)

Commander McManus
(*The Coast Watchers*, 1946)

RIGHT MAN, RIGHT PLACE, WORST TIME

Admiral Halsey's thank you to Eric Feldt The *Courier Mail* 28 April 1954 (Trove)

Coastwatchers Memorial Lighthouse, Madang

Eric Feldt at opening of Coastwatchers Memorial Lighthouse
(Brenda Tait, Feldt family photo)

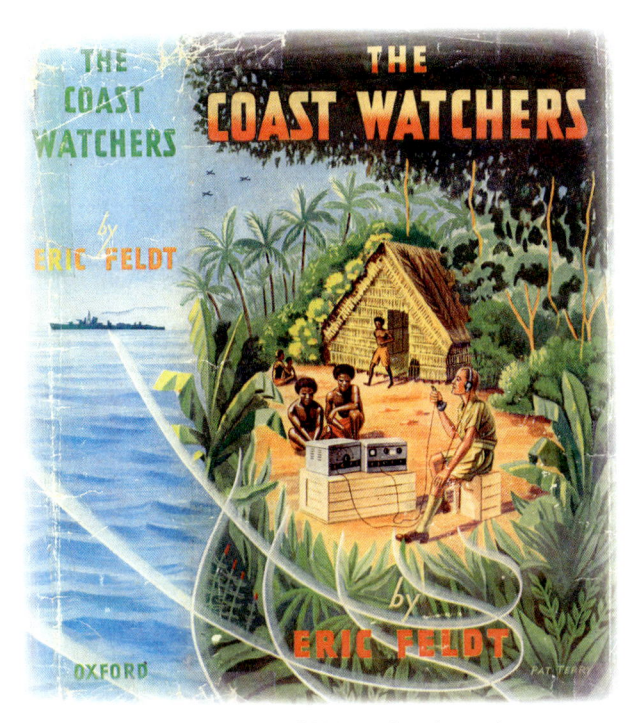

The Coast Watchers, 1946 Australian dust jacket

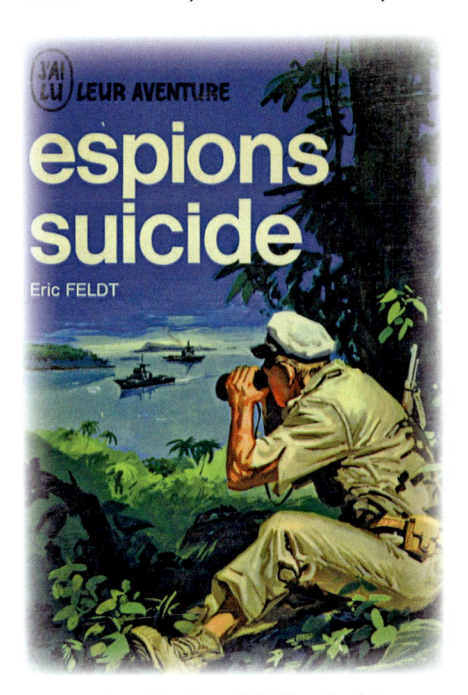

The Coast Watchers, 1964 French edition

Commander Eric Feldt portrait by Norman Carter 1957 (AWM ART17504)

CHAPTER 8

THE COASTWATCHERS AND THE JAPANESE INVASION OF THE N.E. AREA

The mighty Japanese military forces flooded south and shattered the Feldt Fence of Coastwatchers. Parts of the fence fled before the storm, parts were destroyed and, remarkably, some parts remained standing — or more accurately, dodging and weaving.

In the New Ireland area, the Coastwatchers position was precarious. On Anir, Leading Telegraphist J.L. Woodroffe had recently replaced Chief Yeoman Lamont. As previously mentioned, Lamont arrived in Rabaul just before it was captured and went south with Hugh and Connal's group. Lamont bravely and unselfishly stayed with his sick comrades as the rest of the party went on. He was never seen again. Whether his demise was from disease or by the hand of the enemy is unknown.

Guy Allen on the Duke of York Islands was also never heard from again. C.C. Jervis on Nissan sent a coded signal, which was to be his last, saying a ship had stopped outside the entrance to the lagoon. Woodroffe on Anir was off the air.

Ken W. Chambers on Emirau escaped by launch only to be driven ashore by a destroyer when passing Rabaul. He joined another party, found another launch and escaped to the Trobriands, and from there to Port Moresby. The Admiralty Islands were evacuated after everything that could be of use to the enemy was destroyed.

As tragic as the loss of these Coastwatchers was, Eric found some irony in the Japanese perceiving the strategic importance of these islands. In eliminating the Coastwatchers so quickly they had paid them a backhanded compliment.

At Kavieng, when invasion was imminent, the DO, Major J.H. McDonald, moved most of the civilians to a camp in the jungle on the western side of the island. Cornelius Lyons Page in the Tabar islands and Bill Kyle at Namatanai continued to transmit their messages. On the New Guinea mainland, PO Pursehouse, the Coastwatcher at Finschhafen, headed inland as the Japanese approached.

An incident in New Britain was to have significant and tragic results. The small island of Gasmata, on the south coast, manned by ADO John Daymond, PO Eric Mitchell and medical assistant Dickie Squires, was directly on the air route from Rabaul to Port Moresby. Their report of a large number of aircraft flying towards Port Moresby gave a warning of the port's first air raid, and this resulted in minimising casualties.

However, the Australian Broadcasting Commission in Australia broke the news that the enemy had been sighted off Gasmata. This uncensored release of information alerted the Japanese that a reporting station was thereabouts. In a message to Keith McCarthy, Eric Mitchell complained of the stupidity of those who had let the report go to air and that the Japanese were sure to take action. On 9 February 1942, two weeks after the fall of Rabaul, the Japanese landed a force at Gasmata and captured Daymond and Squires. Mitchell who had set the teleradio up in the jungle reported their capture and that the enemy were now looking for him. Keith signalled for Mitchell to come across the island and join him, but silence was the only reply.

Back in Townsville, Eric wanted to position a Coastwatcher near Salamaua before the enemy invaded. He had Leigh Vial in mind, and Vial himself was a willing volunteer for a coastwatching assignment. He had been a young Assistant District Officer and was among the small number of those evacuated from Rabaul by the RAAF. When he arrived in Townsville he had conveyed his desire to be a Coastwatcher to Eric. For Vial to be commissioned into the Navy, though, would entail an involved process requiring forms, interviews and a medical examination, and would take a long time. The tedious requirements led Eric to later vent his frustration in his book.

> The Red Tape Plant is, of course, one of the wonders of biology. It flourishes in offices; the larger and older the office, the heavier the infestation. It grows apace, strangling and paralysing, its seed proliferated by letters from an already infected office, invisible seed which falls as the envelope is opened, and grows at once. Each segment, like the tapeworm, has full male and female organs of reproduction so it propagates continuously.[1]

The Navy, being an old service, was steeped in red tape. The Air Force, on the other hand, was a young service and could clear the way for Vial to be commissioned. Eric turned to them and Vial was commissioned as a Pilot-Officer in two days. In less than a week, Eric's team had him supplied with teleradio, codes and food. The RAAF flew him to Salamaua and he hid himself in the jungle on the hills a few days before the Japanese arrived.

> Vial sat in the hills, watching Salamaua airfield. In addition to aircraft from there, he saw all those flying from Lae towards Port Moresby. For six months his warning voice was familiar to all who listened on 'X' frequency, a quiet, unhurried voice reporting aircraft on their way, their types, numbers, course and height. As most raids came from Lae or Salamaua, his voice was the voice listened for, and at last a correspondent dubbed him the 'Golden Voice', a title which embarrassed the modest Leigh Vial considerably. At the end of his watch, he was awarded the American Distinguished Service Cross for his work.[2]

While the Coastwatchers on the Papuan coast remained, those from the outer islands, such as the Trobriands and Samarai, were evacuated. In anticipation that the Japanese would strafe any suspected coastwatching posts, Eric instructed all Coastwatchers to move their teleradios to small shacks some distance away. If the shack looked like a dunny that would be all the better, because the Japanese would see no point in bombing an outhouse.

In the Solomon Islands, the Japanese were beginning to put a dent in the Feldt surveillance fence as they proceeded with their drive southward. In 1942 the northern islands, including Buka and Bougainville, were part of the Australian Mandated Territory of New Guinea while the southern ones were under British rule.

A few days after the fall of Rabaul, a native police boy on watch on a hill above Kieta on the east coast of Bougainville reported seeing a Japanese flying boat just outside the harbour. The district officer, J.I. Merrylees, his staff and other civilians, boarded a small schooner and sailed to Port Moresby.

Inestimably, fortune smiled on Australia and America when Jack Read and Paul Mason, among others, decided to stay.

William John 'Jack' Read was born in Hobart, Tasmania in 1905. He took up duty as ADO at Buka Passage just a month before Japan entered the war.

> He was of medium height, wiry in build, with dark hair and clear grey eyes, straight gash of a mouth above a long, firm chin. His voice was deep and a little harsh, his laugh explosive. His manner was blunt and straightforward, with more firmness than tact in it. He had been in New Guinea for twelve years and had experience in many parts but had not been before in Bougainville.[3]

Jack's DO post was on Sohano, a small island in Buka Passage. Also at Buka was a small detachment of AIF. In September 1941, a 1400 ft airstrip had been built on the island and 25 commandos of the First Australian Independent Company, under the command of Lieutenant John H. Mackie, had been sent to guard it. Large quantities of gasoline, oil and 250 pound bombs were stored nearby.

In the event of an enemy attack, Corporal Bill Dolby was to destroy it all.

With the Allied position rapidly deteriorating, Jack sought advice from locals as to the best place to make a supply dump. Aravia was chosen, but access was not exactly easy. It involved a 20-mile drive down the coast to Baniu Plantation, then a two-hour climb inland to reach the village, more than a 1000ft above sea level. Lieutenant

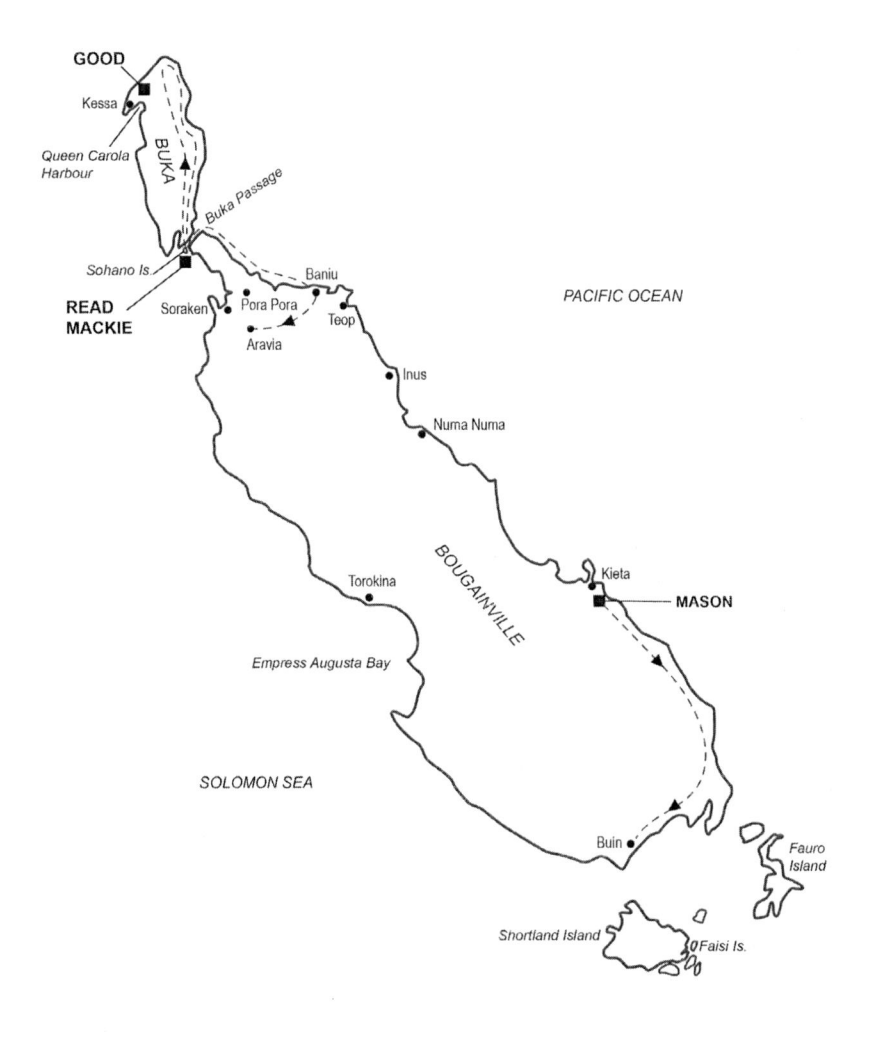

Coastwatchers of Buka and Bougainville

Mackie also set up a few scattered dumps in the hills behind Soraken.

Enemy reconnaissance planes began circling Buka Passage a couple of days after Rabaul was captured. Jack decided it was time to abandon his post at Sohano and collected supplies and equipment for transfer to a safer location. Corporal Dolby set off explosive charges to blow up the fuel and ammunition depots.

Jack left in the government launch *Nugget* with a few police boys and headed for Baniu. On the way, a small Japanese float plane flew over and fired rapid bursts of machine-gun fire at them. Luckily the pilot missed the *Nugget* by a couple of hundred yards. He flew off but reappeared a short time later with five large flying boats. They were not after small ships and flew on to bomb Buka Passage, including Sohano and the Buka airstrip.

Yet again the Allies were incredibly lucky that the pilot's aim was poor, and Jack lived to fight and sight another day. Jack was to reflect on his fortunate escape in later years: 'Since then, I have often thought that the Japanese pilots might not have been so easy on us if they had guessed the big part our teleradio was destined to play in their defeat at Guadalcanal.'[4]

News arrived the next day that Kieta had been occupied by the Japanese, but this turned out to be false. A few days later, Jack received a letter by runner from Drummond Thomson, manager of Numa Numa Plantation, saying that Kieta was definitely not occupied. The letter also said that the natives had gone on a looting spree after the Europeans had departed, but Dr Kroening had stepped in and established order. Thomson insisted that Jack go to Kieta and sort out the mess. Jack sent two of his assistants back to Sohana for more stores and took the launch to Kieta, where, on entering the harbour, he saw a white flag flying over the government building.

Jack was met by Sergeant Yauwika of the native police, a man who had served with Jack in other parts of the territory. Yauwika and his police had tried to stop the looting and destruction by the local population and the hundreds of natives from nearby villages who had joined in. They were unsuccessful until Dr Kroening added his support. Dr Kroening was the DMO and had lived in the area since it was German territory. His leanings were known to be towards Germany. Jack thanked Kroening for stepping into the breach left by Merrylees, but, as ADO, Jack would carry on where Merrylees had left off. As they talked, Sergeant Yauwika and his police marched to the flagstaff took down the white surrender flag and raised the Australian flag in its place.

Although not imminent, Jack realised the fall of Kieta was only a matter of time. He immediately began to establish hidden supply dumps and rid the town of anything that might be of value to the enemy. Most of the tinned food and rice that had been carried off to the villages was gradually returned by the natives.

As no attempt had been made by DO Merrylees to remove anything in the District Office before departing, Jack made sure everything was removed before he finally left Kieta to its fate. He left Sergeant Yauwika in charge. The actual Japanese occupation of Kieta did not take place until July 1942.

On 24 February Jack met with Drummond Thomson and Paul Mason at Inus Plantation, where Paul was the manager, to discuss the situation.

Paul Edward Allen Mason was born in North Sydney in 1901.

> He was a short, fair man who gazed benignly through his spectacles and spoke slowly, generally pausing considerably before replying to even a casual remark. He had been in the islands for over twenty years, was over forty and less like a tough guy to look at than any other man on Bougainville, missionaries not excepted.[5]

One of Paul's hobbies was radio. He had taught himself all there was to know about the workings, could do his own repairs, send and receive Morse and understand signal procedures. He had been a Coastwatcher since 1939.

Paul revealed that he had received two messages from Eric that read in part:

> You will be of great value if you can remain and keep contact for over six months. Suggest you prepare a base two days inland and retire to it when necessary. Make a garden and stock up with fowl and pigs. If you want essential spares and stores, advise your requirements and we may be able to drop them.[6]

Six months was a pure guess on Eric's part. Only they would know to what extent Eric's hope that the two men would stay had influenced them, but to Australia's good fortune Jack Read and Paul Mason decided to accept the challenge and stay.

Although Jack was staying, he strongly encouraged missionaries and civilians, especially women, to evacuate. Some did, but others elected to stay. Jack and the remaining men with teleradios decided to pool their resources with Lieutenant Mackie and establish five coastwatching posts, subject to Eric's approval. These were to be set up at Kessa, Numa Numa, Inus, Buin and Aravia, and this was achieved by 6 March.

Percy Good at Kessa Plantation reached a decision to stop coastwatching and gave his teleradio to four of the soldiers of the First Australian Independent Company so they could establish a coastwatching post in the hills. Their radio operator was Signalman D.I. Sly.

Over the 7 and 8 March, Jack and Paul heard calls coming from the Kessa radio but were unable to understand the transmission or to have signals they sent get through to Kessa. On Monday 9 March they heard a call with an urgent signal to deliver. Again, they were unable to establish effective communication so Jack dispatched a native runner to Kessa, which was a three-day journey.

Late on Wednesday 11 March, Jack heard from Fred Archer at his plantation on the west coast of Buka. He reported that six Japanese cruisers and two destroyers had anchored at Queen Carola Harbour on the previous Monday. Obviously that was the message that the soldiers had been trying to transmit. Jack immediately sent the information on to Don Macfarlan at Tulagi.

Jack was disappointed that the soldiers had been unable to transmit the important information. It seemed that Signalman Sly did not have sufficient knowledge of how to operate the teleradio. Jack decided to head closer to Buka Passage to see if he could remedy the situation. On Thursday he heard from Archer that the enemy ships had put to sea on Tuesday night. Jack passed this update on to Don at Tulagi.

When Jack reached Sorem, on the northwest coast of Bougainville, he discovered that the four soldiers who had been manning Kessa were there. Signalman Sly said that on Monday morning his lookout had seen Japanese ships heading to Queen Carola Harbour, but because he was unfamiliar with the radio transmitter he could not send the message. A few hours later they were almost taken by surprise by an enemy landing party. They just had time to dismantle the teleradio and hide it in the jungle greenery.

Father Hennessy, a local missionary, intercepted the Japanese patrol and managed to stall them so that the soldiers could escape to hide deeper in the jungle. After the patrol returned to their ship, the soldiers beat a rapid retreat to Sorem. They had left the teleradio behind so Jack sent a native police party to retrieve it while he went to Bonis Plantation.

Fred Archer also made his way to Bonis and filled in more of the story. Percy Good had also received a visit from the Japanese patrol at his house on Kessa Plantation. Good still had plenty of radio spare parts and there was an outline on a wall where the teleradio had been. He told them that he had owned a radio in the past but no longer had one. They placed him on parole not to leave or to engage in any hostile activity.

On 13 March, an Australian radio news broadcast did the unthinkable and announced that a Japanese naval force had visited Queen Carola Harbour. Jack's teleradio message to Tulagi had been picked up and used as the basis for the news report. Those in Bougainville hearing the broadcast feared the worst for Percy Good. Assuming that a show of force might be necessary, Jack organised an armed expedition of about twelve.

They were just about to board *Nugget* when a native scout arrived bringing news that Japanese warships had just returned to Kessa. Unable to risk continuing, they hoped against hope that Good would somehow survive.

On Wednesday 18 March, a police constable brought confirmation of their fears. Percy Good had been killed and buried near his house. The ships had departed on Monday night.

At midnight, Jack's team took to *Nugget* for the trip north. Local natives showed them Good's grave and Jack ordered his body be exhumed. A bullet had entered through his left ear and exited above his right eye. His jaw was broken and abrasions marked his face and neck.

> We stood trancelike — shocked and angered. There was a strained silence: not a word was spoken as the body was reburied in its shallow grave.[7]

In Australia, measures had been taken after the deaths of the Coastwatchers of Gasamata to stop the thoughtless release by the media of potentially damaging information to all and sundry, including the enemy. After the death of Good these were strongly reiterated and reinforced. This time the seriousness of the situation was understood and no further revealing information went to air.

Since the Japanese had invaded the North East Area, Eric had been concerned about the status of the Coastwatchers. Despite Eric's urging that they be enlisted in the Navy, the Naval Board had decided that civilian Coastwatchers were to cease reporting once the enemy occupied their area. Now civilian Coastwatchers were reporting from enemy held land and all the services were gladly making use of the information they sent. Very early in the piece Eric had asked that all Coastwatchers be given naval rank. Rupert had given full support to the recommendation, but nothing was happening.

> '... it seemed to have become enmeshed in the red tape forest and needed an explosion to shift it . I knew that Long, a personal friend, would not mind if I fired a delayed action shell at him in the hope that it would explode somewhere beyond him and blow the red tape away.'

On 21 March Eric cabled Rupert: "Is any progress being made to appoint Read, Mason and Page to naval forces or are they expected to give their lives as Good has done without recompense or protection."

Rupert used the cable in one of his battles with naval red tape. Fourteen days later Read was commissioned as a lieutenant, Page and Mitchell as sub-lieutenants and Mason as a petty officer. Eric was also able to obtain a war pension for Percy Good's widow. Having naval rank ensured pensions were paid to the wives of Coastwatchers should they become widows. Eric thought at the time that being dressed in uniform would afford his men more respect and better treatment should they be captured by the Japanese. Ultimately, this turned out to be a naïve and erroneous assumption.

During March, the enemy took over the Shortland Islands and established a seaplane base at Faisi.

Since giving the earliest warnings of enemy aircraft approaching Rabaul, Con Page had continued his coastwatching from the Tabar Islands. Cornelius Lyons Page was born in Mudgee, New South Wales, in 1912, and moved to New Guinea with his parents when he was nineteen. He had been working as the manager of Pigibut

Plantation on Simberi Island, one of the three islands in the Tabar group, the others being Tatau and Tabar. With Con was his partner, a young Tabar woman called Ansin Bulu.

The Japanese had detected his signals shortly after they invaded Rabaul and Kavieng. Five days after taking Kavieng they sent a warship to Simberi and raided the plantation. They found it deserted. Con had moved with his teleradio to a hut in the jungle. Once the ship had gone, he signalled its departure.

In Eric's estimation, Con continuing as a Coastwatcher was potentially suicidal. After conferring with Rupert, he sent a signal to Con saying, 'You have done magnificent work. Your position is now dangerous if you continue reporting and under present circumstances your reports are of little value. You are to bury your teleradio and may join either party on New Ireland or take other measures for safety. Good Luck. Feldt.'

Con ignored the warning and continued to send signals about the occupation of Kavieng, the guns and defence positions. It was obvious he had no intention of leaving. Eric reasoned that a period of silence might fool the Japanese into believing he had left and sent another message. 'Your reports appreciated, but it is more important to keep yourself free. Do not transmit except in extreme emergency. You will be ordered to make reports when they will be of greatest value.'

The position in March 1942 was that the Japanese held Rabaul, Kavieng, Gasmata, Finschhafen, Lae and Salamaua. It was a most demanding and stressful time for Eric.

Myriad emotions and thoughts must have besieged him as he worked from his back room in Townsville. Some of his Coastwatchers had sent what was presumed to be a last signal. Not a word had been heard from others, many of whom were men that he had personally asked to enrol — Allen, Jervis, Woodroffe and Lamont. For many weeks this was also true for his friend Hugh

Mackenzie and his Port Moresby assistant Connal Gill. Others like Daymond and Squires were known to have been captured, and Mitchell was likely to have met the same fate. Some like Con Page refused to obey Eric's orders to leave a hopeless situation. There were those, like Bill Kyle, Jack Read and Paul Mason, who he had asked to stay on because of the probable value of their observations, knowing the enormous risks they would be facing. There was Keith McCarthy, who he had asked to perform mission impossible. One fatality was certain — Percy Good. Most of these men were well known to Eric and several were his good friends.

In the midst of all this Eric received an official reprimand. It was because he had used the word *sked*, which was then a new word coined for radio use, derived from *schedule* to denote an agreed time of transmission.

> This apparently was most offensive. The thought that some senior officer, charged with the defence of Australia, had nothing better to do while the country's existence hung by a thread cured me of any tendency to use slang for the next half hour. I used only old Anglo-Saxon four letter words or their derivatives, coupled with that good Norman word which was the first William's title before he became the Conqueror.[8]

The enemy's success was such that by the end of March, Con Page was a dot in an ocean of Japanese occupied territory. The natives, who originally had been faithful, were beginning to waver in their loyalty and some were enrolled by the Japanese as police.

Food was running short for Con. Supplies at the plantation were nearly all consumed by the end of April. The RAAF, impressed by Con's courage, agreed to make a drop, but it was late May before it could be done. Food supplies and naval cap and badges were dropped at night. The supplies indicating outside support temporarily restored his prestige a little with the natives, but not for long.

His appointment as Sub-Lieutenant RANVR, along with appointments for Read, Mitchell and Mason, without signing any forms, interviews or medicals, was a happening without precedent. Eric was vindicated. 'At last the red tape was cut', but Eric knew Con could not escape the native police. Eric sought help from one of the recently arrived American submarines. These were old subs that had taken a beating in the Philippines. A rescue rendezvous was arranged for early June. Con waited in a boat at the agreed place for three nights in a row, each night flashing his torch and hoping to see the submarine surface. Unbeknown to him the sub had developed a serious mechanical fault and had to crawl back to Townsville. Because of the reefs surrounding the islands, sending another submarine was not an option until the next full moon, a whole month away.

Con and Ansin Bulu moved into caves to hide. He signalled that the Japanese and natives were using dogs to hunt him. Con messaged that his only chance of escape would be a flying boat landing on the west side, where there was a small island. Eric appealed to Air-Commodore Lukis for the RAAF for one last try. It was extremely dangerous for a Catalina and its crew of nine to fly to Tabar. The Japanese were known to have speedy planes stationed at Kavieng, only 80 miles away. 'The Air-Commodore's big heart made his head assent.'

The time, 5.30pm Tuesday 16 June, and exact location of pick up were signalled to Con. With Squadron Leader Frank Chapman as the Captain, the Catalina took off for Tabar. According to a document on the Anzac Portal website, Eric was onboard to guide the pilot. The plane flew over and around the agreed pick up site, searching carefully, but there was no sign of a European. Natives sitting on the beach gave no acknowledgement.

The article on the Anzac Portal is an unattributed document telling the story of Cornelius Page. ['The stubborn Coastwatcher — Cornelius Page' AWM 54 Item 629/1/11].

Did Eric go on the Catalina? He makes no mention of it in his book, but perhaps it was something he did not wish to disclose. To have gone would have been a caring and brave act, but at the same time a rather reckless one, putting his leadership of the Coastwatchers in jeopardy.

Two years later, Sub-Lieut. Stan Bell, who was attached to US Naval Headquarters, Emirau, visited Tabar and questioned the natives about Con's fate. An educated native had written an account and Bell obtained it. Con had been captured around 16 June 1942. He and his friend and fellow Coastwatcher Jack Talmage, a plantation owner from Tatau Island, were in a small hut in the jungle. A hostile native disclosed their position to the Japanese who surrounded the hut and captured the men as they slept. They were taken to Kavieng and later executed.

Soon after, Bell returned to Tabar and this time found Ansin Bulu, looking emaciated and aged beyond her years. She handed him a note written on a grubby, crumpled piece of toilet paper, in faint pencil:

To C.O. Allied Forces.

For Lieut.-Com. E.A. Feldt, RAN

From Sub- Lieut. C.L. Page, RANVR

9th July.

Re the female Ansin Bulu,

Nakapur Village,

Simberi Island, Tabar,

This female has been in my service 7 years. Has been of great value to me since Jan. Japs looted all she owned value 50 pounds, put her in prison and God knows what else.

Her crime was she stuck.

Sir, please do your best. Sub-Lieut. C. L. Page

Eric noted that Con had said not a word about himself.

Ansin had been captured a week before Con and was in Kavieng jail when he and Talmage were brought in. She was released from prison shortly afterwards and the note had been smuggled out to her with instruction to give it to the first white man she met. This happened to be Bell. 'She had concealed it for nearly two years, with that fatalistic patience of the native, and at last delivered it into the right hands.'

During his time in New Guinea, Eric's and Bill Kyle's paths had often crossed and the two had become good friends. Eric considered Bill to be his best friend, and Nan Feldt was also very fond of him. Alan Fairlie Kyle, known as Bill, was born in Toowoomba, Queensland, in 1898. He had married the previous year, 1941, in Sydney, somewhat later in life than common.

> Bill Kyle was very short, rather plump, with wide set grey eyes. He had served in World War I as a youth and had been in New Guinea fourteen years. Despite his size, he was a good athlete who had played first-grade cricket in Sydney. In himself, he was a mixture of idealism and worldliness, a man who could take a strong dislike and not trouble to conceal it, and who formed deep friendships to which he gave fanatical loyalty.[9]

When the war in the Pacific began, Bill was ADO at Namatanai on New Ireland. With him as PO was Edmund Reginald Gregory Wade Benham, born in Dubbo, New South Wales, in 1914, also married.

> Greg Benham was about thirty, tall, with a slouchy gait - a man who moved easily through a pleasantly frictionless life, the smoothness of his relationships with others being of his own making.[10]

Bill and Greg stayed at Namatanai until they saw the Japanese convoy arriving off Rabaul. They set off down the east coast, gathering planters and missionaries, and reached Metlik, near Cape St. George, on the southern tip of New Ireland. Bill signalled that he had a boat and a party of 10 and asked for instructions. Due to an error, his message went to Port Moresby and was not sent on to Townsville. When Bill received a reply for him to arrange the evacuation, but for him to remain, he thought it had come from Eric, his best friend. He instantly agreed. Bill urged Greg, who was unwell at the time, to go. Greg declared that if Bill was staying so was he.

They compromised the positioning of their post by setting up on a ridge overlooking St. George's Channel. Although moving further inland would have been safer if the Japanese landed, by maintaining contact with the coastal natives they hoped to preserve their loyalty, which may have otherwise been lost.

A month after the fall of Rabaul, 10 AIF commandos, trying to escape from Kavieng were driven ashore near Cape St. George. Bill and Greg knew that if they continued to feed the soldiers they would run out of supplies for themselves so Eric authorised for food to be dropped to them. Their receiver was also malfunctioning so arrangements were made for a replacement to be dropped as well. This was the very first of many drops of supplies to Coastwatchers.

> Like all pioneering efforts, it had its difficulties. We had some experience in dropping supplies in New Guinea in peace-time and knew, for instance, that a half-filled bag of flour landed well, whereas a full bag burst like a bomb. But some articles had to have parachutes, so we turned to the RAAF. In peace-time, they had devised two supply dropping equipments; one, a harness of webbing in which a packing case could be lashed; the other, a cylinder for dropping liquid. The RAAF had only one of each in Australia. They gave us both. The radio receiver was packed in a case and lashed in the webbing equipment, but the liquid container was found to be unusable. In Port Moresby, F/O. Neal came to our rescue and the remainder of the supplies was fixed to condemned personnel parachutes.[11]

Wing-Commander Pearce, in Moresby, organised the drop. A Hudson bomber would be used in daylight for the radio and a Catalina for the other supplies at night. The latter would then go on to bomb Rabaul. Eric offered to go as a guide in both planes. Pearce said he could not go in either as that would only mean one more person killed if the planes did not return. A good sketch would do.

The pilots reported successful drops, but during the day three Japanese destroyers were anchored off shore and had fired at the Hudson. The ships were gone by the time of the night drop.

Nothing was heard from Bill and Greg for some time, and with a heavy heart Eric accepted their loss. Then, six weeks later, he was surprised and delighted to hear them come back on air again. They were at Muliama on the east coast, and the soldiers were with them. They had recovered some of the supplies and the receiver but had spent time evading the Japanese. More than once they had been betrayed by Chinese and natives. On the first occasion, they were on the ridge overlooking St. George's Channel, and the enemy got to within 20ft of Bill. He had to break through the side of the hut and dive down the mountain. On another occasion they were staying in a deserted house and walked out the back steps as the Japanese came in the front door. Bill thought the only reason they had not been captured was because the Japanese were 'mug bushmen'.

They had had trouble with the teleradio. However, another group had joined them. DO Major J.H. McDonald and the civilians from Kavieng had moved from their camp in the jungle on the western side of the island across to join Bill and Greg on the eastern side. A member of this party was able to get the radio going.

The first signal they received was Eric's, which included telling them that Bill was now a Lieutenant and Greg a Sub-Lieutenant RANVR, and that payments were being sent to their wives. Shortly after, Eric was able to arrange for a boat captained by Harry Murray, a planter from Kavieng, to evacuate the group, which numbered 23. Bill once again asked for instructions.

Eric took several factors into consideration. Naval forces were readying for a battle in the Coral Sea and a Coastwatcher at Muliama might provide vital information. The information Eric had to hand was that Allied forces from the New Hebrides would soon be launching a counter attack on Rabaul. Such an attack would benefit from Coastwatchers in key positions on New Ireland and, assuming a successful outcome, would mean a positive reversal of fortune for the Allies.

Eric sent instructions for them to come out if they considered the position untenable. They replied that they would stay. For a second time, Bill and Greg watched as others sailed away to safety.

About this time, a message was received that although the coastwatching post on Anir had been burnt, Woodroffe was alive and hiding in the hills. A drop of food and teleradio was made to Anir, but no reply was received.

Another supply drop was made to Bill and Greg a few days after the boat of evacuees had left. They continued to successfully send signals until the end of May when Bill sent news that the Japanese had started a civil administration at Namatanai. Eric viewed this development extremely gravely. He feared this would further weaken the loyalty of the natives and increase the likelihood of them assisting in the hunt for the Coastwatchers.

Due to the seriousness of the situation, Eric appealed for a submarine to rescue the two men. This was granted and a rendezvous set for the night of 30 May 1942. Eric anxiously awaited the return of the submarine until, four days overdue, she made contact. She reported engine trouble but expected to dock the next morning. Eric was there to see the sub arrive but, to his great disappointment and dismay, without Bill and Greg.

The submarine had kept the rendezvous for two nights but the Coastwatchers had not appeared. The sub had continued on a prearranged journey and limped home three weeks later.

"After all our high hopes, the shock of the bad news was like a kick in the guts, for Kyle was my closest friend."

Eric was not about to give up. Pilot-Officer Cecil John Mason, a former planter, now in the RAAF was available to go if another submarine could be found. On the same trip as searching for Bill and Greg, he could also try to rescue Woodroffe from Anir. Eric went to Brisbane to personally appeal to the US submarine commander. The Admiral, with all his staff present, saw him. Eric found his attempts of persuasion were not working, until he presented a poignant letter Bill had sent out with McDonald's escapee group. Parts of the letter are as follows:

Muliama

28/4/42

Dear Eric,

....

Got your radio — don't worry about us — with extra food and medicine we can last for some months unless there is more patrol activity than there has been to date. However, I hope you can eventually get us out or we counter-attack, as they seem to murder anyone they find with teleradios

Hope to see you soon, Eric, old son, and many thanks for looking after us, also for writing to the ball and chain. Give Nan my love and tell her she had better lay down a cellar in good time for my return. All the very best and let us know for Gawd's sake any helpful news or any prospects of getting out. It gets a bit wearing as we have no reading matter or anything, the nerves are not the best after the little bitches have chased us round and round the mulberry bush.

Au revoir,

Bill

The Admiral's heart was in the right place and he authorised a submarine. On 3 July Cecil Mason, armed with a rifle, went ashore in a collapsible canoe. He landed near Muliama and soon met a native. Too late, he saw the villager was wearing an armband with the emblem of the rising sun. The native denied any knowledge of Bill and Greg but said there was a Japanese post at Muliama. Mason returned to the submarine that night.

The following night, he landed on Anir and found a friendly native who confirmed that Woodroffe was alive and living in the bush. Mason gave him a note to give Woodroffe, saying he would return at midnight the next night and for Woodroffe to meet him at his landing place.

Mason accidentally fired his rifle when getting back into his canoe and shot a hole in it. Stranded, he used his torch to signal the sub, which sent a rubber dinghy to pick him up. The canoe was able to be repaired for further use.

Not long after Mason returned to the submarine, a steady light was seen on shore. It appeared to be coming from a lantern. Mason who had not slept for 36 hours was exhausted and the approaching dawn was a concern for the sub's captain. It was decided to try again the following night, as Mason had planned.

Mason reached the shore by 10pm the next night. The submarine moved off and returned near midnight. As they came in, a Japanese patrol boat appeared. The sub quickly submerged. After two hours, all was clear and the sub surfaced to retrieve Mason. There was no sign of him or Woodroffe. They waited until dawn was dangerously close and then returned at midnight for the next four nights, but in vain.

Nothing more could be done to try to rescue the men. All Eric could do was to arrange for supplies to be dropped at a known friendly village in New Ireland in case his best friend and the others were still fugitives in the jungle. 'This was done regularly — a forlorn hope.'

Eric later learned that Mason and Woodroffe had been captured, but no details of how nor of their demise came to light. In 1943 he found out that Bill and Greg had been captured just 18 hours before the planned rendezvous on 30 May. Like Con Page and Jack Talmage, they were executed near Kavieng.

Bill Kyle and Greg Benham were each awarded the British Distinguished Service Cross for their courageous and unselfish service. The award was not published at the time, as it was vital that the Japanese not know of their outstanding achievements in spying, relaying information and evading detection for so many months.

As the war progressed, it became apparent to Rupert that there was a need to combine all intelligence operations. General MacArthur had arrived in Australia in March, and on 18 April 1942 MacArthur was appointed Supreme Commander of Allied Forces in the Southwest Pacific Area (SWPA). His authority was needed for covert organisations to be housed under one umbrella. MacArthur conferred with his Chief of Intelligence, Colonel Charles Willoughby, and on 8 June authorised the formation of the Allied Intelligence Bureau (AIB).

The establishment of AIB took place over the next month. Space was found on the fifth floor of 121 Collins Street, Melbourne. Willoughby suggested Rupert for the job of heading up the organisation, but he was needed in his role of DNI and combining both positions would be too demanding. Next choice was Eric, but at that time there was no one who could take his place as head of the Coastwatchers and, as with Rupert, taking on both roles would be impossibly difficult.

The position of head was filled by Colonel Caleb Grafton Roberts, the Army Director of Intelligence. Caleb Roberts was the son of renowned Australian artist Tom Roberts.

Robert's title was Controller of AIB. The AIB was divided into four sections: A, B, C and D. Section C was divided into three subsections. Subsection 1 was North East Area, which Eric was in charge of. It was the most active, and the only section of AIB doing really useful work. Eric was appointed Acting Commander shortly after.

Colonel Van. S Merle-Smith, US Army, acted as a link between Colonel Roberts and Willoughby and MacArthur. Despite many officers in the AIB being Australian, MacArthur kept control through finance. Major Allison Ind, US Army, was made Deputy Controller and Finance Officer.

One of the few descriptions of Eric comes from Ind, about their first meeting in Melbourne in the early days of AIB:

> One of our first and most important visitors was a slender individual in the neat, dark uniform and spotless white cap of the Royal Australian Navy. His blue-grey eyes had a youthful twinkle; they and his smooth, unlined face belied the iron grey of the hair. This was Lieutenant Commander Eric Feldt... There was an upward tilt to his lips and an upward tilt to his words, but there was no nonsense about him. So, it was that in a surprisingly short time we had made a compilation of names, check marks and neat columns of notations that constituted Allied Intelligence Project No. 1A: the collection of all possible information about the enemy on the ground, in the air, and on the seas surrounding Guadalcanal.

They appear to have developed a mutual regard for each other for Eric said of Ind in his book:

> The Finance Officer was Lieutenant Colonel Allison W. Ind, US Army, cheerful and co-operative, who helped us through our financial tangles, and gave us means to obtain our unorthodox supplies without delay.

With the formation of AIB in July 1942, it became apparent that differentiation needed to be made between Eric's two areas of activity — his naval intelligence duties and his command of the Coastwatching. Eric thought that continuing with the name Coastwatching would be too revealing. 'For preference, it should be a name that, in the interest of security, should not indicate the nature of the activities to a casual listener.' Eric decided *Ferdinand* would be a suitable name. Walt Disney had released an animated short movie in 1938 called *Ferdinand the Bull*, based on a children's book *The Story of Ferdinand* by Munro Leaf. The hero was Ferdinand, a bull who, rather than fight, preferred to sit under a tree and smell the flowers.

It was meant as a reminder to Coastwatchers that it was not their duty to fight and so draw attention to themselves, but to sit circumspectly and unobtrusively, gathering information. Of course, like their titular prototype, they could fight if they were stung.[12]

Allison Ind watched as: 'Quite shamelessly he appropriated the symbol of the benign old toro with flowers entwined in his horns as the motif of his "escutcheon" for Ferdinand.'

Ind kept the original drawing Eric sketched.[13]

Colonel Charles Willoughby, (later Major General) said of Eric that he was 'A very remarkable officer, modest, silent, deliberate — but with the capacity of speed in an emergency.'

The unique nature of coastwatching in the NE Area meant different items were required. Trade articles for the natives, such as twist tobacco, knives, calico and beads, were not normally stocked in naval stores. Eric was told unorthodox items were to be obtained through the Naval Board, which they were, but only four months after the request. Long before their arrival, the necessary articles had been obtained by irregular means.

Another necessity for their activity was parachutes to drop the supplies. These were in short supply because there was no silk, but fortunately the RAAF designed a parachute made from artificial silk which could be used for supplies.

The need for a more portable teleradio to replace the AWA 3B was well recognised. Nothing was being manufactured, so specifications were drawn up and an order placed. However, something went wrong and, months later, teleradios arrived, similar to the 3B but not as good. In the meantime, the RAAF developed teleradios of the type Eric had envisaged which could be supplied to the Coastwatchers.

The other need was for personnel to work at Headquarters with Eric. In his book, Eric laments his actions at this time and says he made a grave error. He regretted his failure to train more office staff as it eventuated in his having to carry much of the workload himself.

Perhaps he liked to oversee as much of the Coastwatcher operations as possible, including the minutia, or perhaps, as he said, he envisaged staff would be coming from Coastwatchers withdrawn from active duties. This was the case with Connal Gill, who had become his assistant, and Eric hoped that others would do the same. He misjudged this, for most of 'those in the field stayed there, determined to go on while they could, often living on their nerves, so that, when they finally came out, their health was so bad that they were not fit for anything, even light office work. It would have been better if I had taken on an office staff and trained it from the start.'

This begs the question of whether Eric with all that was happening and the responsibility he was carrying had the time to train office staff as well.

Besides, the Townsville headquarters was often filled to overflowing with new recruits learning the requirements for active service. Preference was given to personnel who had lived or worked in New Guinea and the Solomons. The basic prerequisites were knowing how to live in the jungle, how to handle the natives, and how to fend for themselves.

Every day their training in the office consisted of reading all the signals exchanged between the men in the field, becoming acquainted with the ACH organisation and seeing how the incoming information was handled. They learnt to interpret the trends the natives were taking, what difficulties might be expected, how essential a code was, and that, without a teleradio, all was lost. Realising their lives depended on it, they learnt to code and decode, to operate a teleradio and how to make simple repairs.

> The office looked like a slice of chaos with all the officers milling around in it; but they were learning their jobs the best way, by teaching themselves. Paddy Murray, carrying on his office work in their midst, did not go mad, but nearly.

The first officer to arrive was Sub-Lieutenant Malcolm H. Wright RANVR who had been a PO in New Guinea …

> He was a dark, cheerful young man with a soft voice, and the most efficient scrounger in *Ferdinand* who stole pencils off Paddy Murray's desk with such a charming smile that the latter forgot to take them back.

The next to join was Pilot-Officer Cecil John Mason whose fate in trying to rescue Kyle, Benham and Woodroffe has been told. Others who came together were Lieutenant Gordon H.C. Train RANVR, and R.A. 'Robbie' Robinson, Harold R. Koch and G.H. 'Rod' Marsland, who were all Flying Officers in the RAAF. Then came Keith McCarthy, who was now a Captain in the Army. He had joined another section of AIB, but was glad to transfer back to *Ferdinand* and reality. Lieutenant B. Fairfax-Ross of the AIF was next. He was followed by Lieutenant Peter Figgis, who had escaped from Rabaul with Hugh and Connal.

> He was a large, dark young man in his early twenties who never took anything, not even Peter Figgis, quite seriously.

The next two were Sub-Lieutenant P.J. Mollison RANVR and Lieutenant H. Hamilton AIF, both of whom had been patrol officers.

> They all crowded into the office in Townsville, jostling, reading, arguing, appealing for decisions above the hubbub, each sharpening the others' wits in the apparent anarchy.'[14]

Most of the members of the Harris Navy became members of *Ferdinand* and were given officer ranks in the RANVR.

As Allied forces began to build up in the South Pacific, Rupert foresaw the need for a *Ferdinand* leader to be closer to the action. Eric was vital for leading the operation from Australia, so Hugh Mackenzie was the obvious choice. He was sent to Noumea with the title of Deputy Supervising Intelligence Officer (DSIO). Lieutenant Train was later sent to him as an assistant.

When the Japanese forces flooded south, Coastwatchers in the north west segment of the Feldt fence were not in the initial direct path of the destruction. They were, however, cut off from communication. Transmissions from Tupling on the Ninigo

Group and McColl on Wuvulu did not have sufficient strength to reach Port Moresby because of the intervening mountain ranges. Signals were normally sent via Rabaul, but its fall put an end to that. Tupling and McColl remained on their lonely islands. Eric was left wondering about their safety, until Harris, at Saidor, picked up a signal from Tupling. The two Coastwatchers were instructed to evacuate and bring all civilians with them. This they did, and joined Harris on the Rai Coast, becoming part of *Ferdinand* as Petty Officers RANVR.

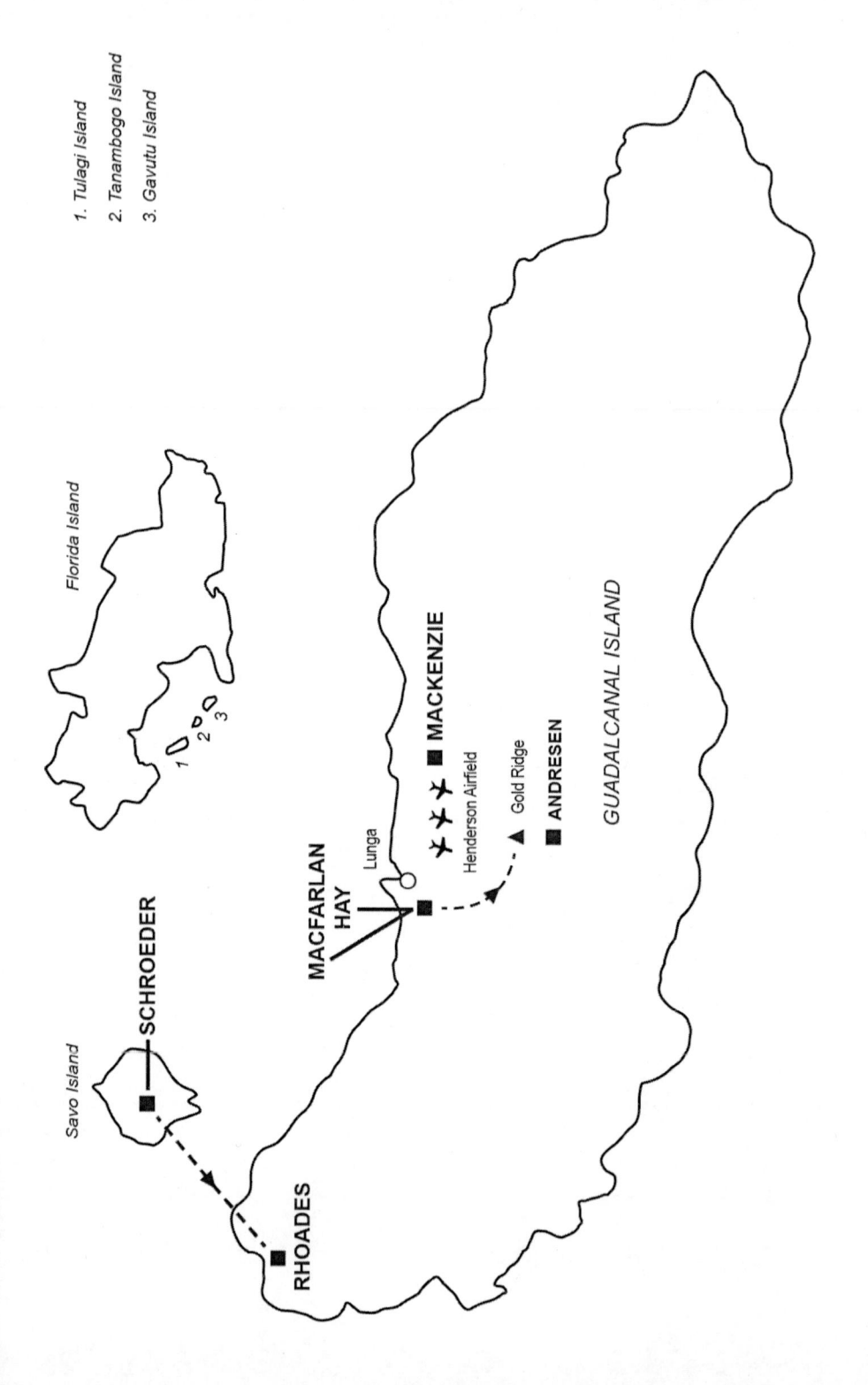

Coastwatchers of Guadalcanal

CHAPTER 9

THE COASTWATCHERS OF BOUGAINVILLE, GUADALCANAL AND OTHER SOLOMON ISLANDS

The Japanese continued their invasion south towards the British governed Solomon Islands. These are made up of a double chain of mountainous islands. Choiseul, Santa Isabel and Malaita are the main islands of the eastern chain. The main western ones are Vella Lavella, the New Georgia group, the Russells and Guadalcanal. A deep-water channel, New Georgia Sound, separates the two island chains. During World War II this waterway became known as The Slot. A single island, San Cristobal, lies at the southern end of The Slot. Centrally located in the The Slot is Florida Island, a small island with an even smaller island, Tulagi, to the south of it. These two islands lie just north of Guadalcanal. Tulagi Harbour is on the northern aspect, of Tulagi Island, facing Florida. In the harbour are the smaller islands of Gavutu and Tanambogo.

The Administration of the British Solomons was based at Tulagi, with the Resident Commissioner, William E. Marchant, in charge. Coastwatcher and Naval Intelligence Officer, Don Macfarlan, was also stationed in Tulagi. The RAAF was on Tanambogo.

During the Japanese invasion, bombings on Tulagi steadily increased, with the radio station being a prime target. Its imposing latticework mast appeared to belong to a top-class communications centre, but it was in fact a decoy. In its time it had housed a radio, but this had become old and useless. The real radio, positioned inconspicuously by the RAAF on Tanambogo, was left unharmed by the Japanese.

Marchant decided to move to Auki on Malaita. With him went the radio operator, T.W. Sexton. This would enable transmission of Coastwatcher information to Vila. At this time, the civil administration was turned into a military one by the stroke of a British pen. The resident Commissioner was given the rank of Lieutenant-Colonel and district officers became Captains in the British Solomon Islands Protectorate Defence Force (BSIPDF).

There were a number of Coastwatchers in the Solomon Islands.

DO Forster evacuated from Tulagi to San Cristobal, taking a large group of Chinese with him. Several monitored events at Guadalcanal. One of them was DO Martin Clemens, a BSIPDF officer who was born in Scotland in 1915. Eric described him as being a tall, engaging, ambitious young man. He had native police under his command. Other Coastwatchers were Australian Naval Officers in *Ferdinand*, or became so later. Macfarlan moved from Tulagi to Guadalcanal as previously planned. At Berande, near Lunga, he met Ken Dalrymple Hay, a planter and veteran of WWI, who had decided to stay. Hay had removed large quantities of supplies from Tulagi and was busy ferrying them inland. Macfarlan joined him and added his supplies to be carried inland. Their provisions even included a refrigerator. They moved to Gold Ridge where they found Albert M. 'Andy' Andresen, a miner who had been in the Solomons for 25 years. Macfarlan had no experience of jungle life but took advice from Hay and Andresen and learnt how to survive the rigours well.

On the western end of Guadalcanal was the manager of Lavoro Plantation, Frederick Ashton 'Snowy' Rhoades. He had been appointed a Coastwatcher in the early days, and of his own volition decided to remain and report. Eric thought that of all the Coastwatchers only Snowy looked the part. He had unruly hair and bushy eyebrows, below which his cool blue eyes peered out. His face was lined and he had a mannerism of holding his head like a prizefighter. Snowy was as tough as he looked.

To the north-west of Lunga is the small island of Savo, where Lafe Schroeder kept a trade store. Elderly, frail and unwell, Lafe had volunteered to stay and had been given a teleradio made from bits and pieces by the RAAF signal staff on Tanambogo. Coastwatching on Santa Isabel Island was DO Donald Gilbert Kennedy, who was born in Springhills, New Zealand, in 1898, and was a Major in BSIPDF.

> A determined man of middle age, with a strong personality ....he had spent most of his life in the Pacific, largely in the Solomons. He was one of those to whom command came naturally, a full-blooded, dominant man, who at last found himself in a position where he could really use his talents.[1]

At times when transmission from Malaita to Vila became difficult there was a backup in the form of the only female Coastwatcher, Ruby Olive Boye, born in Sydney in 1891. She was on Vanikoro Island, 300 miles south east of Malaita, and was the wife of the manager of a timber company there. She had learnt how to operate the radio and transmit voice reports, and became the link to Vila when Malaita had transmission troubles. Eric welcomed her into *Ferdinand* and she was eventually appointed an Honorary Third Officer in the Women's Royal Australian Naval Service (WRANS). She was to later be awarded an MBE for her bravery in remaining at her post.

The next phase of the Japanese plan of advance was to conquer Port Moresby from the sea. At the same time, they planned to take Tulagi. In Australia, the Fleet Radio Unit, Melbourne (FRUMEL), a signals intelligence unit, had been able to interpret Japanese communications sufficiently to have discovered their intent.

> As signals were progressively interpreted it was clear that Japanese naval forces were steaming toward various assembly points. The best estimate for the invasion was the first week of May.[2]

This knowledge meant that the American and Australian Naval forces were able to be in the vicinity at the approximate time to attempt to foil Japanese plans. Actual sightings from the Coastwatchers helped to verify the presence of the enemy fleet.

On North Bougainville, Jack Read had set up Lieutenant Mackie and his AIF men at Matahai in the highlands behind Inus Plantation. From here they had sweeping views to the west of Buka. Mackie sent out small patrols to gather local information. On 2 May, he sent a message saying that many enemy warships were anchored in Queen Carola Harbour. Jack was scouting for a new location for himself, one that would afford a panoramic view of both Matchin Bay and Queen Carola Harbour. However, the highlands were often covered in cloud, and this was the case on 2 May. The next morning the clouds had cleared.

> By a stroke of luck the sky cleared early the next morning just long enough for me to spot the vessels preparing to put to sea. I immediately sent a message to that effect. Presumably this fleet concentration was associated with the battle of the Coral Sea and the Japanese seizure of Tulagi.[3]

Further south, on 1 May, Japanese aircraft made a heavy raid on Tulagi. On 2 May Donald Kennedy reported two enemy ships at the southern end of Santa Isabel anchored in Thousand Ships Bay. With the knowledge that the Japanese were close at hand, those remaining on Tulagi and Florida Islands, including the RAAF, beat a hasty retreat to Vila.

The Japanese landed at Tulagi on 3 May. The information Donald reported was passed on to the US Naval Forces, who sent the aircraft carrier *Yorktown* under Rear Admiral Frank Fletcher to 'welcome' the invaders. Sixty US aircraft sank a destroyer, three minesweepers and four seaplanes. Donald Kennedy, Schroeder and Don Macfarlan sent accurate reports to Fletcher about his raid.

The *Yorktown* then sailed off to join the rest of the Allied fleet for the Battle of the Coral Sea, 7-8 May. Schroeder, on Savo, had a 'grandstand view of the battle' and sent accurate and thorough reports. Although the outcome of the Battle of the Coral Sea was a tactical victory for the Japanese, it was a strategic victory for the Allies for it prevented the enemy from landing troops at Port Moresby. The battle is also credited as having a positive effect on the more highly successful Battle of Midway a month later due to the damage inflicted on Japanese ships and aeroplanes.

The Japanese set about building up Tulagi, their efforts being hampered to some extent by bombings by Allied aircraft from Port Moresby and the New Hebrides. Ten days after the initial invasion of Tulagi, two downed US airmen were brought to Martin Clemens on Guadalcanal. They were the first of many that the Coastwatchers were to save.

In early June, the enemy circulated pamphlets to the natives, written in English and a native language, saying that British rule had been replaced by Japanese and that natives must report the locations of any Europeans. On Guadalcanal and surrounding islands, not one native responded to the demand.

In late June, Japanese detachments landed on Guadalcanal and began building an airstrip near Lunga. Don Macfarlan and Snowy Rhoades gave detailed reports of the construction. Air reconnaissance confirmed their observations.

Meanwhile, on Bougainville, Jack Read was maintaining native support despite the native people of Buka and the villages on the Bougainville side of Buka Passage becoming pro-Japanese immediately after their subjugation by the enemy. Jack attributed the local loyalty in part due to his presence in the area but also to the respect they held for his former position as a District Officer. They continued to bring their various disputes to Jack for his advice and judgement. They also depended on the Australians to buy their garden produce. Jack had the collected government money from the district offices at Buka and Kieta and also had brought such trade goods as tobacco and calico.

The Japanese treatment of the natives was of assistance to Jack and his team as well, for the enemy demanded produce, labour and women without giving any payment in return.

About this time, one of the Army scouting parties discovered an excellent observation post for Jack's coast watching activities.

> The location was in the mountain range directly behind Soraken — about 2,500 feet above sea level — and commanded a panoramic view of everything north, east, and west of an imaginary line from Soraken Point to Baniu Bay. The site covered all of the passage and Buka Island. It was about 12 miles from Sohano and clouds would rarely be a problem.[4]

In order to reach this location, it would be necessary to cut through very dense bush in uninhabited mountain country. Jack decided to keep this new post at Porapora in reserve as a safe guard for future developments.

On 7 June, Jack received his first supply drop, which was arranged for Kunua Plantation. They lit two smoke fires on the beach and watched excitedly as a Hudson bomber from Port Moresby appeared and parachutes began floating down. Jack felt extremely grateful to the brave air crew and to all others responsible for the operation. Not only did the drop bring supplies but it also had letters from home, including one from Jack's wife, lifting his spirits. It also boosted the moral of the police boys '... who, in spite of their avowed loyalty, must have been harbouring some misgivings about our future. They now realised that we were not forgotten.'[5]

Paul Mason, meanwhile, was having a more unsettled time at his coastwatching station at Inus overlooking Kieta Harbour. Four AIF men had been assigned to Kieta — Warner, McGarrell, White and Johnston. Another four soldiers — Wigley, Otton, Ross and Swanson — were sent to Buin and assigned to coastwatching duties there.

The Japanese raided Kieta on 31 March. Paul warned the AIF men of the impending attack by sending a letter by runner. Two of the soldiers, despite the warning, stayed in the town and barely escaped. By midday the raiding force had left Kieta. The Japanese looted the AIF supplies during the rampage so the four soldiers decided to join up with Mackie again and headed for his camp. Paul was left with just two houseboys.

He sent a signal to Wigley at Buin saying that they were next on the list for the Japanese to invade. However, these soldiers also failed to heed the warning. The AIF men were just getting dressed when the enemy arrived on Easter Sunday morning. They smashed the teleradio by hurling it to the floor and fled via the back door. Their escape was successful but it meant leaving everything behind. They hacked their way inland through 25 miles of thick jungle.

Having been secretly informed that a group of natives intended to loot a government supply facility guarded by one police boy at Daratui, inland from Kieta, Paul went to investigate and obtain some provisions. He returned to his coastwatching base and fell ill with a severe attack of malaria. Not long after, the four tired, hungry and bedraggled soldiers from Buin stumbled into the camp. Paul's houseboy whipped up plenty of hot drinks and food to revive them.

Paul had decided that a coastwatching position near Buin would be of considerable advantage to the Allies and applied to move there. In early April he received permission from Eric to do so. His request for Wigley and Otton to join him under his command was also granted. After travelling south, and after some further investigation, an observation spot was chosen on Malabita Hill, from where they could see the entire Buin–Tonolei area. Paul then set up the teleradio station at Lagui, about 9 miles north west of Buin. This was in-keeping with his practice of, wherever possible, keeping the observation site and transmitting post separate.

While Jack Read had supply deposits available in the north of Bougainville, there were none in the south for Paul. He began running short of stores and requested a supply drop from Eric but had not decided on a safe location. A few days later he received a signal that provisions had been dropped at Mamarega, about 70 miles west of his camp. Eric's record says that a Hudson was despatched to make a moonlight drop but was unable to find Mason's position though had dropped the supplies anyway. Paul rode by bike and walked for 10 miles when it got a flat tyre until he reached Piano where it could be fixed, and then he rode on again. He searched for two days when he got to Mamarega but could not find the supplies. Empty handed, he rode the 70 miles back. A not too happy Paul notified Eric that the supplies were not at the specified location. Eric informed him that there had been a mix up in communication and the drop had been made at Mutapina Point on Empress Augusta Bay.

Paul arranged with Eric for another drop to be made at Tabararoi Village on the Molika River on 2 June. Unfortunately the Catalina scattered the parachutes fairly widely, and mostly in the river, so it took three weeks to recover all the chutes. On the upside, one package contained his Petty Officer's cap and badges.

Japanese patrols came and went from the Buin area. In the middle of June, Paul learned that members of the local village of Langui had contacted the Japanese. Knowing that this was putting his activities in jeopardy, he decided he needed to assert his authority. Paul and his team visited the village and explained that betrayal would not be tolerated. They emphasised this by holding the *Tultul* of the village and explained he was going to take the punishment for the entire village. 'I gave the *Tultul* ten pats on his backside and we had no more trouble from this group of natives from then on.'[6]

Eric signalled to Paul and Jack that the enemy was bringing in dogs to hunt them. In the north no dogs were ever seen or reported to Jack. Luckily for Paul in the south, the dogs were killed by a bomb from one of the Allies infrequent Catalina raids.

In July, Eric, in Townsville, learned that the Allies were planning an attack on Guadalcanal and Tulagi when he received a visit from Lieutenant Colonel Merrill Twining. Twining was the assistant operations officer for Major General Archie Vandegrift, the commander of the Marines' First Division. Eric was able to provide him with a comprehensive intelligence brief on Guadalcanal. Twining had been concerned about the size of the Japanese forces on Guadalcanal and he thought the US estimates were on the high side.

When he requested an estimate, Eric, saying nothing, gave him a slip of paper on which he had written in pencil the *Ferdinand* numbers, which were about half the US calculations. This encouraged Twining that the attack had prospects for success.

The exact date of the Allied attack had not been planned, but when Don Macfarlan reported that the airstrip at Lunga would be finished in about a week, the decision was made to attack even though some of the US forces felt they needed more time to prepare. An airstrip on Guadalcanal was much too close to Port Moresby and would be a huge advantage for the Japanese.

The importance of potential information from Jack Read and Paul Mason during the attack was such that signals from the two Coastwatchers were to be sacrificed to decrease the chance of their being detected by the enemy before the attack. Eric instructed Jack and Paul to maintain radio silence unless there were matters of major importance or it was vital to their own safety. They were not to resume reporting until told to. He also ordered them to move inland.

When Kieta was invaded by the Japanese in July, the natives transferred their allegiance to the invaders. Paul signalled Port Moresby about the situation and was censured for doing so. He then kept silent until, with supplies getting low, he requested a drop on 4 August, at Kataku on the Miwo River. However, there were problems with the drops, stemming from a lack of reliable maps of the Buin area. It was largely unsurveyed and open spaces suitable for supply drops had not been charted. This time the Catalina unloaded the provisions into the Puriata swamp, about 20 miles west of Kataku. Paul's group recovered just one parachute. A later drop nearer his camp was successfully carried out.

Eric's attempt to protect Jack and Paul from discovery from the enemy was well reasoned. Only Rabaul and Kavieng had air bases capable of handling bombers. Major enemy air strikes during the American attack on Guadalcanal and Tulagi would come from these two towns. Planes flying from Kavieng would pass over Buka Passage and would be seen and reported by Jack. Those from Rabaul would be on a flight path over Buin and would be spotted and reported by Paul. It could also be anticipated that any ships engaged in the Japanese counter-attack would anchor at Buka and Buin. Eric was doing his best to have the game covered:

> Experience had shown that in meeting an air attack, time was the most vital factor. There had to be no delay between the sighting of enemy aircraft and the receipt of the news by Allied forces. The US forces were told the frequency on which the reports would be sent ('X' frequency) and to avoid delay in coding and decoding, Read and Mason were instructed to make reports of aircraft in plain language. "Regretfully, I reflected that the use of plain language would disclose the organisation to the Japs, who would probably set out after Read and Mason and kill them, but a lot of Japs would have been killed first."[7]

New call signals had been arranged for Jack — JER — and Paul — STO. As well as their messages going directly to the US

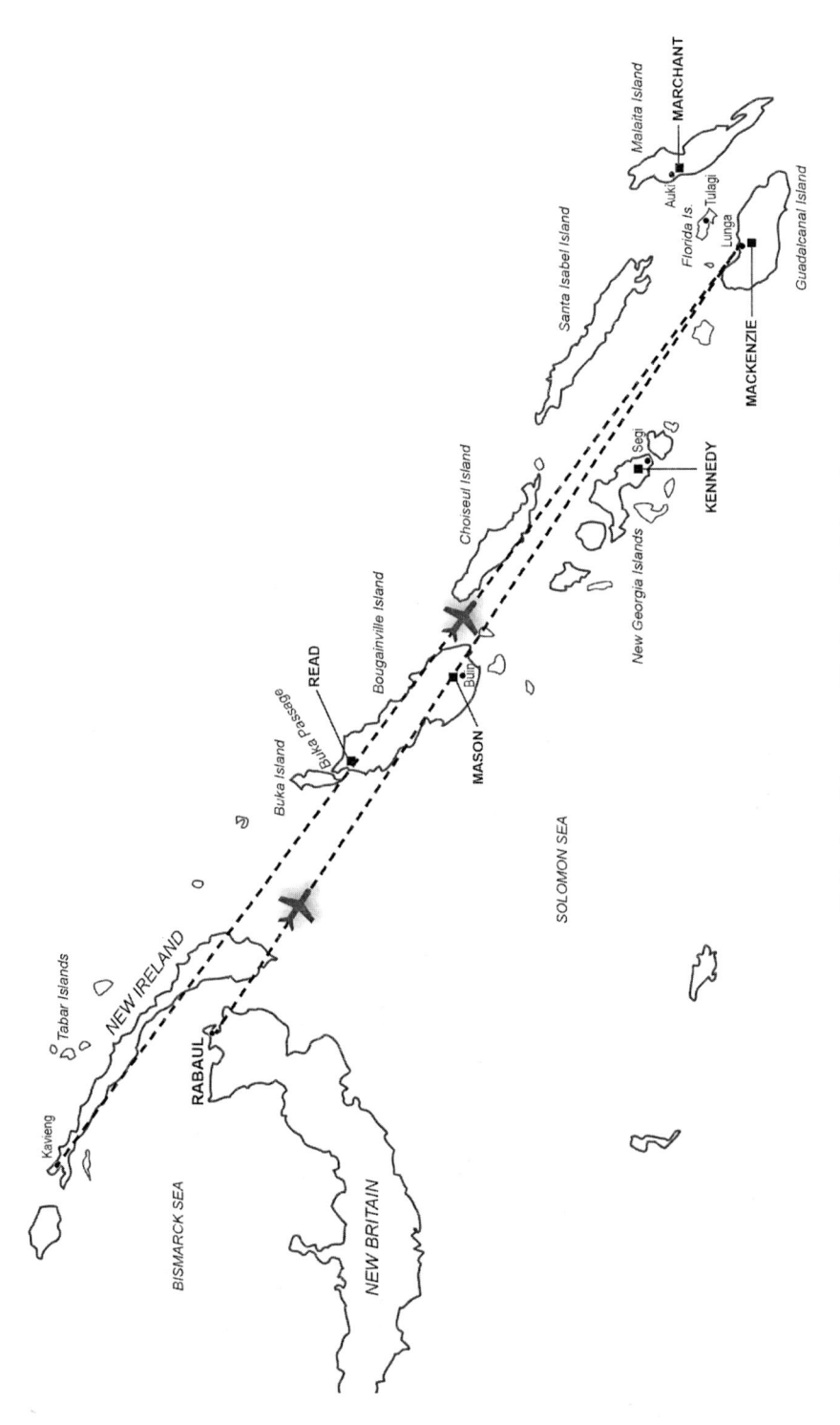

THE COASTWATCHERS OF BOUGAINVILLE, GUADALCANAL AND OTHER SOLOMON ISLANDS

Air Routes of Japanese Attacks on Guadalcanal

forces, it was arranged that Marchant on Malaita would send them on to Hugh Mackenzie on Vila to also pass on. An alternative channel would transmit through Port Moresby, Townsville and Canberra on to Pearl Harbor, where a powerful transmitter would broadcast them to the Pacific.

Meanwhile, in Vila, Hugh Mackenzie had met three young district officers from the British Solomon Islands Administration, who for various red tape reasons were stuck in Vila. Hugh recommended they be appointed Sub-Lieutenants RANVR, to which the High Commissioner consented.

> Dick Horton was unremarkable in appearance, and it was only after some acquaintance that one realised he was a man whose directness had made a mark on the memory. Henry Josselyn was small, cheerful and assured; Nick Wadell was big and slow in speech and movement.[8]

The three new Coastwatchers, Horton, Josselyn and Waddell, were assigned to go as guides for the Marines in the landing at Tulagi. Waddell had an attack of malaria and was unable to go. Horton and Josselyn landed with the first wave on Tulagi on 7 August and were each later awarded the Silver Star for taking part in the heavy fighting.

In the first week of August. Eric ordered Jack and Paul to break radio silence and report all enemy aircraft heading to the southwest. Jack was ordered to his observation post at Porapora, and Paul was ordered to his at Malabita Hill. Both suspected that an Allied attack in the Solomons was imminent.

> Dawn of the 7th August, 1942, was a surprise for the Jap. With the first light, dive-bombers from carriers attacked Tulagi, Gavutu and Tanambogo, while a battleship, cruisers and destroyers bombarded gun positions ashore. Other cruisers, including two Australian ships, bombarded Guadalcanal, while transports moved into both areas. So complete was the surprise that float planes near Gavutu were sunk at their moorings by gunfire from ships. Landing barges,

lowered from the transports, pushed their square snouts ashore, dropped their ramps and disgorged marines out for blood, while heavy gunfire held the Jap in his trenches. Tulagi was overrun in a few hours; Gavutu taken but not wholly subdued, on the first day. On Tanambogo, the Jap held out for four days, sweeping the causeway which connected it with Gavutu with deadly fire and turning tanks over with their bare hands before they were overcome. There was no resistance on Guadalcanal; the Japs, mainly members of construction units, left their still hot breakfasts and fled.[9]

Four hours after the attack had begun, Paul Mason was on duty at Malabita. He heard the drone of approaching planes. He counted as they flew overhead and immediately signalled: 'FROM STO, TWENTY-FOUR TORPEDO-BOMBERS HEADED YOURS.' The warning was immediately heard by the US forces at Guadalcanal. 25 minutes later Pearl Harbor broadcast the signal across the Pacific. It was to become one of the most famous warnings of the War in the Pacific.

This signal gave the Allies an enormous advantage. Their fighter planes could be high in the air at an altitude right for an attack on the enemy aircraft. The ships could either be prepared for fighting, or others, like the transports, could disperse to avoid being targets. When the battle was over, only a small number of bombers made the return journey to Rabaul, with very little damage having been inflicted on the Allied ships.

The next morning, Jack Read, who had not yet relocated to Porapora, was about to make the move. At 8.40 am Sergeant Yauwika's keen ears were the first to detect a dull sound coming from the north west. Within seconds they all heard it. The noise of a multitude of planes grew louder. Some of the police boys climbed trees to get a better view. Jack was stunned by what he saw:

> In a matter of moments, the largest aircraft formation I had ever seen raced across a break in the jungle. With their propeller blades glistening in the sun 27 Japanese dive-bombers roared across the sky in the direction of Tulagi. Minutes later another squadron of 18 aircraft of the same type passed only a few hundred feet over our heads.[10]

Jack immediately reported: FROM JER. FORTY- FIVE DIVE-BOMBERS GOING SOUTH EAST. The message went to Port Moresby, relayed to Townsville and then to Tulagi, where it was received within 10 minutes. At 9.10 am Pearl Harbor signalled the news to the Pacific.

Jack sat by his radio, hearing nothing until two hours later when a voice from an aircraft carrier announced preparations for the attack and that transmission would cease during the battle. A few seconds later, the radio operator, overcome with excitement was back on the air exclaiming: "Boy! We're shooting 'em down like flies! What a sight! I can see one…two…three…eight of 'em splashing into the sea."[11]

For Jack, 400 miles away, the feeling of excitement was mutual. Several minutes later the operator announced in a much calmer voice that at least 12 enemy planes had been shot down and little damage had been done to the transport area. The contribution his coastwatching crew had made to the success of the Allies left Jack feeling more than a little proud.

That afternoon, Paul Mason reported further aircraft, and again the fighter planes were waiting for them. Once more the assault was repelled and Paul, listening in to the fighter control, was also feeling proud and excited by the result.

This was to be the start of almost daily Japanese air raids over Guadalcanal and Tulagi. They continued over the next six months. Possession of Guadalcanal was much too valuable to the Japanese for them to give it up without one hell of a fight.

One of the many stories of bravery to come out of Guadalcanal was that of Jacob Vouza, a Sergeant-Major of the native police who was captured, bayonetted and left for dead by the Japanese. He refused to divulge any information about the Americans. In a letter to Hector McQuarrie under whom he had previously served Vouza gave his version of what had happened:

Well, I was caughted by the Japs and one of the Japanese Naval Officer questioned me but I was refuse to answer and I was bayoneted by a long sword twice on my chest, through my throught, a cutted the side of my tongue and I was got up from the enemies and walked through the American front line and there my officer Mr. Clemens who D.O. at Guadalcanal during the war, later he is Major and his Clerk a native from New Georgia he was Staff Sgt his name was Daniel Pule... they came up to the front line and took me to the American hospital at Lunga Guadalcanal and there they done the treatment and the wounded was healthed up, only 12 days I was in hospital. After I wad discharged from the hospital I wad do my fighting with the Japs and paid back all what they have done with me and now, here I'm I, still alive today...

Vouza was awarded, the American Silver Star, the Legion of Merit, the British George Medal and MBE. Clemens worked successfully to obtain a knighthood for him in 1979.

A week after the US Marines occupation of Lunga, Hugh Mackenzie, with Train, Eedie and Rayman, arrived to take up residency and established a radio station so Coastwatchers' messages could be passed directly by telephone to the forces. Three Marine radio operators were assigned to Hugh so a 24-hour watch could be instigated.

The best locations had already been taken so Hugh had to make do with what was left, which happened to be a Japanese dugout on the north-west edge of the airfield. The Marines had named the airfield Henderson Field after a pilot killed during the Battle of Midway.

The aerials were slung between palm trees and the teleradio was housed in the dugout under a roof made from rotting sandbags supported by the trunks of coconut palms. When it rained, which was often, water soaked through the sandbags and dripped into the trench below turning the floor into black mud that stuck to everything. To keep the parts of the radio dry, the group had to donate their raincoats, while they themselves became saturated.

A tattered Japanese tent nearby became an office in the day and sleeping quarters for the operators at night. Hugh and Train slept at the Base Radio Station nearby. All the men lived on GI rations. Such was the headquarters of the DSIO, uncomfortable and uninviting. It was, nevertheless, a pivotal part of the Coastwatchers' contribution to the Battle of Guadalcanal.

The Americans worked hard to complete Henderson Field. The first few days after Hugh's arrival were quiet but on 18 August a message was received from Jack that aircraft were on the way. Hugh passed on the warning and an air-raid alarm was sounded. Many Marines ignored it and consequently some were killed. The following day Hugh notified of another raid. This time the Marines took to the trenches immediately even though the planes were two hours away. After that, whenever a warning was received from Jack or Paul, Code Yellow was sounded when the aircraft were half an hour away and Code Red when the raiders were within 10 minutes of striking.

A squadron of Grumman Wildcat fighters arrived at Henderson Field on 20 August. The next day, with forewarning, they were in the air to greet and beat the enemy planes. The Japanese usually attacked from 25,000 ft and Wildcats needed 45 minutes to get above them. Jack's warnings gave two and a half hours' notice, Paul's two hours, Donald Kennedy, who had moved to Segi in the New George Group, gave 45 minutes.

Almost every day Jack had the rewarding experience of watching a precision formation of Japanese planes flying southward followed by, five to six hours later, what was left of them straggling home in small groups. Some of the planes, unable to reach Rabaul, landed at Buka airfield, but many of them crashed as they endeavoured to do so.

Each evening Hugh, whose code was HUG, held a scheduled broadcast to the Coastwatchers. He would announce 'the score' for the day's air battle. The results were usually 20 to 1 in favour of the

Allies, and sometimes the complete contingent of fighter escorts had been annihilated.

Poor living and working conditions were not all Hugh had to contend with. As well as radio operators, Hugh had been assigned two Marines as coders, but they had been unable to learn the code. As many messages still came in coded, Hugh and Train had been on duty or on call since they had landed. In September, Lieutenant L. Ogilvie and Sub-Lieutenant K. Harding arrived, easing the strain on Hugh and Train.

After the arrival of the Marines at Lunga, Martin Clemens of the BSIPDF had come down from his base at Vungana in the mountainous interior and joined the Marines. He became attached to Lieutenant-Colonel E.J. Buckley, the US Divisional Intelligence Officer, and was also appointed the British Liaison Officer. Clemens' experience as a district officer stood him in good stead with the native police and he was able to organise several scouting and patrolling excursions that were of great assistance to the Marines.

However, Hugh and Clemens did not see eye to eye. On 6 October, Hugh sent a letter, SECRET AND PERSONAL, addressed to 'Cocky and Eric': 'Clemens with Buckley's authority is systematically endeavouring to undermine my authority and to gain control of the coastwatching system... He drafts signals to be sent by C.W.'s over Buckley's name and telephoned them through in a lordly manner. If I have objections Buckley swings his superior rank on me ...'[12] Hugh also struck difficulty with Lt. Col Buckley in acquiring essential supplies for the Coastwatchers and were at times sent away empty handed.

In an official telegram to Rupert Long the next day Hugh asked for confirmation that Clemens had no authority to supervise or control the organisation of other Coastwatchers. Rupert sent a reply confirming that Hugh had his full authority to supervise or control Australian Naval Intelligence Coast Watching Stations in the Solomon Islands.

As Hugh was a lieutenant, Eric asked Rupert for him to be given a higher rank, of at least a lieutenant-commander. Air Force servicemen with three months experience and no prior experience had higher ranks. Rupert did his best and the Navy eventually granted Hugh the rank of Acting Lieutenant Commander late in 1942.

Hugh's relationship with the US Air Force was always cordial for they appreciated the early warnings. After he presented the telegram from Rupert to the Marine officers, liaison with them showed improvement. Although the parties continued to share information, the situation was clarified that Clemens was no longer part of the coastwatching organisation.

Other aspects of Hugh's existence took a turn for the better. Horton and Josselyn, who Hugh had met at Vila, arrived. They were good at scrounging and set about trying to improve living conditions.

Hugh had had his eye on a derelict Japanese light truck that appeared to have died on the side of a muddy road. Attempts by others to coax it back to life had failed. Eric explained: 'Hereditary traits persist. Mackenzie is descended from a long line of Highlanders who lived by stealing each other's cattle and, on seeing the truck, felt an urge.'[13]

He sent Ogilvie and Rayman, who was a mechanic, to attempt resuscitation. A few hours later they were revving through the mud to the envy of many onlookers. A Seabee officer remonstrated with Hugh that the Seabees' need for a truck were much greater than those of Coastwatchers. Hugh agreed that he really did not need a truck, but a jeep would be a true asset. A swap was instantly made and Hugh took possession of the jeep on which he had painted RAN in the biggest letters possible.

Dick Horton described Hugh as being: 'a most likeable man, very cheerful and quite fearless, and had his own peculiar brand of unsystematic thoroughness.' When an alarm sounded, Hugh, as senior officer, would take over the teleradio while the Marine radio operators would dive into their slit trenches. Feeling obliged by duty, Horton, Train and Josselyn would crowd in next to him while he happily tuned into the fighter network and listened as he gave a running commentary of the dogfights overhead. Undaunted by bombs falling close by and rocking the dugout, Hugh dismissed suggestions that there were safer places for them to gather.

One day a bomb exploded so close to the dugout that part of it caved in. Hugh was forced to reconsider, at least for the safety of his treasured teleradio. Ogilvie suffered a chest injury in that incident and had to be evacuated. Hugh was badly shaken but managed to carry on his DSIO duties.

It was obviously time to shift camp. A vacant space among the palm trees further from the airfield was chosen. Huts and tents were erected for working and as sleeping quarters. A spacious hole was excavated by a borrowed bulldozer. It was given both a floor and a roof made of steel plates. Sandbags covered the roof and lined the entrance. Battery operated lights, telephones, tables, stools and packing cases furnished the dugout, making it an elegant new home for the teleradio (and the men).

Shortly after the team moved to the superior new dugout, a bomb destroyed the old one and another demolished the Base Radio Station where they had previously slept.

On the north-west of Guadalcanal, the Japanese had been landing reinforcement troops, which posed increasing danger to Rhoades and Schroeder, who had been forced to retreat to inland caves. Hugh was becoming more concerned for their safety and two requests to General Vandegrift to despatch a ship to rescue them had not resulted in any action. Hugh began to wonder if the General viewed the two Coastwatchers as expendable. He was determined to make sure they were not.

Knowing he would be incurring Vandegrift's wrath, Hugh borrowed the launch *Ramada* from Benbough, who was Acting

Resident Commissioner while Marchant was away on leave. He sent Dick Horton to bring back Rhoades and Schroeder and anyone else who was with them.

Dick set off at dusk and arrived at Tangarare Mission at daybreak. Snowy Rhoades and Lafe Schroeder were waiting on the shore. With them were nuns and clergy from the mission, totalling a dozen people, plus two downed American airmen and Rhoades' teleradio. The return trip in daylight was perilous. During the journey, the appearance of Japanese barges and troops on shore was a danger to them and Dick sent a message: 'Calling HUG — Air cover needed urgently.' Hugh responded with 'Mackenzie calling -wilco-wilco -over and out'. About five minutes later three single-seater fighters appeared and strafed the troops and barges while Dick and the heavily laden *Ramada* continued on safely.

Both Shroeder and Rhoades were fatigued and suffering from malaria. After they had provided information about the Japanese build up, Lafe was sent back to Australia immediately and Snowy sometime later.

The anticipated call to report to General Vandegrift came and Hugh received the expected reprimand for organising the unauthorised rescue. Reportedly, the General did not hold back with his comments and Hugh took the dressing down, buffered by the knowledge that his actions had been instrumental in saving 16 people (and a teleradio).

Early in October, Don Macfarlan and Andy Andresen came down from Gold Ridge to Lunga. Fortunately they did not encounter any of the Japanese patrols that were in the area. Ken Hay remained at Gold Ridge with the teleradio as his obesity meant he could not run if they came across Japanese. Don was suffering from severe malaria and was dispatched to Australia. Andresen stayed on Guadalcanal.

Donald Kennedy had moved to Segi on the southern shores of New Georgia as a result of betrayal by a native medical practitioner who had been captured by the Japanese and tortured. Relocation was a brilliant choice. The seas around Segi were uncharted and dotted with numerous reefs known only to the local natives, whom Donald believed to be loyal. Before he left Santa Isabel Island, he gave a teleradio to Geoffrey Kuper, a native medical practitioner of mixed race, who continued to report from the southern end of Isabel.

Segi was a plantation with the residence situated on a ridge in a good defensive position. There were no tracks leading to it on land, the beach could be watched, and approach from the sea was unlikely. Although assigned to BSIPDF, Donald Kennedy remained a part of the coastwatching organisation. He was fortunate to live in more style than his fellow Coastwatchers. The plantation house was comfortable, the plantation cattle provided beef, the garden grew vegetables, and fish were plentiful in the sea.

Donald's reports, from 160 miles away, tied in well with those coming further afield from Jack Read and Paul Mason. They enabled a check of the speed of the enemy aircraft and an extremely accurate estimated time of arrival.

As the war progressed, the Japanese came closer to Segi. In October they occupied Gizo, 80 miles to the north-west. Donald's scouts observed it during the day and reported to him by canoe at night. He signalled the information and Allied bombers attacked so frequently that the Japanese eventually evacuated, leaving behind a large supply of aviation fuel, which the scouts quickly appropriated and hid.

Japanese destroyers bringing supplies to Guadalcanal travelled down The Slot at night and had been given the name Tokyo Express by the Allies. Barges with provisions also travelled under cover of darkness. In order to protect the route, the enemy occupied Viru Harbour, 9 miles from Segi. The Japanese continued their occupation of staging posts for the route, unintentionally encircling

Donald Kennedy. His native scouts watched Viru Harbour and Wickham Anchorage, while Harry Wickham's scouts watched Munda. As information came in, Donald reported it to Hugh, who sent it on to the Air Command. With the receipt of such accurate intelligence, heavy bombing by the Americans inflicted severe damage on the posts and personnel.

Donald increased his native force and called on their help when a Japanese barge deviated off course and headed towards Segi. In his estimation, the only way to preserve the secrecy of Segi was to wipe out all the occupants of the barge. With his native army, he ambushed the barge at an anchorage, killed all the Japanese and collected supplies, guns and ammunitions. He distributed the latter two acquisitions to his troops. Later, two other unsuspecting barges veered off course and met the same fate at the hands of the Kennedy Army.

Next came a warning from his scouts at Viru that a patrol of 25 Japanese was trekking overland to Segi. Donald's force attacked their camp at night, but the patrol escaped into the dark, leaving equipment and diaries. It was clear from these that the purpose of the patrol was to hunt and capture him. In the skirmish, Donald was shot in the thigh and two of his scouts were also wounded. He treated his wound himself and continued on duty.

Segi became a hub for the rescue of downed airmen. Pilots chasing Japanese planes fleeing from air battles over Lunga or on bombing missions to Japanese posts were at times forced to parachute out near New Georgia. Japanese airmen also had to bail out of ailing aircraft. Donald's scouts were sent to locate and retrieve all downed pilots. Their reward was a bag of rice and a case of tinned meat for each airman brought in, as well as daily pay for all those who took part in each mission. Overall, they rescued 22 US airmen and captured 20 Japanese POWs, the latter being kept in a stockade until a Catalina could fly in to pick them up. Their tally of Japanese killed in the forays was 54. A small number of others were taken prisoner.

Hugh Mackenzie saw the need to have Coastwatchers on Vella Lavella and Choiseul to provide surveillance of the vessels coming down The Slot and bringing supplies and reinforcements to the Japanese on Guadalcanal. In early September, he sent a request to Eric for Josselyn and Waddell to be assigned to these posts and to be transported there by submarine. Eric set about arranging the sub and the two Coastwatchers were flown to Brisbane.

Eric was all too aware that 'the strain on a single Coastwatcher was too great for endurance over a long period.' He informed Hugh that the parties would be increased by adding Sub-Lieutenant J. H. Keenan RANVR, who had been a PO in New Guinea, to Josselyn; and Sergeant C.W. Seton AIF, a planter from the Shortland Islands, to Waddell. The four men gathered in Brisbane and collected three months supplies of food and arms, and a teleradio for each party. They tested the equipment and packed it in watertight coverings. Included with the food was a separate three-day ration consisting mainly of dehydrated and tinned food. The pack had been specially designed by an Australian firm for another branch of the AIB.

On 6 October the four embarked on the US submarine *Grampus*. On arrival at Vella Lavella they were concerned to see a Japanese destroyer at anchor a few miles north of their landing place. Josselyn used the periscope to search for a break in the reef through which they could reach the shore. Seeing none, he decided they would have to take a chance. The submarine surfaced that night and they loaded their gear into two rubber boats and a collapsible canoe. Josselyn paddled the canoe, towing the rubber boats. Keenan was in the second boat, paddling when he could, which wasn't often as it had sprung a leak and he was busy trying to plug the leak and bail out water. Unable to find a passage through the reef they battled the breakers and reached the beach just before dawn. Hurriedly,

Coastwatchers in the Solomon Islands

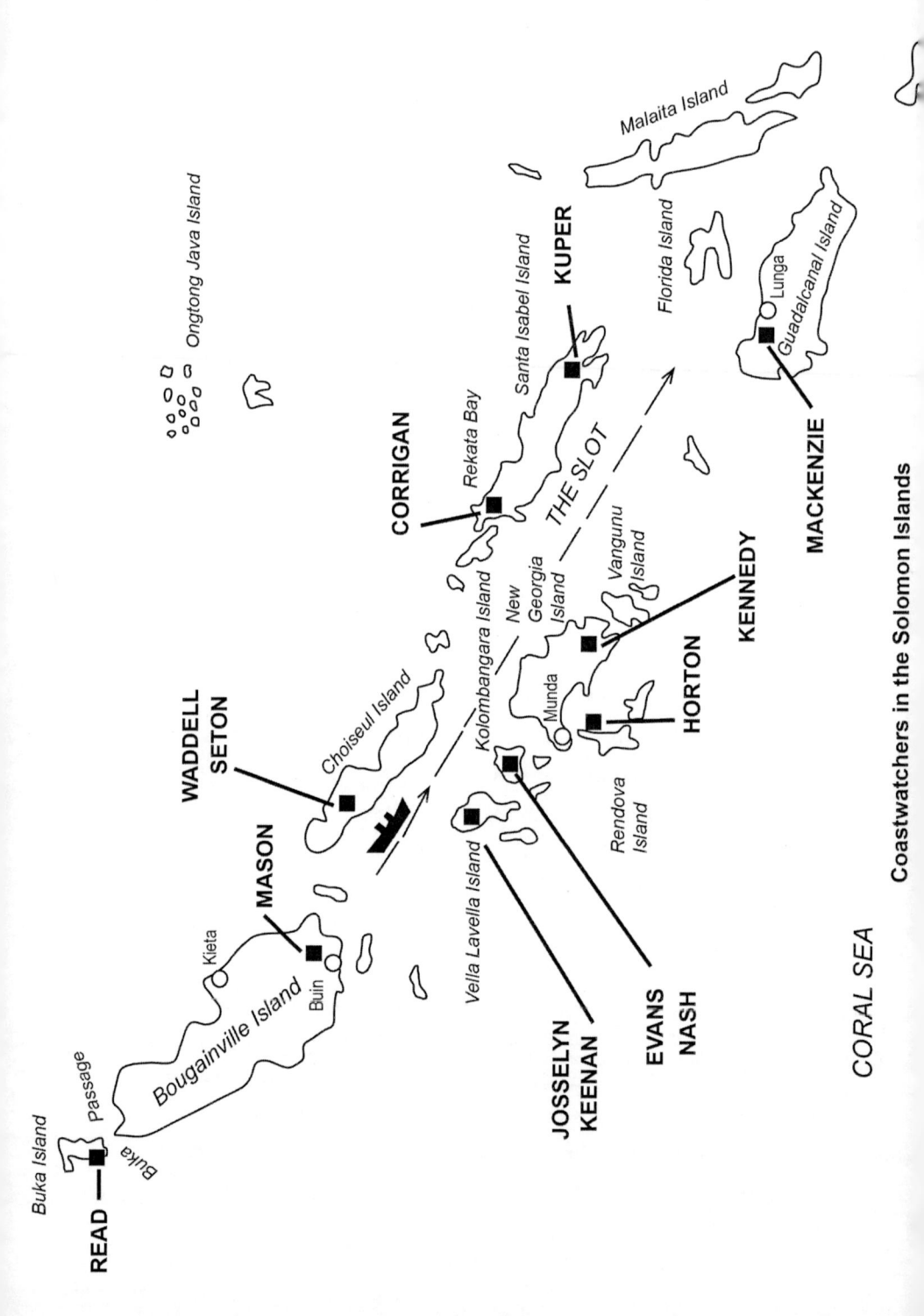

they carried their gear ashore and hid it in the nearby vegetation. Exhausted, they lay down and fell asleep.

When they woke, they spent time drying their clothes, guns and ammunition and checking their possessions. Some had been lost in the breakers, including, most unfortunately, the binoculars.

They were a few miles from Mundi Mundi Plantation and they set out to reconnoitre it. It was uninhabited so they chose a camp site on the edge of the plantation. Days of intense physically hard work followed as they used the rubber boat to move their supplies along the shore at night. They journeyed up the Mundi Mundi River, which was well concealed by overhanging trees, and finally carried the stores to the chosen camp site, where they built a lean-to shack made of corrugated iron taken from the plantation. After 9 days of exhausting toil, the task was finished.

On 22 October they sent a message to Lunga and received a reply. The next day when they tried to call, the transmitter failed to function and all their efforts to repair it were in vain. They were deeply disappointed because it had been thoroughly tested in Brisbane and now large formations of Japanese bombers flying overhead could not be reported.

Only one course of action was possible and that was to take the transmitter to Donald at Segi, where he, with his excellent knowledge of radios, might be able to repair it. If not, he could have one flown in to replace it.

It was decided that Josselyn would make the journey to Segi, which was over 100 miles away with Japanese posts along the way. The only means of doing so was by native canoe, which he did with the help of friendly villagers. Travelling at night and resting during the day, he made his way from village to village, changing canoes at each one. The natives paddling the canoe would use the previous night's canoe to return to their own village. They managed to sneak by the enemy posts and arrived at Segi, where Donald repaired the transmitter and Josselyn made the return journey by the same means.

During his absence, Keenan, assisted by local natives, had scouted the island for a better observation post. He had chosen a ridge in the jungle that overlooked The Slot and had built a hut for themselves, a storeroom, a hut for native assistants and a lookout position in a tree. They installed the radio and soon had plenty to report as aircraft went over almost daily and destroyers and barges made frequent voyages through The Slot.

The *Grampus* cruised near the Shortland Islands and attacked a cruiser and six destroyers, torpedoing the cruiser and was depth charged in return. On 19 October, she approached the southern coast of Choiseul and an easy landing place for Waddell and Seton was selected. At 1am the two Coastwatchers left, with Seton in the canoe and Waddell paddling in the second rubber boat. Despite paddling their hardest, tidal currents swept them past the chosen landing site and onto a reef. Both rubber boats grounded and were swamped as waves broke over them. The weeks of inactivity on the submarine had decreased their fitness and the Coastwatchers were exhausted by the paddling.

Battered by the waves, they frantically hauled the boats ashore as dawn broke. One by one the packs were carried up the beach and into the scrub. Then, too tired to eat, they concealed themselves in the bushes and slept.

That afternoon they were found by a native who knew them both and was overjoyed to see them. An observation post was selected on a nearby hill and natives helped them carry their gear to it. A hut was built, hidden by trees, and their first transmission was sent ten days after they had landed. Two ex-police, Gorata and Levara, had served with Waddell before and became part of the team, organising scouts in the villages. The scouts' duties were to warn of any Japanese activity, bring in any downed airmen and give instructions that all natives were to avoid contact with the Japanese.

Dick Horton and Andy Andresen were sent to the Russell Group in early October but were recalled due to the large build-up of Japanese on Guadalcanal. They brought back a downed pilot and made arrangements for the locals to help any others who were shot down.

The Battle of Guadalcanal raged on with both sides bringing in reinforcements. The Marines were successful in defending the perimeter of Lunga. They endured the bombing and shelling, along with illnesses such as dysentery and malaria. They took part in many fierce battles, suffering many losses of life and limb, but they fought on determinedly. Air battles continued despite the heavy losses of the Japanese planes. The balance of sea power was so unclear that both sides could send ships to the island.

On Bougainville, Jack Read and Paul Mason continued their stupendous surveillance.

The Japanese had occupied Buin or, as the natives reported, they had brought their beds. Paul could see they had brought more than their beds as they unloaded equipment of all types. The area between Buin and the Shortlands became an anchorage for ships of every description. Although some Coastwatchers had been supplied with a sheet of silhouettes of enemy warships in the early days, Paul was not one of them. He sent an urgent message to Eric, who arranged for several pencilled silhouettes to be dropped. After that, Paul's identifications were remarkably accurate. Eric also sent messages of support to his Coastwatchers with the supply drops. This was greatly appreciated by Paul:

> From time to time, Lieutenant Commander Feldt sent us encouraging letters with our supplies. Because I had no personal contact with other naval officers, or any of the authorities I was working for, these messages heartened me a great deal.[14]

Paul also stated how Coastwatchers like himself and Jack 'continually operated under a great amount of stress' and Hugh's messages about the number of enemy planes destroyed helped lift his spirits and improve moral. 'It was not that we expected "pats on the back," but we could tackle the job with fresh enthusiasm when we knew our reports were helping the Allies score a goal or two.'

He was very appreciative when he was later commissioned as a Sub-Lieutenant in the Naval Volunteer Reserve, for although there was no additional pay, he felt the Royal Australian Navy had shown recognition of his achievements.

Denied reclaiming the airfield at Lunga, the Japanese began construction of Kahili airstrip at Buin, forcing hundreds of locals to take part in the work. Paul sent one of his native team members, Lukabai, to join the construction gang. Twice a week, Lukabai returned to Paul's base with a detailed report on the developments for Paul to send across the airwaves.

For Jack Read, the almost daily occurrence of enemy planes flying towards Guadalcanal was too much for one person to observe and report on his own, so he enlisted the help of Signaller Sly of the AIF.

The enemy also started to make more use of Buka airfield. With the increased Japanese activity and occupation, both Jack and Paul moved their bases further inland.

In October, General MacArthur awarded the US Distinguished Service to Jack Read, Paul Mason, Donald Macfarlan and Snowy Rhoades. The citations were not published because that could reveal to the Japanese the value of the Coastwatchers. The award of high US decorations to Jack Read and Paul Mason implied that lesser awards could be granted to others in the field. Mackie, Wigley, Sly and Otton of the AIF received the US Silver Star, and Sergeant Yauwika of the native police was awarded the Australian Commendation Medal.

By the end of October 1942, the Japanese High Command had nearly completed preparations for a full-scale attack on Guadalcanal to drive out the Allies. Large numbers of troops were massing in the Carolines. Transports were ready to convey them and warships had assembled in readiness as escorts.

As insurance, the enemy decided to put an end to the troublesome Bougainville Coastwatchers who might spot and report the vessels as they approached. It was at this time, dogs were shipped to Buin and kept in a wire cage prior to the hunt for Paul. His scouts reported they were all killed by a bomb dropped by a Catalina at night. Paul signalled his gratitude.

When a patrol of over 100 moved from Buin towards him, Paul took his team to the rugged mountain country. After a day and a half of hunting, the patrol gave up and returned to Kahili. Notified by his scouts, Paul returned to his camp and reported the incident before the last Japanese was back at base. He also reported an increased number of ships in the harbour.

Jack was warned by his scouts that a patrol from Buka Passage was heading out looking for him. He signalled that he was moving inland and was told to keep radio silence to decrease the chance of his discovery. His team climbed through a tropical downpour to reach a village on a mountain top. As the rain cleared, visibility returned and there came into view a convoy of 12 large passenger ships, each over 10,000 tons, heading south-east. Despite the threat of a patrol, this was far too important to keep silent about. Jack and his team quickly set up the teleradio and reported the ships that were carrying part of the invasion force aimed at recapturing Guadalcanal.

In the second week of November, enemy battleships and cruisers were attacked off Savo Island by four cruisers under Rear-Admiral Callaghan, who was killed in the battle. It was the beginning of the Naval Battles of Guadalcanal.

The Naval Battles of Guadalcanal, 13–15 November 1942, thwarted the last attempt of the Japanese to retake Guadalcanal.

During various battles, the Japanese lost two battleships, a heavy cruiser, three destroyers and eleven transport ships. The Americans lost three cruisers and seven destroyers, and seven warships were damaged. The difference in the effect of these losses was that the US could replace their ships but the Japanese could not. The Allies had gained naval supremacy and were able to bring in reinforcements to Guadalcanal more easily and safely.

Reorganisation of the *Ferdinand* signalling system was undertaken, with a radio being installed at Santo in the New Hebrides. Messages from Hugh could be sent directly to Santo. Later, Vila also received these signals, which were passed to Colonel L'Abbe, US Army, and to Admiral William F. 'Bull' Halsey's US Navy Headquarters in Noumea.

Hugh visited Santo, Vila and Noumea during the reconfiguration of the signal system. In Noumea, Admiral Halsey personally expressed his appreciation of the Coastwatchers' work.

He arranged for Hugh to speak about the Coastwatchers to senior officers on the staff. Eric portrayed the event thus:

> 'Mackenzie is not at his most insouciant on a lecture platform ... hesitant in speech, a little red in the face while he scratched his behind for inspiration (a regrettable habit of his), and in fumbling words, gave credit to everyone but himself.'[15]

However awkward Hugh's presentation was, it had a positive effect. Back on Guadalcanal, the Coastwatchers were recognised as a separate unit under the orders of the Commanding General. There would be no staff officer intervening, and supplies and equipment were to be made readily available.

After the defeat of the Japanese in November, a Coastwatcher was not needed on Gold Ridge, but Ken Hay did not come in until January 1943. He had been looking after an elderly nun, the sole survivor of a Japanese massacre. She had walked out unaided, but Hay, because of his obesity, was exhausted by the time he reached the roadhead. He sent a native with a note to the Americans saying he was 'knocked up'. To an Australian this meant too tired to go any further, to an American it meant pregnant. Unsure what to expect, an American officer set off in a jeep to collect Hay. On taking one look at Hay's considerable circumference, he exclaimed 'My God! It's true!' To his credit, Hay good-humouredly told this story about himself.

In December, the Marines under General Vandegrift on Guadalcanal were replaced by the Army under General Patch. The Marines had fought many gruelling battles against Japanese troops, with thousands of men having been killed, wounded and dying of diseases. Hugh found in Patch a considerate and helpful ally who gave him free rein to run the coastwatcher organisation his way, and direct access if he needed it. Hugh felt some of the strain lift from his shoulders.

As the Allies had taken over Guadalcanal, the Japanese began to seal it off by making new bases in the Solomons. More Coastwatchers were needed to observe their activities. Hugh sent a message to Townsville asking for six more men to man the posts and added that he might need more later. Eric and his team 'felt like a conjurer who had run short of rabbits with his trick half done' but they set about searching for more recruits.

CHAPTER 10

THE COASTWATCHERS – TOWNSVILLE, THE *PALUMA*, AND PAPUA NEW GUINEA

The war also raged in Papua and New Guinea. Unable to gain Port Moresby by sea, the Japanese sought to take it by a land invasion. On 21 July they landed troops at the beachheads of Gona and Buna and sent them on a trek over the Owen Stanley Range. So ensued the various intense battles of the Kokoda Track. A month later, on 25 August, the enemy tried to capture Milne Bay as another step towards Port Moresby, but their intelligence had underestimated the Allied garrison, a predominantly Australian force. It was here that the Japanese suffered their first defeat on land during the Pacific War.

The Japanese troops successfully fought their way over the Owen Stanley Ranges and on 26 September 1942 were within 25 miles of Port Moresby when they were recalled by the Japanese Imperial Headquarters in Tokyo. The reason for this was that Guadalcanal was going badly for them. However, as it was customary for Japanese to fight as they retreated, more fighting took place on the Kokoda Track. When the exhausted and starving enemy troops reached the beachheads, Japanese Headquarters did not evacuate them and instead sent reinforcements and supplies to Buna. Invading New Guinea was still on the Japanese agenda, so the battle continued.

Prior to the enemy's invasion of Papua and New Guinea, the Allies GHQ had plans to recapture Rabaul and they wanted Coastwatchers in position to observe the town from all directions. It was decided that several teams of Coastwatchers would be required for such a mission. This raised the problem of transportation as a submarine could not carry them all. They needed to find a suitable boat, one large enough to carry the men and their gear but small enough to hide in creeks and inlets. A speed of 15 knots was desirable and an endurance of 1500 miles was necessary.

Locating such a vessel was difficult. HMAS *Paluma*, the examination vessel at Thursday Island, met all the requirements except speed, which was 10 knots. Although the Navy were desperately short of small craft, they lent her to *Ferdinand*, who kept her for more than two years. However, once the Japanese occupied the beachheads it meant that *Paluma* was unable to pass Buna, so the plan was abandoned.

Despite this, refitting went ahead in Townsville as *Paluma* was likely to be a useful vessel for other ventures. Extra accommodation was added, two 50 calibre machine guns were mounted aft, a teleradio was installed, and she was painted in camouflaging green and grey.

Before long, *Paluma* was called on for a most important assignment. Supplies and heavy equipment were needed for the Allied troops fighting at Buna. Tanks and cannon were too heavy to move across the Owen Stanley Range or to fly in by plane, but could be brought in via a sea route. The waters between Milne Bay and Buna were uncharted and known to be full of reefs. The Navy was about to survey it, but it would be months before a chart could be completed. The question was asked: 'Could *Paluma* lay buoys and place lights by early November?' Lights would also be needed at Sewa and Cape Nelson as anchorage sites. Eric studied the information and assured GHQ that *Paluma* could do the job.

Lieutenant Ivan Champion, who had rescued Hugh and the soldiers from Palmalmal, had the best knowledge of the area and was chosen to lead the expedition. Keith McCarthy was selected to command the shore parties, with Mollison for Sewa Bay and Fairfax-Ross for the forward reconnaissance. Rod Marsland was engineer, Harold Koch, first officer, and soldiers of the Independent Company, the crew. As American soldiers were expected to operate throughout the area, Lt.Col.H. W. Millar of the US Army joined the team to gain local knowledge.

The Navy gifted *Ferdinand* a new code, specially devised by the cryptographers and much safer than 'Playfair'. It was called the 'Bull' code.

Although the days in Townsville were very busy, the nights were more relaxed. Eric described the conditions at the time:

> Townsville was by this time so crowded by Australian and American troops that the mechanics of everyday life were severely strained. Hotels, restaurants and pictures were crowded out; shops sold out of their wares, now largely irreplaceable, the Yanks having more money than the Aussies, being the best customers. Even the bordellos had such an oversupply of patronage that it was not unknown for an impecunious Aussie to line up at one early in the evening and later sell his place in the queue to an affluent late-coming Yank.[1]

Eric told of how beer was available but not in unlimited supplies, though there was sufficient for Robbie Robinson, 'who loved beer with a deep and abiding love', and Keith McCarthy to drink and 'to put the world to rights.' Finally, they left and strode out into the gloom of the brownout, which in Townsville was a shade above black. Striding confidently along, they walked straight into the brick wall of an air-raid shelter. Next morning, they looked at each other's faces, then in horror at their own reflections... 'We'll have to tell a tale or everyone will think we were elephants (rhyming slang. Elephant's trunk = drunk) when they see us,' said one.

'They mightn't be far wrong at that,' said the other.

'Better say a lorry hit us. An Air Force lorry would sound best.'

The next day their story received sympathy in the *Ferdinand* office, but an incensed Paddy Murray set out to bring the careless lorry driver to task and wondered for a long time afterwards why he never found him.[2]

All those involved in *Paluma's* mission worked excitedly to make her ready for the voyage:

> The preparations of the *Paluma* reached fever heat. She lay alongside a wharf while Robinson checked off supplies being handed aboard, Koch directing the soldiers in the stowage. Fairfax-Ross, with more soldiers, stored arms and ammunition, all clashing, getting in each other's way and cursing and all cursed by Marsland and his engineers when they infrequently bobbed up, covered in carbon and grease, from the engine room. McCarthy tripped people with aerials and Mollison muttered imprecations while he untangled the wires. Everyone was swearing and snarling at everyone else so it was clear that the work was going well and the everyone had his heart in it.[3]

For Eric, the refitting of the *Paluma* was probably a welcome diversion from his high level of responsibility and heavy workload. It was also likely to have been an entertaining interlude for Nancy, who gave the crew a gift of a kitten.

> Last aboard was a kitten presented by my wife. Terrified, she took to the bilges and it was two days before hunger overcame fear and she reappeared. She was everyone's pet and twice men went overboard to rescue her. Given the name 'Emma Lady Hamilton,' she stayed in the ship for a year until she was seduced away by some Nelson of a Tom in Port Moresby[4]

Despite all the feverish activity, *Paluma's* preparation was behind schedule and GHQ made inquiries about her progress, which became more pointed as time went on. She set sail on 26 September, but at Cairns her water tanks burst and she was forced to stay a week while repairs were made. Eric received further questioning from GHQ, this time from Colonel Merle-Smith. He replied that this was just a patch of bad luck and that she would run to the timetable thereafter. GHQ were doubtful but Eric's prediction was right and *Paluma* ran like clockwork after she left Cairns.

At Port Moresby, H. Hamilton and three natives joined, and Peter Figgis left by another ship to set up a teleradio at Milne Bay. *Paluma* travelled up the coast at night and moved into inlets in the day, but some of her work needed to be done in daylight hours. Mollison was landed at Sewa with a teleradio, lights and a motor dinghy. *Paluma* journeyed on to Cape Nelson, where Corporal Lionel Veale was the first to sight an enormous reef, which now bears his name: Veale Reef. This was marked by a buoy with a rung on it that a light could be attached to guide ships in the night. At Porlock Harbour, 40 miles from Buna, Fairfax-Ross, Captain Rich of ANGAU and three soldiers were landed to make their way to Oro Bay and set up a post there. Hamilton and his team were put ashore in the Cape Nelson Area with a teleradio and lights. *Paluma* then rechecked the route, laying buoys where necessary.

The Japanese, 50 miles away at Buna, took no notice of the insignificant vessel that appeared to be plodding about aimlessly. They did not realise that it held the key to opening their back door. In making way for sea transport to carry tanks and guns that aircraft could not, *Paluma* was ensuring the fall of their bastion.

Other small ships and a survey vessel arrived and joined in the search to locate reefs.

On 4 November, Ivan Champion announced that the channel was ready for the passage of ships, but it was not until early December that he piloted the first ships through to Oro Bay. *Paluma* acted as pilot vessel under Marsland's command. Champion boarded the first supply ship and piloted it through the channel, *Paluma* then transported him to other vessels for him to do the same. From *Paluma* the light was hung on the buoy on Veale

RIGHT MAN, RIGHT PLACE, WORST TIME

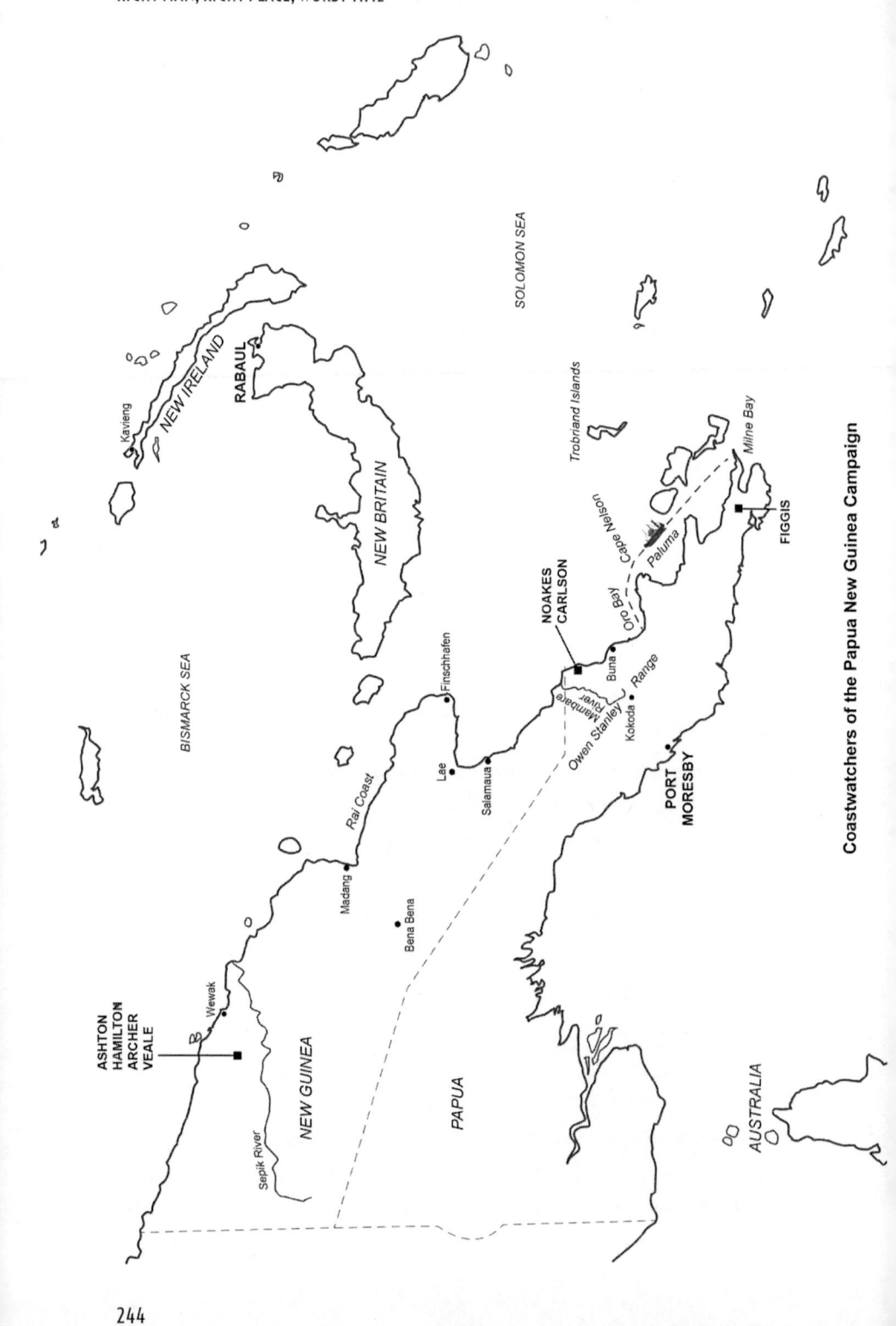

Coastwatchers of the Papua New Guinea Campaign

Reef, by no means an easy task. To hang a light on a buoy bouncing about in the waves in the dark was definitely a challenge. 'McCarthy took an involuntary swim the first time he essayed it. He had his revenge in song and picture, in his own version of *Danny Buoy*.'[5]

For more than a month the stealthy operations were repeated night after night. The movements of the ships were under the control of NOIC Port Moresby using the *Ferdinand* teleradios and the 'Bull' code. Tanks and field guns were landed at Oro Bay, enabling the hard-pressed infantry to finally put an end to the Japanese at Buna.

By the end of October, Port Moresby was considered free from the threat of immediate invasion from the Japanese. *Ferdinand* and Eric moved there on 1 November, leaving Connal Gill and Paddy Murray in Townsville as the supply centre.

GHQ had also moved to Port Moresby and Willoughby presented Eric to General MacArthur, who conveyed his appreciation of the work of the Coastwatchers.

In Townsville, Connal's health failed due to overwork. He had never fully recovered from the malaria he had contracted during this escape from Rabaul. Others joined the staff, but Paddy Murray was the only original member left.

Another section of AIB had sent four teams to New Guinea to engage in surveillance and sabotage, but as there was little opportunity for the latter it was decided to place them under Eric's command. Two other teams that were ready to operate were also added. Eric knew most of the men, in fact he had asked for some of them before AIB was formed and so was glad to have them. This section had a new, more portable type of teleradio, like those Eric had tried to obtain six months earlier.

Among those who joined *Ferdinand* were his old friend Lea Ashton, now a Lieutenant in the AIF. With him were Lieutenants Archer and Mac Hamilton of the AIF, the latter being with Keith McCarthy in the evacuation from New Britain. Others were Lieutenants H.L Williams, a PO; LH Searle, a planter; Lyndon Charles Noakes, a geologist with the former New Guinea Administration, and his signaller, Sergeant L.W.T. Carlson. All AIF. A further group consisted of Lieutenants K.W.T. Bridge and C.J. Millar, AIF; W/O Robson, RAAF; and Sergeant R.K. Henderson, a signaller. Millar was a PO and Robson a medical assistant from New Guinea.

There was friction between some of the four AIB teams and the Australian New Guinea Administrative Unit (ANGAU) because their activites in the same areas had been clashing with each other. Eric spent some time conferring with ANGAU and finding duties and assignments for the new members of *Ferdinand* which did not clash.

Lyndon Noakes was already stationed near the mouth of the Mambare River, 40 miles north-west of the Japanese at Buna, and it was decided he should remain there. Bridge was asked to scout towards Salamaua. The enemy were sending supplies to Buna from Salamaua by barge at night and hiding them by day. The Coastwatchers could prove useful if they were able to discover the locations of the hideaways. However, the Japanese, in order to provide more supplies to Buna, planned to make a landing at the mouth of the Mambare and establish a bridgehead. If successful this carried the added danger that the enemy could travel up the Mambare in barges for thirty miles then swing south and attack the Australian flank.

One morning, Lyndon, with Carlson and a few natives in his camp, on a small ridge about two miles from the mouth of the Mambare, heard the sound of friendly planes strafing enemy barges. He headed through the jungle to investigate. The pilots had done considerable damage to the barges they had spotted, but Lyndon made the greater discovery that the Japanese had indeed landed. Sneaking through the mangrove swamp, he took careful note of their tents, supply dumps and location in relation to a sand beach easily seen by air. He returned to his camp and coded a message, which Carlson sent. 'Next morning at daylight the Bostons and Beaufighters "did it over."'. Japanese supplies and tents were wrecked, barges were sunk and men killed. When their planes departed, the Japanese moved the remains of their stores to a new location.

Lyndon Noakes was slim, youthful and a natural bushman. Stealthily he made his way along the muddy banks of the crocodile infested river, through the spiky mangrove roots and crept through the dense dark jungle with its thorny vines. Undetected, he discovered a new Japanese encampment. After taking careful note of its position, Lyndon silently retraced his steps to his camp.

He was pleased to report the new location and the fighters were happy to return the next day and smash that as well. A few days later, the Japanese brought in more supplies and set up another new camp site. Lyndon found that too, and so did the pilots by following his exact information. After the planes had wreaked destruction, Lyndon could not see any survivors. Still, he remained suspicious and searched for several days. He came across their last remaining launch at a place so well camouflaged in a tree-covered creek that, despite his meticulous description, it took three sorties by the pilots to finally destroy the site.

More barges landed and Lyndon discovered them. This cat and mouse drama played out for a month. 'One man and his party against the determined efforts of the enemy'. He and Carlson were often only half a mile from the nearest enemy post. Finally, the Japanese gave up and decided to pull out to another area. The bridgehead never eventuated and the potential damage to the Allied soldiers at Buna had been eliminated.

Lyndon signalled Bridge to watch for new activity in his area. When the enemy landed at the mouth of the Waria River, near Morobe, Bridge was ready to signal immediately. It was a large force, which sent out patrols, and this prevented him from getting close to the camp, though he was near enough to observe and describe the location. Heavy daily air assaults on the base ensured that it was unable to provide any support to Buna.

One unfortunate outcome of the air attacks were casualties among friendly natives who were mistakenly shelled at times. On one occasion, Bridge's team were strafed by Allied aircraft, killing one native and wounding another.

Lyndon and Carlson were withdrawn to Australia to recuperate soon after Buna was conquered, but Bridge remained for some time.

In November there was optimism that the beachheads were about to be recaptured, and the Allies made plans to follow up by retaking Salamaua and Lae. In anticipation of this, Coastwatchers were positioned in support. It was expected that the Japanese would use their airforce stationed at Rabaul to attack the theoretically advancing Australian and American forces. Warnings of the air raids would be invaluable, just as the ones from Bougainville were for Guadalcanal. During the month, 16 Coastwatchers took up their position on the Rai Coast, at Talasea, Witu, Cape Gloucester, Rooke Island, Arawe and Finschhafen, covering the flight paths from Rabaul and Kavieng to Salamaua and Lae in the Huon Gulf. They had six teleradios, five launches and plenty of supplies.

As it turned out, Allied optimism was misplaced.

The Japanese resistance at Buna was so dogged that they held on for three months. It finally fell in January 1943. The Japanese, seeing the fall of the beachheads as probable, strengthened their hold on the northern areas of the territory and occupied Wewak, Madang, Finschhafen, Cape Gloucester and Arawe. This meant that many of the 'strategically placed' Coastwatchers were in Japanese-infested areas and in great danger.

On 16 November, Coastwatchers set off in launches to meet up with Bell and Hall who had been coastwatching the area at Rooke

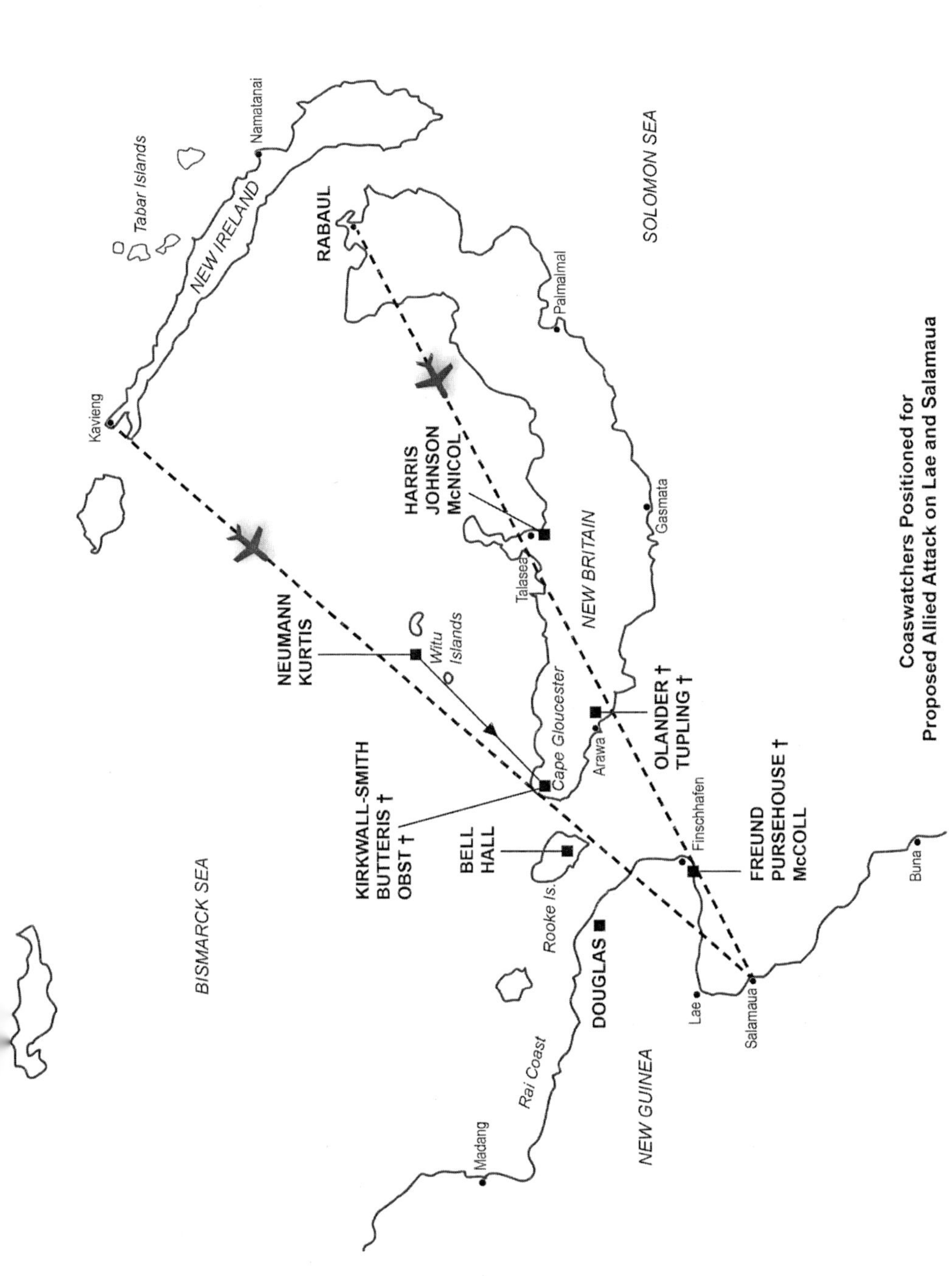

Coaswatchers Positioned for
Proposed Allied Attack on Lae and Salamaua

Island. The teams moved from there to their assigned positions. Harris, Johnson, McNicol and two native police went to Volupai, opposite Talasea; Neumann and Kurtis in *Umboi*, the best launch, went to Witu; Kirkwall-Smith, Obst and Butteris reached Cape Gauffre near Cape Gloucester; Olander and Tupling found that the way to Arawe was blocked by reefs and stopped at the Itni River.

On the New Guinea mainland, Pursehouse, Freund and McColl were at Sattelberg, north-west of Finschhafen, At the last moment, Douglas became ill with asthma and malaria and was omitted from the New Britain teams. He was dropped at Sio and walked slowly to Sattelberg.

The first report came from Bell, who spied five destroyers going southwards through the Vitiaz Straits. The Air Force responded rapidly and sank at least two of the destroyers and drove the others back. A US Flying Fortress was downed during the attack and crashed into the sea near Finschhafen. Two sergeants survived and were taken by friendly natives to the Coastwatchers at Sattelberg. Supplies were dropped to them and it was decided they would walk out with Douglas, who had decided to take the longer but easier route out. The shorter way was over the rugged mountains north of Lae. The longer journey meant returning to Sio and walking north to Bogadjim, then inland to Bena Bena from where they could be flown out.

On 19 December, the Japanese High Command implemented their plan to capture Wewak, Madang and Finschhafen by sending troops to occupy them. At the same time, enemy troops were landed at Cape Gloucester and Arawe.

The previous day, Bell reported that Hall was sick and that he was taking him to a hospital near Madang. When he reached Sio, he found Douglas and the two airmen and took them up the Rai Coast in his launch, only to find that the Japanese were already in Bogadjim.

That left only one way out for the men — over the 10,000ft Finisterre Range. Bell and Hall, who had recovered, were instructed to remain at Saidor while Douglas and the airmen set out on their long walk to Bena Bena. From there they were flown to Port Moresby. The journey took two months.

Ferdinand had further trouble when Paterson in Port Moresby was stricken with an attack of acute appendicitis. His assistant, Connor, had been transferred to Oro Bay a few days before and had been relieved by Sub- Lieutenant C.Looker RANVR, who had not yet learnt the ropes. Eric was doubly busy until Looker, assisted by Carden, grasped what was required, which fortunately did not take too long.

Neumann, at Witu, had trouble with some of the natives and moved near to Cape Gauffre, and was there when the Japanese landed at Cape Gloucester. He committed the cardinal sin of not reporting his move to Eric or any of the other Coastwatchers.

Kirkwall-Smith, Obst and Butteris, with four natives, had settled into the rest hut in a friendly village on Cape Gauffre. They did not see the convoy that landed the enemy troops at Cape Gloucester as it had arrived at night from the north. Natives told them about it the next day. Kirkwall-Smith signalled the news and then went by canoe to investigate. The Japanese had been told of the Coastwatchers' presence and that evening a patrol opened fire on the village. Obst, Butteris and their natives escaped unharmed, but without their guns, and fled into the jungle. They spent the night in a small hut in a native garden.

Having seen the Jap camp at Cape Gloucester, Kirkwall-Smith was returning, keeping his canoe close to the shore to decrease the risk of being seen. Suddenly a large barge came into view around the next point and opened fire. He and his natives dived into the water and swam ashore. They hid in the jungle and spent the night there.

The next morning he headed back to the village, unarmed and in bare feet that had been cut by coral during his escape.

Obst and Butteris had made their way back to the village earlier in the morning. The villagers told them that the Japanese had gone but, unbeknown to them, a small patrol was lurking nearby in the jungle. Obst may have been feeling unwell or was of a trusting nature. Whatever the reason, he returned to the rest hut and lay down on the floor. Butteris, less certain, stayed in the jungle, watching.

About a dozen Japanese soldiers leapt from their hiding place and ran through the village to the hut. Obst was shot in the head and dragged from the hut and tortured as he lay on the ground. Butteris seeing the torment unfold was filled with abhorrence and anger that he could not suppress. Courageously and crazily he rushed full speed at the nearest soldier and with one punch knocked him to the ground. The other soldiers quickly surrounded him. He struggled but was overpowered and tied up. Mercifully for Obst his pain and suffering were over as he succumbed to his wounds and died.

The Japanese took Butteris and two natives to Cape Gloucester by barge. One of the natives managed to escape by slipping overboard when night fell and swimming ashore. Butteris and the other native were taken to Cape Gloucester and beheaded.

Kirkwall-Smith heard the horrific story from friendly natives, who also told him the *Umboi* was hidden not very far away. Surprised that he had not been notified, he knew that reaching her was his only chance for escape. His own launch, hidden in a creek near the village, had been discovered by the enemy. He hobbled determinedly on his badly cut feet and reached the *Umboi* and Neumann late the next day. Neumann signalled Kirkwall-Smith's report and then they set out for Long Island in the launch.

Blue Harris and his group were in serious danger. Although he was willing to stay at Volupai, the risk was too great and he was ordered to depart. His launch took him to Witu, where the engine failed.

Neumann was ordered to pick up the Harris party, but he had sailed to Saidor before he received the message. Now Bell was ordered to take *Umboi* and rescue Harris, but the native crew refused to sail. Then Neumann developed cellulitis in one of his arms and Bell needed to stay and treat him with a sulpha drug, receiving instructions via the teleradio from the naval doctor in Port Moresby. To add to Bell's woes, one of the Allied planes bombed and strafed his position. There was only one casualty, Schultz, a mixed-race man, who was wounded in the leg. This was the final straw for those natives who were determined not to sail in *Umboi*. They slipped her mooring ropes one night. The next morning she made a sorry sight, a forlorn wreck stuck on the reef.

At Witu, an enemy air patrol spotted a member of the Harris team and strafed and bombed the post. Luckily no one was injured and the teleradio escaped damage. On hearing Blue's predicament, Eric turned to his old friends, the Catalinas. With Keith McCarthy onboard as a guide, Flight Lieutenant White landed the Catalina in Johann Albrecht Harbour on a moonlit night on 18 January 1943. As those on board watched anxiously, a canoe came towards them. In it were Harris, Johnson, McNicol, two policemen, the teleradio and Blue's dog. 'Blue Harris had been lucky — he had gotten away at the last possible moment.'

At the Itna River, Olander had decided to go to Arawe by canoe. The sea between the two places was uncharted and full of reefs, making it impossible to use the launch in the dark, while Japanese patrol planes ruled out sailing during the day. Night travel would be possible with a full moon so Tupling was to follow in the launch at that time. Olander signalled his intention, and then nothing more was heard from either of them.

A year later, natives told of how Olander had arrived at Arawe in his canoe, unaware that the Japanese had occupied it just before his arrival. They shot him as he landed. Natives who had sided with the Japanese led them to Tupling at the Itna River, where he too was killed.

From their base near Sattelberg, Pursehouse and McColl conducted nocturnal reconnoitring of Finschhafen. Creeping forward stealthily in the dark, they counted the enemy guns and estimated the number of troops in the camp. After two nights of observation they sent in reports of their findings.

Coastwatchers Greathead and Fryer, assigned to northern New Guinea, had their objectives and situation altered by the Japanese occupation of this area. Getting to their posts now meant travelling long distances on foot.

As January 1943 was coming to an end, Eric considered the *Ferdinand* situation. Their last venture, undertaken to support an Allied advance that never happened, had been the best organised and executed operation *Ferdinand* had carried out up till then. Because of the Army's miscalculation of their ability to quickly overcome the Japanese at the beachheads and their having no forewarning of the Japanese intention to invade the northern regions, the requested venture had been a failure for *Ferdinand*, apart from at Finschhafen. Furthermore, Eric had lost a quarter of the men who had taken part in the venture. Four out of 16 of his Coastwatchers were dead, while the others had been driven out or were in danger.

The previous year had been a tumultuous and traumatic one for Eric and his Coastwatchers. Some of his men were missing and he had gone to great lengths to try to save others, and had sent encouragement when he could as he understood the enormous difficulties they had endured and was hugely proud of their achievements. At the same time, he was interacting with, and co-ordinating operations with, the Navy, Army and Airforce at both an operational and intelligence level. The strain on him at times must have been tremendous.

At the end of January 1943, though, his thoughts were not for himself but for his Coastwatchers, many of whom had been in the field for a year and were greatly in need of relief. The long drawn out campaign at Buna had left two divisions of Australians and one American division with diminished numbers, exhausted, wounded and suffering from tropical illnesses of malaria, dysentery, hookworm and tropical ulcers. They were in no condition to take part in a battle to recapture Lae and Salamaua. They would need to recuperate, and reinforcements would need to be added. This would require time.

The realisation that a rapid outcome to the war in the N E Area was not viable posed problems for the Coastwatchers; there was a limit to their endurance and they could not be left at their posts indefinitely. New officers with knowledge of the area would need to be found and soldiers would need to be given training, especially in jungle survival.

Eric was also aware that the Japanese were becoming more aggressive in their hunt for Coastwatchers. This was particularly so on the New Guinea mainland where the Japanese army was sending patrols out to comb the hinterland.

Another alarming but not unexpected factor was that natives in and near the occupied areas were turning their allegiance to the Japanese. For the Coastwatchers to function optimally, loyalty and assistance from the natives was essential.

Hugh had requested more staff at Lunga and this placed more demands on Rupert to arrange the entry of selected personnel into the Navy as Eric asked for them. Already in *Ferdinand*, R.A.

'Robbie' Robinson was despatched to Hugh. A firm friendship followed.

One new recruit was Alan Campbell, manager of Burns Philp's plantation interests in the Solomons, commissioned as Lieutenant RANVR. Seven others were enlisted as RANVR or transferred from other services to *Ferdinand*. All were sent to Hugh in Guadalcanal.

Last to come on board was Eric's friend from his DO days, 'Wobbie' aka Captain Eric Robinson AIF who had left New Guinea to keep a pub in Sydney and had gone to Milne Bay in time for the battle.

Arrangements were made for relief of the Coastwatchers on the Rai Coast. Large numbers were no longer needed there and the majority were instructed to walk to Bena Bena. As Bell and Hall were the fittest, they were asked to remain until a party was sent to relieve them.

An offensive was planned for when the Allied troops were rehabilitated. Airfields would be needed on Woodlark Island and in the Trobriand Group. It was not known if the Japanese had occupied Woodlark, 200 miles north-east of Milne Bay and in no man's land.

Eric knew Woodlark Island and, as there was nobody else available with that knowledge, he 'ordered' himself to go. He took command of *Paluma* for the venture and left McCarthy in charge in Port Moresby. Three US engineer officers and one medical officer were assigned to examine the islands and select sites for airstrips and camps.

Perhaps Eric welcomed this opportunity to be working in the field again and enjoyed this break from his heavy schedule, and perhaps he knew he needed it, but perhaps it was a continuation of his responsibility and long hours in a different setting.

It is unclear how many others were on board *Paluma*, but Eric showed the US officers the rather cramped conditions and explained that everyone on board worked their passage. They were very accepting, and Colonel Mills 'did a trick at the wheel' during one of Eric's watches.

They embarked at Port Moresby and sailed to Guasopa Harbour at the south-east end of Woodlark, arriving at dawn. *Paluma* was 'snuggled close to the trees of a small inlet, hidden under a camouflage net' before full daylight. The engineers examined the land during the day and the *Paluma* carried them on to the next destination at night. After 10 days they returned to Port Moresby via Milne Bay.

After the Woodlark expedition, Eric flew to Brisbane for discussions with the Controller, Colonel Roberts. Keith was left in charge in New Guinea. All the coastwatching posts behind Allied lines in Papua were taken over by the Army so that the Port Moresby base was able to devote its attention to *Ferdinand* teams only in New Guinea and the Solomons.

In Brisbane, Eric found himself being bombarded by requests for urgent information about the Japanese forces at Wewak. Eric was exasperated by this as all his previous requests to have Fryer's group landed by Catalina on the Sepik had been refused. Instead, they had to be landed at Bena Bena in early January and were currently walking the 300 miles to where they were to operate. If air transport had been granted when asked for, they would have already been in position to provide the information. Fortunately, Lea Ashton's party was available and he, Mac Hamilton, Geoff Archer, Lionel Veale and four natives were flown by Catalina and landed on the Sepik at the end of February 1943.

The discussions in Brisbane led to the agreement that the headquarters of *Ferdinand* would be moved to that city. Setting up an office and a camp to accommodate Coastwatchers not in the field, amongst other requirements, would take time.

Meanwhile there was severe discontent among the Army officers and other ranks in *Ferdinand*. Under the Army system, promotions could only be given in the unit in which a soldier served. Those seconded to *Ferdinand* could not be promoted when deserved so they lost seniority against those who had not been seconded. To solve this problem, a separate Army unit for surveillance, 'M' unit, was formed and all Army personnel were transferred to it. The Army took nearly six months to form the unit and make the first promotions, 'having its own forest of red tape to pass through.' The frustration led to another classic Eric observation:

> Seniority has no counterpart in civil life. Only in the barnyard, in the pecking order observed by fowls, can a parallel be found. No one wants seniority but all resent it in another. When there is a new order on earth, when there are neither rich nor poor nor titles or profits, there will be seniority. And it will be much worse. There will be no felicity in Heaven if there is seniority amongst the Blessed, while Hell will not be intolerable if we are all equally damned.[6]

Another concern for Eric was that Hugh was in urgent need of leave. He was now the 'oldest inhabitant' of Guadalcanal. Eric discussed this with Rupert who arranged for Lieutenant Commander I. Pryce-Jones to be sent to Guadalcanal to become familiar with the specialised organisation that was Hugh's domain. Once Pryce-Jones had learnt how things operated, he would take charge while Hugh left for his well earnt and long overdue rest.

It was also agreed with Rupert that Eric should visit the Solomons to familiarise himself with activities there, to ensure uniformity in *Ferdinand* procedures.

In New Guinea, Japanese patrols from Madang had forced Greathead back to west of the Ramu River, which he reached in about the middle of March. One of their team, Chambers, fell ill and provisions were running low so a request was sent for supplies to be dropped. Difficulty in getting a plane meant that delays occurred, but at last a Liberator was obtained and Leigh Vial, whose coastwatching at Salamaua had been so valuable, went as a guide to the dropping spot. The aircraft crashed into a mountain during its flight over the highlands of central New Guinea, killing all onboard.

The relief party for Bell and Hall at Saidor on the Rai Coast was led by Fairfax-Ross.

> He had grown a large red moustache, which was the butt of all and the envy of some. This hirsute adornment was not an unqualified success: while on a supply dropping mission an updraught from suddenly opened bomb bay doors had blown it up his nose and nearly suffocated him. In spite of this misadventure, he continued to wear it.[7]

Lieutenant D.A. Laws accompanied Fairfax-Ross's team. He was a radio technician who was to service the teleradios and then return with Bell and Hall. On 9 February the group were flown into Bena Bena, and after two weeks of trekking through the mountains they met up with Bell and Hall at a village inland from Saidor.

The Battle of the Bismarck Sea had changed the situation for the Japanese. Unable to send ships from Rabaul and Madang to Lae and Salamaua, their obvious option was to use barges. The barges from Madang sailed along the Rai Coast at night and hid in creeks and inlets by day. Staging points were needed and Saidor was chosen as one. Three weeks after Fairfax-Ross arrived, the Japanese landed a force there, which he reported. Aircraft bombed the villages where the enemy were living but little damage was done because the thick jungle hid them well.

The natives were impressed by the number of Japanese and scared by the severe punishments they inflicted for disobedience. Some assisted the enemy, some remained loyal to the Coastwatchers, and most tried to be neutral.

Late in March, patrols of Japanese were led by natives to where the Fairfax-Ross team was camped. The Coastwatchers were able to shoot their way out but Fairfax-Ross received bayonet wounds to his hand and knee. They retreated to the highlands where Fairfax-

Ross developed pneumonia, which responded to sulpha drugs. They continued their withdrawal once he had recovered.

The journey, which had taken two weeks on the way up when the men were fresh, was now much more challenging. The natives were frightened and unhelpful, food was running low and boots were wearing out. A supply drop to them on the track went wrong and was deposited in enemy territory in the Markham Valley. The villagers denied them food and shelter, avoided them where they could, and at one location even fired arrows at them. The trek for the exhausted and hungry party took three weeks. Eventually, with the help of a friendly chief, they crossed the Japanese occupied Markham–Ramu Valley and trudged into Bena Bena. They joined the small force stationed there in expectation that the enemy would try to take the town, which fortunately they did not. Later they were flown out to Port Moresby and sent to Australia to recuperate.

Hall, who was later awarded the Distinguished Conduct Medal for his coastwatching services, decided not leave with Bell, who walked out with Laws and Shultz. For Bell and Laws, who had been through many dangerous situations, walking out to safety appeared to be relatively easy; however, nothing was heard of the three for a year after they had left. When the area was reconquered, it was learnt that they had been double-crossed by their apparently friendly native carriers. At a prearranged signal, the carriers had turned on the unsuspecting Coastwachers and murdered them.

The team sent to investigate the Wewak area, with Lea Ashton in charge, had with them two native police and two Wewak natives who had been trained by another section of AIB in spreading propaganda. On the following day after the Catalina landed the men on the Sepik, it returned with their supplies and equipment.

> Lea had been an assistant resident magistrate in Papua, but caught by the lure of gold, had resigned fifteen years before to go mining at Edie Creek, He had continued mining and was now fortyish and

greying, but his brown eyes were still bright, his step still springy and his voice still drawled lazily and attractively. When the Pacific War broke out, he had fought the Japanese at Salamaua as a member of NGVR. Geoff Archer, quiet and dour, a young miner from Bulolo, had fought beside him and together they had transferred to AIB. Mac Hamilton's hair was a little thinner than when he had come out with McCarthy from New Britain, but otherwise he was unchanged. Veale, the hard-working open-faced Corporal, was glad to be ashore; he was easily seasick and the *Paluma* had tried him sorely.[8]

The expedition was beset by difficulties from the start. Their provisions for several months required over a hundred carriers to move them, and the natives did not want to go in that direction as there were rumours of a Japanese presence. Mosquitoes were in the area in abundance, swamps had to be traversed and it was the land of the native drums, the garamuts.

Each time Lea's team left a village, the beat of the garamuts would sound across the jungle, telling other villages they were on the way. Fearing the drumming would alert the Japanese to their presence, Lea bribed and threatened the natives, trying to get them to stop. To no avail.

The search for a suitable lookout began as they neared Wewak. On the last day of March, Lea found a site on a ridge from which the Wewak Peninsula, the airfield and the anchorage were visible. They camped there, but shortly after midnight they were warned by a friendly native that a Japanese patrol was hunting them and was only two hours away. 'The garamuts had done their work.'

They broke camp and moved westward. They were not welcome in the native villages and obstructions had been placed across the track. They camped at sunset and set off again at dawn. They walked at top speed, and late in the afternoon they felt they were well enough ahead of their hunters to stop and send a signal to Keith in Port Moresby telling him of their trials.

The team stopped at a rest house in a village, set up the aerial and coded a message for the teleradio, which was the new more portable type. They took off their sweaty clothes and put on dry shorts. All except Lionel Veale took off their shoes, which were also wet from sweat and walking through swamps.

Mac was adjusting the transmitter and the others were coding when a shot rang out from the front of the hut. It was followed by a yell and more shots into the house. The group threw themselves out the back door and a few second later a grenade exploded in the house. They dashed towards the jungle and Mac became separated from the other three. All they had were their shorts, apart from Lionel who had his boots on. Lea, Geoff and Lionel decided to make for the Sepik, travelling at night and hiding during the day. On his own, Mac made the same decision.

Using the Southern Cross as a guide, with feet battered by butts of kunai grass and punctured by sago thorns in the swamps, they made their way in the dark. With no food or weapons and bitten by thousands of mosquitos, they kept going. When day dawned, they found places to hide them as they slept. Lea's feet were becoming macerated and Lionel unselfishly gave him his boots. On the third night, they had to cross what seemed like an endless swamp as they floundered through the mud with the mosquitos descending on to them in droves. It took them 10 hours to finally make it across.

The next evening, as they were leaving their daytime hideout, they were seen by hostile natives. Lea, holding a large nut in his pocket, pretended it was a grenade and demanded food. Reluctantly the natives parted with a pawpaw. On the fifth night, they reached Mauri, where Father Hansen at the mission gave them food and clothes. He told them Mac had arrived the previous day and the natives of the team had also escaped.

When Mac had escaped the attack he knew the others had also, but to try to find them in the dark could be a waste of time and might increase the danger to them all, so he had moved off alone. He had followed a creek, knowing that all creeks in the area flowed into the Sepik. At night he waded along the stream, in mud most of the way. As dawn broke, he rolled in the mud, completely covering himself as a means of protection against the mosquitos and tried to sleep.

As he came closer to the Sepik, the creek became larger, and on his last night he often had to swim. 'His guardian angel must have been constantly alert to protect him from the crocodiles.'[9]

Fortunately, an ANGAU party under Captain J.L. Taylor was in the area and Lea's team moved upstream to join them. They also met up with their police, who had also headed for the Sepik after the attack, which they had reached further up. They sent a signal to Keith and, when a Catalina was available two weeks later, it flew in on 31 April with supplies for Taylor. It brought Lea's team out.

The expedition had not succeeded in providing surveillance of Wewak. However, it had given a warning of how dangerous the region was, being strongly patrolled by the enemy and with native allegiance turned towards Japan. Miraculously, this had been achieved without loss of life.

CHAPTER 11

THE COASTWATCHERS – GUADALCANAL, BOUGAINVILLE AND ILLNESS

Before General Vandegrift departed from Guadalcanal, he gave a farewell address in which he said of the Coastwatchers: 'Our small band of devoted Allies who have contributed so vastly in proportion to their numbers.'

The Japanese built up their troops to the west of Lunga. To bring supplies and reinforcements, destroyers of the 'Tokyo Express' left the Shortland Islands about noon to maximise the cover of darkness as they reached their destination. Josselyn and Keenan on Vella Lavella, and Waddell and Seton on Choiseul, reported the vessels as they passed down The Slot, having a friendly competition to see who could spot the most. This gave the dive bombers ample time to attack the destroyers before nightfall.

Over the ensuing months, Coastwatchers on many of the islands of the Solomons kept watch and reported the enemy's movements on land, sea and air, alerting the Allies to their presence and enabling aircraft and battleships to take off on missions to destroy them. A consequence of these actions was that military men on the receiving end of the battles were forced to evacuate their damaged craft and hope to be rescued. The majority were air crew, both Allied and enemy, but others were sea goers. Finding, feeding and arranging their evacuation fell to the Coastwatchers. Arthur Reginal 'Reg'

Evans on Kolombangara was involved in one rescue which would later become famous.

By March, there was a chain of Coastwatchers throughout the Solomon Islands from north to south.

> It was "streamlined coast watching", so rapid and sure that the enemy attempts to prevent our forces being built up were quite ineffective; while information supplied by the Coastwatchers, designating targets to be attacked, allowed our aircraft to harass the enemy so effectively that his bases could not be built up sufficiently to withstand attack.

On 25 February 1943, when Guadalcanal was safely in the hands of the Allies, Hugh sent out messages to the Coastwatchers from personal letters he had received congratulating him on his promotion to Lieutenant Commander.

From Admiral Turner, Commanding Amphibious Forces:

Large share credit our successes against enemy due to splendid men in coast watcher service.

From General Patch, Commanding General at Guadalcanal:

Your magnificent and courageous work has contributed in great measure to success of operations on Guadalcanal.

These messages greatly encouraged the Coastwatchers 'in their lonely posts in the jungle' and 'made them feel that all their privations and dangers had been worthwhile.'[1]

Due to their losses on Guadalcanal, the concentration of Japanese troops on Bougainville had increased. Missionaries who had remained in the hope of continuing their work found that it was prohibited. Planters had withdrawn from the unsafe coastal regions and were living in the hills. Both groups approached Jack Read seeking a way out. The priests asked if the nuns at least could be evacuated and the planters, who had disdainfully refused his advice to leave early in the war, now clamoured the loudest for his help.

Jack radioed the situation and recommended evacuation, especially of women. The problem was that submarines and planes were engaged in fighting a war and could not be spared to rescue civilians. Eventually the US Submarine *Nautilus*, scouting off Buka and captained by Commander William Brockman, was made available at short notice. The evacuation was arranged for the last night of 1942 at Teop Harbour on the north-eastern tip of Bougainville.

Jack sent his scouts to notify all evacuees to assemble at Teop and began the trek from Porapora, taking his teleradio so he could keep in contact with Hugh. Signalman Sly and Sergeant Yauwika went with him. The journey down from the hills was not without incident. A torrential downpour made travelling hazardous and swelled the creeks. In the last river, the water was waist deep and a large log swept along by the current collided with the carriers who were holding the transmitter. By superhuman efforts the team of carriers held the vital equipment up and kept it from falling into the swirling water. Had it fallen, that could have spelt an end to the night's endeavour and even to coastwatching in Northern Bougainville.

Mackie and several of his AIF men and the evacuees assembled on the beach. The wife of one of the plantation owners had brought a large amount of luggage 'enough to sustain an ocean tour in a luxury liner.' All attempts to dissuade her from taking it failed. On the other hand, the American Sister Superior took Jack aside and confided that she and the other nuns had thought his earlier action in ordering them off Buka had been high-handed. Now she spoke on behalf of herself and her sisters, gently stating how they regretted their previous opinion and the trouble they were now causing him. 'Read swallowed the lump in his throat and busied himself preparing the fires and posting sentries at each end of the beach.'[2]

As prearranged, fires were lit on the beach at 10pm. At midnight Jack heard a voice calling from the darkness of the harbour. He hopped into a canoe and paddled out into the night and found the submarine's launch stuck on a reef. He raced back to shore to gather natives in more canoes. Before long the boat was pushed off the reef with minimal damage done. To celebrate being free and to welcome the New Year of 1943, the crew and Jack each had a nip from a bottle of medicinal brandy. Then it was back to the task.

The launch and the rubber boat being towed behind had room for 17 passengers, and 29 had amassed on the beach. It was planned that the women would be taken. If the captain agreed and if there was time before dawn, the launch would return for the men. To shorten the pickup time, if the launch was able to return, Jack and the men waited in canoes 2 miles out from shore. At 4am Jack was just about to give up hope when his natives heard the sound of the boat returning.

Back on the beach, Jack had time to examine the supplies he had requested from Hugh, which had been off loaded from the launch on its first trip in. He was pleased to find a large stock of equipment, food and other provisions. He was touched to find that the crew of the submarine had given presents from their own supplies of tinned food, cigarettes, tobacco, matches, clothing and other articles, 'a gift which warmed the hearts of those who remained.'

Jack's team returned to Porapora and Mackie's men to their camp. This was the first submarine evacuation that Jack had been involved in. It was a relief for him that the rescue had been successful, but the natives were not reassured. Why were the missionaries and planters leaving if the white men were going to win?

Paul Mason's position at Buin had become impossible. He had moved his camp into the rugged inland halfway between Buin and Kieta. Three Japanese patrols set out to find him and one struck his camp. They were three days too late. Hugh ordered that Paul abandon his teleradio and join Jack in Northern Bougainville, a journey of over 100 miles.

At this time, Eric asked that a small patrol of AIF men be sent to meet up with Paul and his team. The patrol set out with Corporal McLean in charge. Just before contact was made, Paul decided to visit a Chinese community, leaving his team to make the rendezvous while he was away. Paul injured his foot while trekking through the jungle and his progress was slowed. He sent Constable Kiabi as a runner to inform the soldiers. Paul hobbled on, his foot becoming progressively more painful, eventually arriving at Atamo, where he took off his left boot for the first time in 36 hours. His sock and his flesh came away to expose an angry, festering ulcer. Paul rested for two days, treating his infected foot. Then, with help from Kiabi, he staggered on again.

On 28 January he reached Jack's Porapora camp. The two had barely known each other previously but they soon formed a firm friendship, no doubt founded on their mutual experiences and high regard for each other.

In February, Mackie asked Jack to send a message requesting that his AIF unit be relieved. There was some difficulty in this as they were part of the Australian Army and not the Coastwatching Organisation. Eric's and Rupert's solution was to place the AIF unit under Jack's command and send a replacement as soon as possible. An offer for leave was made to Jack and Paul, but both refused, opting instead to remain with the natives who had been so loyal to them. As their continuing presence was of such importance, they were permitted to stay.

The USS *Gato*, a submarine under Lieut. Cdr. Foley, was assigned to take in the replacement troops, with Lieutenant Bedkober in command, plus Jack Keenan to reinforce the coastwatching situation. Concerned by the maltreatment of the Chinese by the Japanese, Jack asked if the *Gato* could also evacuate Chinese women and children, and permission was granted.

On 29 March the evacuees gathered on the beach at Teop. Jack paddled his canoe out to the submarine. Lieut. Cdr. Foley had been advised there would be 24 people to be collected. Jack explained that he had 51. After a short discussion between the captain and his navigator, Jack was given the welcome news that they would try evacuate everyone. In less than an hour, all were crammed aboard.

Jack and Paul remained on Bougainville, experiencing increasing enemy hostility until they were evacuated in late July in separate trips by the submarine USS *Guardship*.

Eric went on his planned visit to Guadalcanal in March, calling in first at Noumea, where he met with Lieut. Col. 'Bucky' Harris, USMC of the Intelligence Staff. A short discussion was all that was required because the operation was running smoothly. Eric also met Admiral Halsey and his staff, who expressed great satisfaction with the Coastwatchers and made Eric feel extremely welcome.

Admiral Halsey later said the contribution of the Coastwatchers in the Battle of Guadalcanal, especially the intelligence signalled from Bougainville by Read and Mason, saved Guadalcanal, and Guadalcanal saved the Pacific

At Guadalcanal, Eric quickly found Hugh's camp of tents and huts among the coconut palms next to Henderson Field. The set-up was comfortable, the mud being the only nuisance. Everything was running with precision. Hugh now had adequate staff who helped each other as needed.

However, there was an air of sadness in the camp. The previous week Gordon Train had gone as a guide on a mission to bomb a new airfield in the Shortland Islands. His plane and another one had not returned. Their exact fate was never learnt. Train's red and white dog jumped up hopefully when anyone came into the tent. Then sank down again, keeping his eyes mournfully on the door.

Robbie Robinson, who was Hugh's right-hand man, had had a lucky escape. His love of beer had not diminished since his

Townsville days. In fact it had probably increased. Beer was in even shorter supply on Guadalcanal than in the north Queensland town. On one special day, a delivery of beer arrived. Robbie was enjoying the brew, with the bottle to his lips and his head tilted back. An enemy float plane, known as 'Washing-Machine Charlie' made one of its regular visits and shots were fired at it. That did not concern Robbie sufficiently to interfere with drinking beer. Suddenly a piece of shrapnel grazed Robbie's forehead. If his head had been in an upright position, he would have been killed. This was another reason for drinking beer, said Robbie.

Hugh took Eric to visit the staff of the various units at Lunga. 'At every one, he (Hugh) was greeted as a tried friend, and the Coastwatchers were praised and appreciated.'[3]

Hugh's own staff were like one happy family and Eric was not required to do anything.

A conference was held with the Army and Marine staff, and plans were made for the activities of the Coastwatchers in the forthcoming advance of the Allies. Eric had one more duty on his schedule, which was to meet with the Resident Commissioner on Malaita at Auki.

On the morning of 20 March 1943, Eric climbed aboard a small sea plane and took his seat. As they approached Auki a severe pain gripped Eric's chest. The pilot landed the seaplane but took off again a short time later, landing at Florida Island seaplane base. From there Eric was taken by motor ferry to the naval hospital on Tulagi, where the doctor who saw him made the diagnosis of coronary thrombosis. Fortunately, although Eric's heart attack was serious it was not fatal, but the adverse effects on his health were to spell the end of his captaincy of the Coastwatchers.

Eric was taken good care of in Tulagi hospital. Air-raids were still an occurrence, one of which sunk the New Zealand corvette *Moa* and an American tanker in Tulagi Harbour. Many of the wounded and burnt sailors were brought to the hospital.

Many thoughts must have flooded into Eric's mind as he lay in his bed. Thoughts of Nan, his family and friends would have been to the fore, along with thoughts of the Coastwatchers, from their 1939 inception and throughout the tumultuous year that 1942 had been. Eric would have considered with amazement the enormous contribution his loyal band of men had made to the vital task of keeping Australia and Australians safe. He may have been overcome with feelings of pride and of grief for the sacrifices they had made. However, he would have worried about what was to become of them without himself at the helm. Perhaps part of him was feeling determined to recover and return to the job, and part of him was feeling too exhausted to contemplate doing so. Eric Feldt had been running on empty for far too many months.

It has been said by Dr Brendan Nelson of the Australian War Memorial that if 1788 was the most important year in Australia's history then the next most important year was 1942. For it was the year when Australia was in the greatest danger of losing so much of what was vital to its existence.

The importance had been all too obvious to Eric, who had devoted his heart and soul to doing his best in the fight to save the Pacific and his homeland.

He was not steeped in military background, having been out of the service for 17 years and back in for little over two years. As a practical man used to achieving what he set out to do, his frustration at the slowness of the Navy and Army must have reached boiling point at times. His desire to get things done led him to take on tasks apart from his leadership role. Such activities included sourcing parachutes from a Townsville sail-maker and then helping to fold and pack them, taking the *Paluma* on a reconnaissance patrol, and possibly going as a guide in a Catalina.

What was most telling on Eric was the heavy responsibility of having to ask, or order, his men to stay in enemy infested territory and having to send new men into the field. Many were men he knew personally and many he counted as friends. The majority had been civilians prior to 1942. Eric knew full well what demands he was putting on them by sending them into infection riddled jungles where Japanese forces might hunt them down, torture them and execute them.

How hard it must have been not hearing from his Coastwatchers day after day, sitting in his office tuning into the radio hoping their voices or codes would come in across the air waves. What a relief it would have been when they did; what a worry when silence was all there was; and what distress to learn of their deaths. Seeing in person the sorry state of the exhausted and ill Coastwatchers when they came out on leave must have taken a toll. Like most men of that era, especially those with northern European ancestry, Eric would have shown few signs of sadness and grief.

All things considered, it is not surprising that the stress, strain and workload resulted in Eric having a heart attack. Perhaps his previously near fatal illnesses of scrub typhus and malaria may have weakened his constitution, and smoking may have contributed to the narrowing of his coronary arteries, but it would have taken an extraordinarily strong man not to be deeply affected by what had happened and by what he had tried to do. Australia was fortunate in having this right man at the right time to achieve what he had, and also fortunate that he lived to write the story of the Coastwatchers.

General MacArthur expressed his regret on hearing of Eric's illness, both on a personal level and on 'the loss of his extremely valuable services in directing AIB activities in the NE Area.' He advised that he wished Eric to be sent to Brisbane as soon as his health would allow air travel. On 18 April Eric was flown to Brisbane by a low-flying Catalina with a naval doctor in attendance.[4] He was admitted to St. Martin's Private Hospital, where he was a patient until his discharge on 5 June.

Soon after his arrival in hospital in Brisbane, Eric received a letter from Rupert saying:

> I am afraid that you are another example of the 'willing horse' Eric; doing too much for too long was your trouble. We shall have to take more care of you when you are on the job again. My very best wishes old lad, and don't start getting impatient, there is still plenty of war left.[5]

Hugh appeared to be the logical successor as the head of *Ferdinand* but he could not leave Guadalcanal until Pryce-Jones had taken over from him. In Brisbane, Colonel Roberts, even with his able assistant, Lieut. Molly McCauley, was unable to cope with the extra demands made on him as the result of Eric's illness.

Rupert chose his own assistant Lieut. Cmdr. James Cathal Boyd McManus RAN, who was Staff Officer (Intelligence) SO(I) in Brisbane at the time, to temporarily take over as SIO until Hugh could return. Don Macfarlan was sent to Brisbane to assist him.

Hugh arrived in Brisbane at the end of April and conferred with McManus and Keith McCarthy, who had been called down from Port Moresby. They made plans for the immediate future. Then Hugh departed for his well-deserved leave in Sydney, with McManus staying at the helm in his absence.

Then illness struck *Ferdinand* again. Hugh went down with blackwater fever and had to fight for his life. 'At one time, he looked to be losing, and was given champagne to revive him. His friends said later that it was only the response of his Scotch soul to free liquor that rallied him in the hope of more.'[6]

McManus was appointed Acting SIO and was relieved of his other duties. Rupert had characteristically given his most experienced officer to the Coastwatchers. It was not an easy task for McManus as he had no previous experience in *Ferdinand* and there was no hand over from a predecessor. Eric described him as 'a small, slight, wiry man with very grey hair which had been jet black once.'

Another officer to fall victim to the rigorous work demands of the Allied Intelligence Bureau was Colonel Van S. Merle-Smith, who suffered a nervous breakdown in August 1943 and was taken back to America, where he died three months later on 9 November. By the end of 1944, conflict from within and without the AIB had become too much for Colonel Roberts and he resigned as Controller, and from the Army. He returned to civilian life as Chief Engineer for the Victorian Roads Board.

After his discharge from hospital, Eric rested at home under Nan's gentle care. Home was a flat in an apartment block called *Belleview Court* in Bonney Avenue, Clayfield. Initially he had short episodes of breathlessness with pain down his left arm, typical of angina. These gradually subsided as Eric recuperated. He remained on the Navy sick list until August, when he underwent a medical review. By then he was feeling generally well but was very tired by the end of the day. Emotion brought on an uncomfortable sensation in his chest behind his breastbone. An electrocardiogram (ECG) showed changes due to the heart attack and the doctor assessed that the damage to the heart muscle had left scarring and that Eric's heart reserve was low.

He was deemed not fit for sea duty, but fit for light duties, mainly in an advisory capacity. Eric commenced light work at HMAS *Moreton*, the Navy's administration base in Alice Street, Brisbane. As Eric was unfit to resume his previous role, McManus was appointed SIO in August 1943 and Eric's appointment was cancelled. The Navy promoted McManus to Acting Commander and reverted Eric's rank to Lieutenant Commander. This was a blow but he took it on the chin. 'It seemed harsh, but what the hell — *Ferdinand* was delivering the goods and that was all that mattered.'

It had taken a little time for McManus and the Coastwatchers to adjust to the new situation, but before long his patience, consideration and dedication proved McManus to be an excellent new head of the Coastwatchers. The planned, but not yet completed, move to Brisbane was an extra challenge for McManus, but eventually the Coastwatchers moved into Heindorf House in Queen Street.

In his book *The Coast Watchers*, Eric gives full credit to McManus for his achievement in taking on the leadership role of the Coastwatchers and explains how the new leader took charge. Eric stated that with the support around him, it was mainly McManus who restored *Ferdinand* to normal and received loyalty and warm regard from those with whom he worked. It is not taking anything away from McManus's leadership to wonder if Eric was in the background as a consultant and if this helped in some of his decisions and aided some of his actions.

The Coastwatchers continued without Eric at the head as the war unfurled, and there are many more stories of their bravery, achievements, narrow escapes from danger and of the sad times when the war took its toll. Eric was the first to write about their deeds in his book, and many other books have followed. Their network had covered more than half a million square miles of islands and ocean and it has been said of the Coastwatchers that they were the most important and successful Australian spy ring ever.

Among the Coastwatchers to fall victim to the Japanese were Pursehouse, who was shot near Sio by a solitary Japanese soldier hiding in the jungle; and 'Blue' Harris, who fought to the death on a mission to Hollandia in March 1944. His team was ambushed and five others perished with him. The loss of 'Blue' was almost incomprehensible to the Coastwatchers as he was the most colourful personality of them all: '...men, hearing it, muttered the meaningless blasphemies and obscenities which have replaced prayer in the modern male vocabulary, while far off in the Admiralty Islands, Keith McCarthy went to church for the first time since he had been married.'[7]

In the New Year's Honours list of 1944, the King awarded Eric the Order of the British Empire (OBE). The presentation was made to him by the Governor of Queensland at Government House, Brisbane, on 13 December 1944. Although appearing to be British, this, the only award he received, was in fact an Australian nomination. The way Australians received honours then was through the British system. No official award or recognition of his outstanding service was given to him by the United States.

During his recuperation, Eric filed an official report of his time with the Coastwatchers and, with Rupert's encouragement, began writing a book on the achievements of the Coastwatchers. Eric tapped out the pages on an old typewriter and found that typing was therapeutic and an aid to self-editing. In a letter to Lieut. Cmdr. George Hermon Gill, who was helpful in giving advice on writing and providing details for the book, Eric said:

> Incidentally, I find typing the best thing I can do - it is the only way I can get myself to read it slowly enough to see the grosser and more maladroit expressions with which I conceal my meanings.[8]

In the Author's Acknowledgements in *The Coast Watchers* Eric gratefully acknowledges Rupert; Lieut. Cmdr. G.H. Gill MBE RANVR; Firmin McKinnon of the Courier Mail, Brisbane; Lieut Paul McGuire RANVR; other officers; and Dorothy Welding of Boomerang House, Sydney. Most of all he acknowledges and thanks Nan, 'who coddled me back to sufficient health, in spite of my rebellious self, to undertake the task of authorship, and then put up with me while I wrote.'

On 4 January 1944, Eric was assessed as medically fit for full sedentary duties. He continued writing his book and the first draft was completed with the assistance of Rupert's team in Melbourne on 18 November 1944.

> Some were disconcerted by Eric's tone, but not Rupert'. From the outset Rupert and Eric envisaged the book to be published in Australia, Britain and the US with a follow-on Hollywood movie. Rupert, G.H.Gill and Paul McGuire did much work to obtain official clearance and secure a publisher.[9]

In February 1945, after 12 months of sedentary work at HMAS *Moreton* in Brisbane, Eric was considered fit to resume full duties. He returned to active duties as Naval Officer in Charge (NOIC) Torokina and Commanding Officer of the new shore base HMAS *Lusair* on Empress Augusta Bay in western Bougainville. Perhaps Eric and Gussie shared a laugh about his appointment to a place that bore her name, although of a somewhat higher station in life.

Eric flew to Madang to meet Commander James Esdaile for briefing. James, another of Eric's friends from the Pioneer Class, had been appointed Naval Officer in Charge (NOIC) New Guinea Area. He found that Eric was 'all zeal, ability and co-operation'. From Madang, Eric went as a passenger on the sloop *Swan* to *Lusair*.

With his appointment as NOIC Torokina, Eric's rank of Acting Commander, which he had lost following his heart attack, was restored to him. This brought with it an improvement in his financial situation, and Eric was pleased to be in the islands again.

Lusair was one of 17 naval outposts in Bougainville, New Britain and New Guinea, and Eric was taking over its command from the US Navy. The roles of the naval outposts were logistic support, intelligence and communications. *Lusair* was just north of an airstrip the Americans had built in the jungle. As the war was moving north, it, like many similar airfields, was only used in emergencies.

Eric felt well for the first month of his appointment and then his health began to deteriorate. This time Nan could not be with him to provide care and support. Eric started to lose weight, feel fatigued and developed recurrent discomfort in his left arm. On 25 May he was admitted to the Australian General Hospital at Torokina with a diagnosis of Coronary Sclerosis, or Coronary Artery Disease in today's terminology. On 5 June he was transferred to the Australian General Hospital at Lae. On 9 June he boarded the hospital ship *Manunda* and arrived in Sydney on 16 June. He was admitted to Royal Australian Navy Hospital *Canonbury* where he spent five days before being sent home to Brisbane. On 28 September he was assessed as physically unfit for naval service and was discharged to the retired list on a 30% pension. This seems an extremely unfair allocation. Perhaps to doctors used to seeing returned servicemen who bore obvious injuries, such as missing limbs, blindness or severe shell shock, Eric looked fit and healthy and behaved normally. Perhaps they failed to comprehend the severity of his internal injuries and the level of his disability because he did not appear battle scarred.

On Wednesday 20 February 1946, Eric and Hugh had a pleasing duty to perform. *The Telegraph* (Brisbane, Queensland) reported that a New Guinea native, Private Wamaru, had been decorated, and Eric and Hugh made the presentation.

> A New Guinea native, Private Wamaru, a member of M special battalion, was decorated this afternoon at the Greenslopes Military Hospital for gallantry in the face of Japanese aggression on Bougainville in June, 1943.
>
> The citation was read in pidgin English by Commander Feldt, of the RAN under whose command Wamaru's unit came at the time of the incident.
>
> The citiation read: "Along Buka passage, Japan he go bush. Wamaru he go too, along.
>
> Sgt. Yauwica. He stop. He stop all time. All time he help carry something. All time he stop along Sgt.Major.
>
> By and by Japan man he come up. Wamaru him call out. Japan man he call out. Wamaru he shoot. This about 9 o'clock, plenty musket. Three fellow stop. Two fellow Jap he die, finish. This fellow (meaning Wamaru) good fellow. He all time work. All time he stop.
>
> Commander Feldt, who was accompanied by Lt. Commander McKenzie made the award at 3 Facio Maxillary and Plastic Surgery unit, an attachment of Greenslopes Military Hospital where Sgt-Major Yauwica is an inmate.
>
> Sgt-Major Yauwica was injured in a later accident suffering extensive injuries to the face and loss of his left hand.

Private Wamaru is at present staying at the unit and looking after the Sgt- Major, to whom he was batman at the time.

Eric's book *The Coast Watchers* was first published by Oxford University Press in Melbourne in 1946. Eric ensured its appearance was a worthy tribute to the men it portrays. A lone Coastwatcher, a teleradio and two native assistants sit in the centre of the picture on the front of the dust jacket. In the background a native hut blends into the jungle. Radio waves swirl out from the teleradio across the sea, on the spine and back of the dust jacket, towards two warships, while planes fly high in the sky. Inside the front cover and extending across the front page is a submarine surfacing at full moon while an armed Coastwatcher sits waiting on shore. Two Catalinas flying over land and water adorn the last page and back inside cover. The artist, Pat Terry, accurately recreated in pictures many of the essential elements of the lives of the Coastwatchers.

The book contains 6 maps, one of which folds out to the size of three pages and shows all the coastwatching stations from December 1941 to December 1943. As well, there are an amazing 53 glossy photographs, many of which are of native people. This first edition sold in Australia for 17s/6d. With index, it is 425 pages in length. The American edition, published by Oxford University Press in New York in 1946, is much less elaborate, and is abridged to 264 pages with index. In some ways it is almost a different book. The first chapters, as one example, are completely different, but of course much of the content is the same. Although not known for certain, it reads as if Eric rewrote it for the American market. It contains no photos, just one map and has a less artistic dust jacket. A much later American edition published in 1979 by Bantam Books had more maps, hand drawn illustrations and a foreword by General Douglas MacArthur.

The Australian newspaper reviews appear to have been positive with many glowing in their praise.

From *The Argus* (Melbourne,Vic) Sat Aug 1946 **Behind The Japanese Lines**

> Cmdr Feldt's account has the detail of an official record (much of which the lay reader will skip), but it also has the dramatic suspense of a hundred adventure stories. This is one of the great untold stories of the war.

From *The Advertiser* (Adelaide SA) Sat 28 Sep 1946 **These Men Helped to Save Australia.**

> This fine book, dealing with a so vital and nearly tragic period of our history, well written and pleasingly illustrated should be read with pride by all Australians.

From *Smiths Weekly* (Sydney NSW) Sat 12 Oct 1946 **Eric Feldt's Show**

> It commenced with an idea which became known in the Solomon Seas as 'Eric Feldt's Show.'

From *Mirror* (Perth WA) Sat 19 Oct 1946 **Unsung Australian Heroes Defied, Outwitted Japs**

> Commander Feldt has not dramatized their story. His book is factual, and well-illustrated. Here is a story of Australians who deserve to live in the memory of their fellows. Every schoolboy and girl in particular, should read it, marvel that the Moment found such Men.

The book showed Eric's talent as a writer, while recording his personal knowledge of the Coastwatchers and the significant events in which they played a part. His descriptive prose, candid opinions and lively sense of humour makes *The Coast Watchers* a most readable story. Perhaps one thing Eric did was downplay the importance of his role and the demands it placed on him. As a relatively quiet and modest man it was in his nature to do so.

The Coast Watchers was published in France in 1964 under the title *Espions Suicide* (Suicide Spies). Its popularity lead to a reprint in 1967.

Eric's war was not a battle fought with bullets but one fought with the eyes and ears; the voices and tapping fingers; the intelligence and cunning of himself and his band of intrepid Coastwatchers. It was a battle fought with allegiance from many of the indigenous people, without whom it would have been doomed before it began. It was a battle when the weapons were not guns but teleradios. It was a battle fought against the odds, and one fought to try to tip the odds decidedly in the Allies' favour — and that it most certainly did.

During the course of the war, the personnel in the Coastwatcher organisation numbered 398 Caucasians with a similar number of native Coastwatchers. The actual number of skilled Coastwatchers, in charge, in the field, was 90. They were mostly Australian, with some British, some New Zealanders and a few Americans.[10]

The way in which the Coastwatchers' war was waged changed in the months after Eric relinquished his command. This was not because he was no longer in charge but because the nature of the conflict had changed. Many of the Coastwatchers combined their surveillance with sabotage and guerrilla warfare in a mopping up action to rid New Guinea and the Solomons of residual Japanese. Their native police and scouts, highly motivated to eliminate the enemy from their lands, became skilled assassins stalking their human prey through the jungle.

General MacArthur's headquarters estimated that the Coastwatchers and their teams in New Guinea, New Britain and the Solomon Islands had 5,414 Japanese killed and 74 captured to their credit. The Coastwatchers' losses were 56, of whom 36 were whites and 20 natives. They rescued 601 military personnel consisting of 321 downed airmen and 280 naval men from sunken ships. The civilians saved numbered 450. But the Coastwatchers paramount contribution was their vital warnings, which were of immeasurable value in the Allies' fight to ultimately gain air supremacy.

'Their achievements and scope of work had far exceeded the expectations of even Rupert, Eric and Hugh.'[11]

During his convalescence an appreciative Eric wrote of his men and the assistance they received:

> It can be stated categorically that not one officer or man in the *Ferdinand* organisation put himself before his duty. This was not advertised but it showed out and its influence permeated to all who came in contact with the Coastwatchers and help was rendered when it would not have been forthcoming for any other reason.

CHAPTER 12

POST WAR LIFE

After Peter's death, Gussie continued living in their home in Victoria Avenue, Chelmer, Brisbane, that Peter had left her in his will. On 13 May 1946, Gussie transferred the property to Eric. No records remain of the financial arrangement. From that time on, she lived with each of her four daughters. The electoral role of 1949 shows her living with Emma in Sydney, but she also spent time with Lucy, Ada and Mabel. Gussie died on Christmas Day 1951 at Lucy's place in Brisbane, aged 89. She was cremated, as Peter had been before her.

Although his book was a success, it is unknown whether it provided any appreciable income to Eric. To supplement his small naval pension of 30%, Eric worked as secretary of the United Service Club in Brisbane in 1946 and 1947, but his health deteriorated again.

His naval pension was upgraded to 100% in November 1946.

In May 1949 he applied for a pension with the Department of External Territories, based on his New Guinea service. After two years nothing had eventuated so Eric wrote to his old friend Reg Halligan, whom he had met in 1923. Reg was now Secretary of the Department. Reg quickly arranged for Eric to receive a modest pension. Eric's thank you letter to Reg gives an insight into the life he and Nan were leading.

> We are living quietly in the old family home and I do nothing whatever except keep the place tidy, and play lawn bowls. I tried work but found I couldn't stand it, tried to write fiction and couldn't sell it, so I have given it all away. Whenever an urge comes over me to do something, I think of Errol Knox who had a coronary at the same time as I did. He went back to editing one of the

Melbourne newspapers and in three years was Sir Errol Knox; three months he was the late Sir Errol Knox, so I go on loafing. Nan is well and does not regret leaving NG though a boy would be handy for the washing up, a matter in which I concur, with reason. We enjoyed our life up there but are too old for it now.[1]

Hugh Mackenzie stayed in the Navy after the war. His blackwater fever had made returning to New Britain impossible and as both he and his wife Betty had loved the life on their plantation they missed it greatly. They decided that their home would be in Sydney. Hugh estimated that by 1949 he would be able to retire on a modest pension. In 1948 he was working as a watch-keeping officer in the Fleet Headquarters, which had a cabin on the first floor for the duty officer to retire to at night. On 14 September 1948, Hugh spent the evening drinking whisky with an officer he was training as his relief. The officer went home about 1.30am. Hugh did not appear to be intoxicated.

About 6am a sailor found Hugh lying in a pool of blood on the floor of the court martial room below the cabin. He had fallen from a small first floor balcony and hit the light fitting as he fell. Hugh was in severe pain and was given a brandy while waiting for the ambulance. He had sustained fractures to his left forearm, left leg and three ribs, plus a deep laceration to his left forehead. Hugh was considered lucky not to have fractured his skull or suffered brain damage.

With no recollection of how he came to fall, Hugh thought he must have been sleep walking. He had been a sleepwalker in his childhood but had not done so in recent years. The doctor who examined Hugh at Concord Repatriation General Hospital wrote in his admission notes that this was not unusual as 'after harrowing experiences sleep-walking may recur.'

Despite continuing to feel unwell and being advised his recovery would be slow, Hugh was beginning to see the accident in a positive light. He told a visitor 'I am lucky to be alive. I think that I got out of the whole thing lightly.'[2]

Five days after his fall, Hugh suddenly became ill and began vomiting. He died on 19 September. A post-mortem revealed that he had died from paralytic ileus, a type of small bowel obstruction, not a common complication of a fall, but one more likely in a patient with a history of malaria and blackwater fever, like Hugh. Although ileus is not usually fatal, it appears that there were delays in making the diagnosis and instigating the correct treatment.

Hugh had cheated death after the fall of Rabaul; at Guadalcanal; and when stricken with blackwater fever. It was hard to comprehend that his apparent invincibility had ended in this manner. Hugh had been awarded a US Legion of Merit (Degree of Officer). This popular member of the Pioneer Class and of the Coastwatchers, who contributed so much to the success of the War in the Pacific, is virtually unknown in his native land.

Eric later wrote of his friend:

> The coast watching service was lucky the day it got Mackenzie, for this man ... was to fill brilliantly one of the most dramatic and responsible assignments of the battle for Guadalcanal.

In June 1951 Eric's Department of Veteran Affairs (DVA) pension was reduced to 80%. It was nearly three years before it was restored to 100% in January 1954. It was not until 4 February 1963 that he received a Totally and Permanently Incapacitated (TPI) pension.

In 1953 Eric was one of many recipients of the Queen Elizabeth II Coronation Medal.

The following year Eric had the chance to meet up with Fleet Admiral 'Bull' Halsey again when the Admiral came to Australia as a guest of the Commonwealth and the Australian-American Association. His visit to Brisbane was reported in the *Courier Mail* of Wednesday 28 April 1954:

> **Admiral's thanks to Aust coastwatchers** 'I could get down on my knees every night and thank God for Commander Eric Feldt.'

US Fleet Admiral Halsey told 250 guests at an Australian-American Association reception last night.

Eric's portrait was painted by Norman Carter in 1957 and is housed in the Australian War Memorial in Canberra.

Rupert Long was the first to put forward the idea of a memorial to the Coastwatchers. In 1948, he had suggested to Gordon Laycock, Director of Lighthouses in New Guinea, that a lighthouse be built in their memory. Walter Brooksbank was the one to instigate the idea. In August 1952 he met with several Ex-Coastwatchers in Rabaul and formed the Coast Watchers Memorial Committee, with himself as secretary. Eric, Rupert, Walter and more than 40 former Coastwatchers began the task of raising funds. A new lighthouse was needed for Madang and this was chosen as the site. The residents embraced the cause as it was one which was dear to their hearts. By 1954 the actual site was selected at the southern entrance to Madang Harbour. The 90ft high concrete column was a wonderful streamlined design, a fitting monument for Coastwatchers, and also served as a practical navigational warning for passing ships, also in-keeping with *Ferdinand's* objectives and operations.

Rupert tried to arrange for as many surviving Coastwatchers as possible to attend the opening. Donations from the public raised half the cost and the Australian Government provided the rest. Donors included Fleet Admiral Halsey and then Vice President Richard Nixon, who had seen the Coastwatchers in action when he served in the Navy in Bougainville.

The opening on 15 August 1959 was a grand affair. The evening before the opening a reception was held onboard the frigate *Swan* after which all adjourned to the Hotel Madang. Roma Bates, the widow of former Coastwatcher and Madang District Commissioner Charles Bates wrote of the event:

I wish I could convey to you the excitement and feeling in the air. They were gathered there en masse and everyone made a great fuss over everyone else. We hurried home to make the wreaths. The atmosphere was terrific and it was so heart-warming and wonderful. Throughout Saturday the roads were thronged with natives heading towards the Lighthouse and by afternoon all the enclosures were packed, every tree dripped with spectators.

The Memorial is, without question, the most beautiful and magnificent design to commemorate the work these men did. As they watched the coast, so now does their memorial. The design was surely inspired. Its simple classic lines sweep from a four-finned base to a fuller top surmounted by a bronze guard in the shape of a flame (narrow strips of bronze which outline the shape of a candle flame) and within this guard swings a 1,000,000 candlepower searchlight. The construction is of dazzling white cement. The lighthouse, 90 feet high, stands on a base of red terrazzo tiles, and on this circle, between each set of fins, is a bronze plaque. The plaque between the two front fins is the Honour Plaque with the names of the fallen, on the left side is a plaque which reads:

"In honour and grateful memory of the Coastwatchers and of the loyal natives who assisted them in their heroic service behind enemy lines during the Second World War in providing intelligence vital to the conduct of Allied operations. Not only did they transmit by means of teleradio from their jungle hideouts information which led to the sinking of numerous enemy warships, but they were able to give timely warning of impending enemy air attacks. The contribution towards the Allied victory in the Pacific by the small body of men who constituted the Coastwatchers was out of all proportion to their numbers."

Rupert and his team in Melbourne had worked to make the event memorable. He travelled to Madang with Colonel Caleb Roberts, who had been the controller of AIB. Among the Coastwatchers present were Paul Mason, Jack Read, Lea Ashton, Snowy Rhoades, Wobbie Robinson, Sargeant Yauwika, and Peter Figgis. Also present was Elma Good, widow of Percy Good.

Movietone and Cinesound sent crews to film the opening for their newsreels. Rupert arranged for a recording to be made of various Coastwatchers and other attendees. Eric was first to speak on the recording and mainly read from the plaques at the base of the lighthouse. Others spoke of their past experiences and all expressed their pleasure and happiness at being present.

The opening ceremony commenced at 5pm. The Coastwatchers and their native comrades sat in pride of place. The first to speak was Walter Brooksbank. He was followed by the Administrator, Brigadier Sir Donald Cleland. When Eric's turn came, his voice trembled with emotions as he gave a short speech in English and in Pidgin. The latter was greatly appreciated by the natives, many of whom had not understood the other speeches.

Solemnly, Eric unveiled the plaque which held the names of the 36 Coastwatchers who had lost their lives. He laid the first wreath in remembrance of those he knew so well, men he had personally enlisted, many of whom had been his friends.

Gordon Laycock, the Director of Lighthouses and designer of the lighthouse, had composed a poem for the Coastwatchers, which he read. The truly befitting last line had been inscribed on the base of the light house.

'They waited and warned and died that we might live.'

Senator Gorton, Minister for the Navy, was there to officially open the memorial. As the ceremony came to a close at dusk, he flicked the switch and on came the light, illuminating the lighthouse and making it even more breathtaking than before.

So concluded a most beautiful and moving ceremony.

There was still plenty of celebration for those gathered as they read the plaque and greeted old friends and comrades. There was sadness too in remembering those who had died. For Eric, Rupert and others, Hugh's absence was deeply felt. The Coastwatchers moved to the Hotel Madang for a dinner. All there were extremely happy and grateful to see each other again, which was something they had never thought would happen. Rupert passed around a menu for all the Coastwatchers to sign in remembrance of the occasion.

Unbeknown to his fellow diners, the ceremony was to be a poignant last hurrah for Rupert, for he knew he had lung cancer. Fully anticipating the diagnosis, he did not seek confirmation from a doctor until his return from Madang. There was little that could be done, and Rupert was given three months to live. He survived a little longer than his prognosis and enjoyed Christmas with his family. Rupert finally succumbed to the disease on 8 Jan 1960.

Rupert's intelligence work was more wide-ranging than the Coastwatchers, but they were the dearest to his heart. In late 1944, when coast watching in the N.E. Area was almost finished, the Coastwatchers paid tribute to him for, as with Eric, without Rupert the surveillance network would not have existed. On 15 September 1944 McManus wrote to him on their behalf, thanking him for the personal interest he had shown for the welfare of *Ferdinand* personnel and their families and offering him a samurai sword captured in New Britain in June 1944 by the Ferdinand Guerrillas.

On 15 November 1944, Rupert had replied:

> Being human I am covetous, and have wanted nothing so badly as a Samurai Sword. For such to come as a gift from the finest body of real men it has ever been my pleasure to associate with leaves me bewildered. And yet, Mac, I am grateful because I feel they would not have done it unless they felt that they could number me, at least in part, as one of their team.[3]

Knowing the difficulties and vagaries of war, Eric's simple words held the greatest compliment he could bestow: "How often have we heard the expression during the war: 'Too little, too late.' Commander did enough and he did it *in time*."

One letter came from Dick Horton who was receiving treatment for an eye problem from a friend who was a spiritual healer and who also had telepathic ability. On the evening of the day he heard of Rupert's death, Dick went for treatment. The friend knew nothing of Dick's background or friends. Suddenly she asked if Dick had received some bad news that day. When he replied that he had, she said that someone who had passed over was trying to get through to Dick. She then described 'Cocky' very accurately and said that he was laughing and waving a bunch of flowers, saying it was a joke between them. At first Dick could not think why Cocky would be waving flowers at him. All of a sudden it came to Dick - Ferdinand the bull liked to smell flowers. Dick asked the friend to pass on his understanding of the joke. Apparently Cocky was very glad to have managed to get in touch with Dick again.[4]

Although the Coastwatchers Memorial Lighthouse is a magnificent monument in Madang, there is no memorial in Australia commemorating the Coastwatchers. No site dedicated to their memory exists where Australians and others can go to pay tribute, to say thank you, to leave a wreath or simply remember these remarkable and courageous heroes. Perhaps in time that will change.

In 1958 a wonderful movie called *South Pacific* burst onto the big screen. It was based on James A Michener's short story collection *Tales of the South Pacific*. In the movie the two heroes become Coastwatchers, but this is overshadowed by the beautiful songs, by the romance between the leading men and their ladies and the impact of racial differences. One of the Coastwatchers is a Lieutenant in the US Marines who is guided by a French born plantation owner. An Australian planter would have been more accurate but not nearly as romantic. The two men and their native scouts locate a spot from which they can see the Japanese ships sailing down 'The Slot'. They send back messages that allow the American planes to strafe and bomb the enemy vessels, leading to a resounding victory for the US. The US Commander gives credit to the two men, one of whom has been killed, by saying that they were the ones who made the result possible. It is a nice tribute to the

Coastwatchers, although they are not referred to as such, but it gets eclipsed by the larger plots and the enchanting music.

In 1961 'Camelot' came to the US. Its King (President) had not pulled a sword out of a stone but had been plucked from likely jaws of death by a modern day Merlin, in the shape of an Australian Coastwatcher, and his assistant sorcerers, in the shape of two native scouts. Given up for dead by his US comrades when his PT boat did not return from a nocturnal sortie in 1944, John F Kennedy and his crew were eventually rescued by the actions of Arthur 'Reg' Evans, Coastwatcher on Kolombangara Island, who sent Biuku Gasa and Eroni Kumana to search. Jack Kennedy carved a message on a coconut shell for the scouts to take back to the patrol boat base.

Seventeen years later, the coconut shell, encased in wood and plastic as a paper weight sat proudly on the President's desk in the White House, and Reg Evans was warmly welcomed by Jack and once again thanked for being his saviour.

The media attention given to Reg's visit to the White House brought some revived interest in the Coastwatchers in Australia, even though it was reflected glory from a charismatic American President rather than an appreciation of what the Coastwatchers had done for Australia and for the War in the Pacific.

The Royal Historical Society of Queensland had its interest reawakened in the relevance to Australian history. Connal Gill gave two presentations. The first "The Last Days of Rabaul" was given on 23 March 1961 and the second "New Britain Anabasis" a year later on 22 March 1962. In between the two, Eric delivered a presentation on "The Coastwatchers" on 26 October 1961

In December 1959 Errol Flynn's book "My Wicked Wicked Ways" appeared in bookshops. Flynn had died of a heart attack at age 50 two months previously. Eric wrote an article for *Quadrant* magazine, Volume V, Spring 1961, titled "Errol Flynn at Salamaua" in which he refutes many of Flynn's claims as lies. In his book, Flynn says he was charged with murdering a native near Salamaua in 1929.

The story was that Flynn and his native carriers were attacked when 3 days into a trek inland. Flynn fired a shot which killed one of the attackers. He claims that when he made his way back to Salamaua, he was arrested by a Government official named Hawthorne, who had it in for him, and who was also his prosecutor. The reality is, if there had been a trial, Eric would have been the presiding magistrate. There was no such trial and there was no one called Hawthorne in the Administration at that time.

As mentioned in Chapter 5, Eric recalled Flynn arriving at Salamaua and how, not long after, Alan Cross of Guinea Airways had asked Eric if he knew of someone to manage their branch in Wau. Eric had suggested Flynn as a possibility. He was given the job and flown into Wau. He did not attempt to walk in with carriers as he described in his book. Flynn did not last long in the job and left the district soon afterwards.

When Flynn returned to Wau in 1932, Eric was no longer in the district. Apparently when Flynn left again, he owed money everywhere, including to the local dentist. When he became rich and famous the dentist re-sent him the account. Flynn sent a large glossy autographed picture of himself as payment. The dentist found an ideal place to pin it on a wall in his outside dunny.

Eric's conclusion was that Errol Flynn was a lying crook who in no way resembled the swashbuckling heroes he played in the Hollywood movies.

Cary Grant and Leslie Caron were the stars of a 1964 movie called *Father Goose*, a romantic comedy set in the Philippines about a Coastwatcher and a civilian teacher with seven young school girls.

In 1962 Eric was stricken by pain in his calf muscles when he walked any distance. This condition, called claudication, is due to peripheral vascular disease that involves narrowing of the arteries supplying blood to the legs. It is similar in nature to narrowing of the coronary arteries. Both conditions are more common in smokers like Eric who had been unable to give up the habit he had acquired at the age of 17. Treatment with vasodilating medication from his doctors helped improve the distance he could walk pain free, but it did not eliminate it. Eric still had to stop and rest until the pain subsided before he could continue.

Although suffering from coronary artery disease since 1943, Eric had been one of the lucky few not to have had any further heart attacks during the next 20 years. This perhaps indicates that his 1943 myocardial infarction was stress related. On 5 January 1963 he had an episode of chest pain that was more severe than the angina from which he usually suffered. He was taken to the Repatriation Hospital, in Greenslopes, Brisbane, where he was diagnosed as having myocardial insufficiency rather than myocardial infarction.

Eric spent nine days in hospital and was discharged on 14 January. It was after this that he received his TPI entitlement.

In 1963 he gave away his niece, Patricia Latimer, when she married Peter Geidans in Sydney. Patricia's father had died 20 years previously.

Eric's luck ran low on 30 July 1965 when he had an actual heart attack. He was again admitted to Greenslopes Repatriation Hospital, where he spent a month as an inpatient.

Fortunately, Eric recovered and, in June 1966, was able to record his reminiscences of his life before the Coastwatchers for the State Library of South Australia. The following year he wrote an article for the *Pacific Island Monthly* about the Australian Administration between the wars in which he said.

> Our Administration was admittedly paternal. But I still believe it was the most humane way of governing the country at the time.

In the same year, Eric and Nan sold their house in Chelmer, where they had lived for 21 years. Neighbours during those years have recollections of Eric taking his two dogs for daily walks. Perhaps looking after a house and garden was becoming too much for them and they moved into a unit at New Farm, close to the picturesque New Farm Park and not far from the Brisbane River.

On the evening of 12 March 1968 Eric suffered his third and final heart attack at home in their New Farm apartment. Records show that his death was swift. *The Canberra Times* on 14 March said:

> **War hero dies**
>
> BRISBANE Wednesday — The organiser and commander of Australia's famous Coast Watchers of World War II, Commander Eric A. Feldt, died here suddenly last night.
>
> Commander Feldt, 68, will be cremated tomorrow after a simple chapel service, with no flowers and no military honours at his specific request.
>
> Commander Feldt was Supervising Intelligence Officer, North-eastern Area, during World War II.
>
> He organised the group of men who became known as the Coast Watchers and who worked behind Japanese lines throughout thousands of square miles of the Pacific war theatre.
>
> The Coast Watchers radioed information on Japanese movements to the allies and cost Japan dearly in ships, men and equipment.

The 15 March *Courier Mail* reported his funeral service of the previous day on page 9. Eric had wanted 'no fuss' at his funeral but the chapel was full to overflowing. Former Coastwatchers, including Connal Gill, had come to say farewell to their old leader. They were among the many mourners gathered at the Mt Thompson Crematorium. The minister conducting the service, Reverend Reuben Foote, portrayed Eric as:

> ... a courageous person who played a prominent part in the defence of his country. We give thanks to God for such a servant. Australia owes a debt of gratitude to this person. His memory will go down in the history of our land.

Not present at the service, Keith McCarthy said of him:

> Feldt was a farseeing man, and beneath a rather deceptively mild manner there was a tremendous drive and determination to get

things done. His imagination impelled him to constantly explore new and better ways to do things.

On 20 May Eric's ashes were scattered in the sea off Madang, near the Coastwatchers Memorial Lighthouse. At 5pm, 18 members of the local RSL formed two lines on each side of the gang plank. The Rev. Father Hatters carried Eric's ashes as they were piped aboard the patrol boat HMAS *Samarai*, Jack Read and Snowy Rhoades followed him. Then the two ranks of RSL members filed aboard. The ship steamed slowly to port side off the Coastwatchers Light point, where a large crowd had gathered. Father Hatters conducted the ceremony and scattered Eric's ashes into the water. The official wreath, the RSL wreath and others were dropped overboard. A police bugler onboard played the last post, then three volleys were fired by the PNGVR on shore, followed by Reveille to end the ceremony.

Nan sent a description to Connal Gill and Malcolm Wright, who were unable to attend.

In August that year, Nan was given the honour of launching a new patrol boat HMAS *Madang* at the Evans Deakin shipyard, Brisbane. Nan lived for another 17 years, dying in New Farm, Brisbane in 1985.

At some stage an attempt was made by members of Eric's extended family to initiate further recognition of, or obtain completion of, an existing award recommendation for his World War II contributions. A letter dated 22 April 1996 and addressed to one of Eric's nieces, is about Commander Eric Feldt's Legion of Merit recommendation case from the Second World War. It states that documentation was being forwarded to the Department of the Army Military Awards Branch in Washington for adjudication in the case. No further correspondence was received.

So what of Eric Feldt the man? He was quiet and modest, with a strong sense of duty and responsibility. His intelligence, forward thinking and determination made him an excellent leader. He cared greatly about the wellbeing of his Coastwatchers, and they were extremely loyal to him. Although basically an armchair warrior, he was more than that, being a hands-on contributor who was not afraid to venture into enemy occupied territory. However, he knew that his most valuable contribution was in overseeing the activities of the Coastwatchers. Perhaps at times he may have wondered if Fate had taken a hand in his life, preparing him for this vitally important task.

The war deprived him of a comfortable life as the Warden of Wau and left him to live the rest of his life not well off and not in the best of health. But Eric would have considered himself to be lucky to have made the contributions that he did. Unlike his fallen comrades, he had much to be grateful for. He had a life with Nan. He had written a book in tribute to the Coastwatchers and had lived to see a memorial erected in their honour. He was content to live out his years simply, with Nan and their pets.

Perhaps if Eric's health had permitted him to take on more active roles post war, the Coastwatchers would have become better known. Possibly if Hugh Mackenzie and Rupert Long had not died relatively young the trio may have made a more lasting impression. Perhaps the Coastwatchers' battle was a small part of a much bigger war. But it was a valiant fight and it was so close to Australian shores that perhaps Australians have the right to remember these Australian heroes and their erstwhile leader with pride.

Eric's book concludes with a poem he wrote. Aware in 1946 that his fallen Coastwatcher comrades were already forgotten, was he also prophesising that a similar fate would befall the rest of the Coastwatchers? It has come to pass that knowledge of this gallant band of selfless heroes has virtually disappeared into the mists of time, forgotten by their native Australia and virtually unknown in the world at large.

ENVOI
We shall forget. Save when some little thing,
A scene, a song, a laugh, or words they said
A flash of memory to our minds will bring.
We shall forget our comrades who are dead.
But if we hold the field on which they fell,
Nor fail, nor falter till we bring surcease
To pain and travail. Then will all be well,
And, though forgotten, they will lie in peace.

THE FALLEN COASTWATCHERS

Guy Allen
Lieut. F.A. Barret AIF
Lieut. D.N. Bedkober AIF
Lieut. L.J. Bell RANVR
Captain G.E. Bengough BSIDF
Sub-Lt. G.M. Benham DSC RANVR
Gunner J.I. Bunning AIF
Sgt. W.A.H. Butteris AIF
Sgt. L.W.T. Carlson AIF
J. Daymond
Writer T.J. Douglas RAN
Thomas Ebery
Sgt. W.F.B. Florance AIF
Sig. A.E. Francis RAN
Percy Dacre Good
Captain G.C. Harris AIF
C.C. Jervis
Leonard Kentish
Yeo of Sigs G.T Knight RAN
Lieut. A.F. Kyle DSC RANVR
Ch. Yeo of Sigs S. Lamont RAN
Lieut. D.A. Laws AIF
Sgt. N.B. Martin AIF
F/O C.J.T. Mason RAAF
Sub-Lt. E.F.H. Mitchell RANVR
W.O.2 A. Obst AIF
Sub-Lt. A.R. Olander RANVR
Sub-Lt. C.L. Page RANVR
Captain L. Pursehouse AIF
Trooper G. Shortis AIF
W.H. Squires
Lieut. G Stevenson AIF
J. Talmage
Lieut. G.H.C. Train RANVR
Petty Officer W. Tupling RAN
Flight Lieut. L.G. Vial
Ldg. Tel. J.l. Woodroffe RAN

BIBLIOGRAPHY

Battle for Australia, http://www.battleforaustralia.org.au/

Burrowes, J., The Last Coastwatcher, http://thelastcoastwatcher.wordpress.com

Collins, J.A., *As Luck Would Have It*, Angus and Robertson, Sydney, 1965

Clemens, M., *Alone on Guadalcanal*, Naval Institute Press, Annapolis, 1998

Feldt, E.A., *The Coast Watchers*, Oxford University Press, Melbourne, 1946

Feldt, E.A., *The Coast Watchers*, Oxford University Press, New York, 1946

Feldt, E.A., The Coastwatchers, Journal of the Historical Society of Queensland, Volume 6, Number 4, 1961–62, pp. 762–778

Feldt, E.A., Errol Flynn at Salamaua, *Quadrant*, Spring, 1961, Volume 5. Pp 81–8

Feuer, A.B., *Coast Watching in WWII*, Stackpole Books, Mechanicsburg, 2006

Freund, A.H.P., *Missionary Turns Spy*, Lutheran Publishing House, Adelaide, 1989

Flynn, E., *My Wicked, Wicked Ways*, Aurum Press Ltd, London, 2005

Gill, G.H., *Royal Australian Navy*, 1939–1942, Collins, Melbourne, 1985

Gill, G.H., *Royal Australian Navy*, 1942–1945, Collins, Melbourne, 1985

Gill, J.C.H., New Britian Anabasis, *Journal of the Royal Historical Society of Queensland* Volume 6, Issue 4, 1962, pp. 817–865

Holland, F., *El Tigre,* Ocean Enterprises, Yarram, 1998.

Horton, D.C., *Fire Over the Islands*, Leo Cooper Ltd, London, 1975

Ind, A., *Spy Ring Pacific*, Weidenfeld and Nicolson, London, 1958

Jones, P., *Australia's Argonauts the remarkable story of the first class to enter the Royal Australian Naval College*, Echo Books, West Geelong, 2016

Lindsay, P., *The Coast Watchers: The Men Behind Enemy Lines Who Saved The Pacific*, Random House Australia Pty Ltd, North Sydney, 2011

McCarthy, J.K., *Patrol into Yesterday My New Guinea Years,* Cheshire Publishing Pty Ltd, Melbourne,1972

Powell, A., *War by Stealth Australians and the Allied Intelligence Bureau 1942-1945*, Melbourne University Press, Carlton South, 1996

Ryan, P., *Fear Drive My Feet*, The Text Publishing Company, Melbourne, 2015

Veale, L., *Wewak Mission*, Lionel P.V. Veale, Ashmore City, 1996

Veale, L., *The Final Missions,* Lionel P.V. Veale, Ashmore City, 2005

Willoughby, C.A. & Chamberlain, J., *MacArthur1941-1951*, McGraw-Hill Book Company, Inc, NewYork,1954,

Winter, B., *The Intrigue Master Commander Long and Naval Intelligence in Australia, 1913-1945,* Boolarong Press, Brisbane, 1995

ENDNOTES

CHAPTER 1: PETER, GUSSIE AND THE FELDT FAMILY 1876-1913

1. Augusta Feldt, *Gussie's Story*, Unpublished memoir All other quotes in this chapter come from *Gussie's Story*, by Augusta Feldt, unpublished memoir.

CHAPTER 2: THE NAVAL COLLEGE YEARS 1913-1916

1. Peter Jones, *Australia's Argonauts The remarkable story of the first class to enter the Royal Australian Naval College*, ECHO BOOKS, West Geelong 2016 p.12
2. Ibid, p12
3. Ibid, p26
4. Ibid, p27
5. Royal Australian Naval College Magazine (RANC Magazine), H Thacker printers, Geelong, 1913, p.17
6. Peter Jones op. cit., p42
7. Ibid, p93.

Other quotes in this chapter, unless otherwise indicated, come from *Reminiscences of Commander Eric Feldt* sound recording held by the State Library of South Australia.

CHAPTER 3: WORLD WAR I AND POST WAR NAVY 1917-1923

1. Peter Jones, *Australia's Argonauts The remarkable story of the first class to enter the Royal Australian Naval College*, ECHO BOOKS, West Geelong, 2016, p.113
2. Ibid, p183

Other quotes in this chapter, unless otherwise indicated, come from *Reminiscences of Commander Eric Feldt* sound recording held by the State Library of South Australia.

CHAPTER 4: NEW GUINEA PRE WORLD WAR II: 1923-1927

1. Quotes and information in this chapter, unless otherwise indicated, come from *Reminiscences of Commander Eric Feldt*, sound recording held by the State Library of South Australia.

CHAPTER 5: NEW GUINEA PRE-WORLD WAR II: 1928-1939

2. Peter Jones, *Australia's Argonauts The remarkable story of the first class to enter the Royal Australian Naval College*, ECHO BOOKS, West Geelong, 2016, p. 224
3. J.K.McCarthy, *Patrol into Yesterday My New Guinea Years*, Cheshire Publishing Pty Ltd, Melbourne, 1972, p.91

Other quotes in this chapter, unless otherwise indicated, come from *Reminiscences of Commander Eric Feldt* sound recording held by the State Library of South Australia

CHAPTER 6: THE WWII COASTWATCHERS: THE BEGINNING

1. Eric Feldt, *The Coast Watchers*, Oxford University Press, New York, 1946, p.7
2. Peter Jones, *Australia's Argonauts The remarkable story of the first class to enter the Royal Australian Naval College*, ECHO BOOKS , West Geelong, 2016, p.267
3. Barbara Winter, *The Intrigue Master Commander Long and Naval Intelligence in Australia, 1913-1945*, Boolarong Press, Brisbane,1995, p. 33
4. Eric Feldt, op.cit, p.5
5. Eric Feldt, *The Coast Watchers*, Oxford University Press, Melbourne, 1946, p 21
6. ibid, p 25
7. Barbara Winter, op.cit, p40
8. Eric Feldt, New York, op.cit, p.12
9. Barbara Winter, op.cit, p40
10. Peter Jones, op.cit., p 287
11. Barbara Winter, op.cit.,
12. Eric Feldt, Melbourne, op.cit, p.29
13. Ibid, p.33

14. Ibid, p.32
15. Ibid, p.33
16. Ibid, p.41
17. Ibid, p.36

CHAPTER 7: THE FALL OF RABAUL AND THE AFTERMATH

1. J.C.H. (James Connal Howard) Gill, *New Britian Anabasis, Journal of the Royal Historical Society of Queensland* volume 6 issue 4, 1962, pp.817-865.
2. ibid
3. ibid
4. ibid
5. J.K. McCarthy, *Patrol into Yesterday My New Guinea Years*, Cheshire Publishing Pty Ltd, Melbourne, 1972, p208.
6. J.C.H. (James Connal Howard) Gill op.cit
7. Eric Feldt, *The Coast Watchers*, Oxford University Press, Melbourne,1946, p.48
8. ibid
9. J.K. McCarthy, op.cit.,p 202
10. Ibid, p204
11. Eric Feldt, op.cit., p.58
12. J.K.McCarthy, op.cit., p.206
13. Eric Feldt, op.cit.,p 65
14. Patrick Lindsay *The Coast Watchers The Men Behind Enemy Lines Who Saved The Pacific*, Random House Australia Pty Ltd, North Sydney, 2011, p.124

Other quotes in this chapter, unless otherwise indicated, are from Eric Feldt's *The Coast Watchers*

CHAPTER 8: THE COASTWATCHERS AND THE JAPANESE INVASION OF THE N.E. AREA

1. Eric Feldt, *The Coast Watchers*, Oxford University Press, Melbourne, 1946, p.51
2. Ibid, p52
3. Ibid, p119
4. A.B. Feuer Coast *Watching in World War II Operations against the Japanese*

on the Solomon Islands, 1941-43, STACKPOLE BOOKS, Mechanicsburg, 2006, p.7
5. Eric Feldt, op.cit., p 124
6. A.B. Feuer, op.cit., p 13
7. Ibid, p19
8. Eric Feldt, op.cit., p 53
9. Ibid, p81
10. Ibid, p81
11. Ibid, p83
12. Ibid p95
13. Allison Ind *Spy Ring Pacific*, Lowe and Brydone, London, 1958, p.69
14. Eric Feldt, op.cit., p 99-100

CHAPTER 9: THE COASTWATCHERS OF BOUGAINVILLE, GUADALCANAL AND OTHER SOLOMON ISLANDS

1. Eric Feldt, *The Coast Watchers*, Oxford University Press, Melbourne, 1946, p107
2. Peter Jones, *Australia's Argonauts The remarkable story of the first class to enter the Royal Australian Naval College*, ECHO BOOKS, West Geelong 2016, p. 454
3. A.B. Feuer *Coast Watching in World War II Operations against the Japanese on the Solomon Islands, 1941-43*, STACKPOLE BOOKS, Mechanicsburg, 2006, pp.36-37
4. Ibid, p39
5. Ibid, p40
6. Ibid, p57
7. Eric Feldt, op.cit., p.143
8. Ibid, p114
9. Ibid, p114-115
10. A.B. Feuer op.cit., p.63
11. Ibid, p64
12. Barbara Winter, Intrigue Master, *The Intrigue Master Commander Long and Naval Intelligence in Australia, 1913-1945*, Boolarong Press, Brisbane,1995, p.193-194
13. Eric Feldt, op.cit., p. 155
14. A.B. Feuer op.cit.,, p.104

15. Eric Feldt, op.cit., p.173

CHAPTER 10: THE COASTWATCHERS – TOWNSVILLE, THE *PALUMA*, AND PAPUA NEW GUINEA

1. Eric Feldt, The Coast Watchers. Oxford University Press, Melbourne, 1946, p187
2. Ibid, p188
3. Ibid, p188
4. Ibid, p188-189
5. Ibid, p190
6. Ibid, p216
7. Ibid, p223
8. Ibid, p231
9. Ibid, p235

CHAPTER 11: THE COASTWATCHERS – GUADALCANAL, BOUGAINVILLE AND ILLNESS

1. Eric Feldt, *The Coast Watchers,* Oxford University Press, Melbourne, 1946, p.256
2. Ibid, p266
3. Ibid, p258
4. Barbara Winter, *The Intrigue Master Commander Long and Naval Intelligence in Australia, 1913-1945* Boolarong Press, Brisbane ,1995, p.204
5. Peter Jones, *Australia's Argonauts The remarkable story of the first class to enter the Royal Australian Naval College*, ECHO BOOKS, West Geelong, 2016, p.503
6. Eric Feldt op.cit., p259
7. Ibid, p374
8. Peter Jones op.cit. p.504
9. Ibid, p504
10. Rupert Long, AWA Recording of Coastwatchers at Coastwatchers Memorial, Madang, 15 August 1959
11. Peter Jones, op.cit., p. 558

CHAPTER 12: POST WAR LIFE

1. Peter Jones *Australia's Argonauts The remarkable story of the first class to enter the Royal Australian Naval College*, ECHO BOOKS, West Geelong, 2016, p.576
2. Ibid, p584
3. Barbara Winter *The Intrigue Master Commander Long and Naval Intelligence in Australia, 1913–1945*, Boolarong Press, Brisbane, 1995, p.247
4. Ibid, p280

INDEX

Adler Bay 138
Admiralty Islands 179, 276
Aitape 64, 74, 76, 77, 79, 80, 81, 120
Albert, Alexander 35
Albert, Frank 29, 35
Albert, Otto 25, 35, 36, *163*, 164
Allen, Guy 179, 190, 300
Allied Intelligence Bureau (AIB) 200, 201, 204, 229, 245, 246, 260, 261, 273, 275, 289
Aloha 64, 65, 66, 71, 77, *166*
Ambunti 65, 66, 72
Andresen, Albert 'Andy' 119, *206*, 208, 226, 233
Anir Island 120, 138, 179, 197, 198, 199
Appel, Pip 153
Arawe 248, 250, 254
Archer, Fred 186, 187
Archer, Geoff 245, 257, 261, 262
Armitage, Geroge William Thomas 36, 37, 39, 50, *163*
Ashton, Lea 93, *170*, 245, 257, 260, 261, 262, 263, 289
Aravia 183, 186
Auki vii, 208, 271
Aussi 146, 147, 148
Australia New Guinea Administrative Unit (ANGAU) 155, 159, 243, 246, 263
Awatip 65, 72, 73

Baker, Gladys 156, 160

Ball, W B 134, 135, 139, 141, 144
Ballarat 37
Baniu Bay 212
Baniu Plantation 183, *183*, 184
Battle of the Bismarck Sea 259
Battle of the Coral Sea ix, 196, 210, 211
Battle of Guadalcanal 222, 233, 270
Battle of Midway 211, 221
Baum, Helmuth 96, 97, 98
Bavaria 155, 156
Bell, Lincoln 151, 158, 160, 248 *249*, 250, 251, 253, 256, 259, 260
Bell, Stan 193, 194
Bena Bena 250, 251, 256, 257, 259, 260
Benham, Edmund Reginal Gregory Wade 'Greg' *112*, 194, 195, 196, 197, 198, 199, 204, 300
Bennett, Duncan 62
Bennett, Harry 62
Bismarck Archipelago 61
Blakey, Snow 156
Blandy, R D 122
Blixt, Anna Maria 2
Blixt, August 2, 3, 6, 52
Blixt, Bothilda (née Lundberg) 2, 3, 4, 53
Blixt, Carolina 2
Blixt, Petter Per Larsson 2
Blixt, Sophie 53
Blixt, Sven Peter 2
Boddie, Ronald 23
Boer War 15, 16, 17

Bogadjim 250
Bogia 104
Boia 121
Bonis Plantation 187
Bougainville ix, *60*, 62, 74, 75, 182, 185, 187, 188, 207–237, 248, 265–270, 278, 279, 288
Boye, Ruby Olive 209
Bridge, K W T *170*, 246, 247, 248
British Solomon Islands Protectorate Defence Force (BSIPDF) 208, 209, 223, 227
Brockman, William 267
Brooksbank, Gilbert 116
Brooksbank, Walter 114, 116, *173*, 288, 290
Brown, Frederick 23
Brown, Vessy 94
Bubu River 88
Buckley, E J 223
Buin 186, 213, 214, 216, 233, 234, 235, 268
Buka Island 62, 74, 75, 119, 120, 182, 186, 210, 211, 212, 216, 222, 234, 267
Buka Passage 74, 75, 120, 182, 184, 187, 211, 216, 235, 279
Bull code 241, 245
Bullock, H W 126, 127
Bulolo Valley 86, 88, 94, 95, 96, 98, 100, 101, 261
Bulu, Ansin 190, 192, 193
Buna ix, 239, 240, 243, 245, 247, 248, 255
Burnett, Joseph 26, 29, 36, 39, 123, *163*

Burns Philp (BP) 58, 89, 94, 146, 256
Butteris, W A H *249*, 250, 251, 252, 300

Calder, Norman Keith 36, 39, 50, *163*
Callaghan, Daniel 235
Cameron, Alan 148, 149, 150, 151, 153
Cameron, Bill 89
Campbell, Alan *170*, 256
Cape Gauffre 250, 251
Cape Gloucester 146, 150, 248, 250, 251, 252
Cape Hoskins 124
Cape Nelson 240, 243
Cape St George 194, 195
Carlson, L W T 246, 247, 248, 300
Caroline Islands 235
Carpenters 89, 120
Carr, Howard 131, 134, 135, 138
Chambers, Bertram 22, 29, 39
Chambers, Ken *112*, 132, 179, 258
Champion, Ivan 158, 159, 241, 243
Chapman, Frank 192
Chimbu 157
Choiseul Island 207, 229, 232, 265
Christian, Stan 64, 69, 70, 72
Chu, Leung 151
Churchill, Winston 46
Cilento, Raphael 62
Cleland, Donald 290
Clemens, Martin 208, 211, 221, 223, 224
Coastwatchers Memorial Lighthouse *175*, 176, 288, 289, 290, 292, 297
Collins, Bill 143
Collins, John 25, 26, 28, 33, 34, 35, 36, 37, 39, 43, 45, 46, 48, 51, 54, 58, 114, 115, 123, *163*

Colonial Sugar Refining (CSR) Company 9, 10, 11, 12, 13
Colvin, Ragnar 115, 123
Conder, Alfred Denis 36, 39, 50, *163*
Creswell, William 21, 23, 34
Crichton, Archibald Frederic 17, 49
Crichton, Mabel Christina (née Feldt) 9, 14, 17, 18, 19, 49, *163*, 285
Cross, Alan 85, 89, 99, 294
CSR (see Colonial Sugar Refining Company)
Cunningham, Earnest Semple 'Dick' 33, 34, 36, 39, 42, 47, 48, *163*

Dagmer 4, 6
Dalglish, Robin 42, 46, 47, 48
Daymond, John *112*, 180, 191, 300
Deakin, Alfred 21
Denman, Thomas 23, 25
Dix, Thomas 23
Dolby, Bill 183, 184
Douglas, Ken 146, 151, 158, *249*, 250, 251
Douglas, TJ 143, 159, 300
Downing, Harry 84, 88
Draper, 'Blue' 79, 104
Drotningholm 53
Dufaur 146
Duke of York Islands 76, 179
Dulcy 151, 153
Dumaresq, John 40, 54
Dykes, Jimmy 100

Eastern Highlands *60*, 62
Echlin, Gladys 102
Echlin, Maude Letitia (née White) 102
Echlin, Richard Boyd 102
Eddy, V C 125
Edie Creek 80, 84, 85, 86, 88, 94, 108, 260
Edith 119

Elwell, Charles 23, 30
Emirau Island 125, 132, 179, 193
Empress Augusta Bay 214, 278
Esdaile, James Claude Durie 'Essy' 23, 33, 34, 35, 36, 39, 51, *163*, 278
Evans, Arthur Reginald 'Reg' 266, 293
Evenson, Albert 148, 149, 150, 154

Fairfax-Ross, B 204, 241, 242, 243, 259
Faisi 120, 189
Farncomb, Harold Bruce 33, 34, 35, 36, 39, 51, 54, *163*
Feetham, W O 141
Feldt, Anders 'Andrew' 2, 3, 5, 7, 9, 12
Feldt, Augusta 'Gussie' (née Blixt) vi, 1–20, 22, 26, 28, 30, 31, 49, 52, 53, 58, 118, 161, *163*, 278, 285
Feldt, Carl 'Charlie' 2, 3, 12
Feldt, Eric Augustas 'Kruge' *162*, *163*, *164*, *165*, *166*, *167*, *168*, *170*, *176*, *178*
  birth and childhood 1, 15, 17–20
  Coastwatchers 113–283
  death 296
  education 18, 19, 20, 51
  employment 49–58
  health 72, 76, 98, 106, 107, 108, 271, 273, 275, 278, 295
  marriage 102, *166*
  naval career (WWI) 37–48
  naval college 21–35
  New Guinea career 61–82, 83–112
  sporting activities 26, 33, 34, 43, 45, 51, 52, 55, 63, 95, 100

INDEX

Feldt, Gottfried Anton 'Gotty' 7, 8, 14, 15, 16, 17, 18, *162*
Feldt, Johanna 2, 10
Feldt, Johanna Botilla (née Alm) 2
Feldt, Lucy Victoria 'Tommy' 14, 18, 26, 27, 28, 30, 31, 49, 52, 53, *162*, *163*, 285
Feldt, Minnie Juliet 12
Feldt, Nancy Lynette 'Nan' (née Echlin) vii, 102, 103, 104, 105, 107, 108, 110, *166*, *168*, 194, 198, 242, 272, 275, 277, 278, 285, 286, 295, 297, 298
Feldt, Nils Persson 2
Feldt, Peter Nilsson 1–20, 26, 30, 31, 49, 52, 53, 58, 118, *161*, *162*, *163*, 285
Feldt, Violet Augusta 9, 14, 15
Ferdinand operation 201, 204, 205, 208, 209, 215, 236, 240, 241, 242, 245, 246, 251, 254, 255, 256, 257, 258, 274, 275, 276, 283, 288, 291
Ferguson, Ronald Munro 34
Figgis, Peter 135, 137, 141, 143, 204, 243, 289
Finisterre Range 251
Finschhafen 121, 155, 158, 180, 190, 248, 250, 254
Fisher, Andrew 23
Fletcher, Frank 211
Florida Island 207, 210, 271
Flynn, Errol 89, 293, 294
Forster, Henry William 71
Francis, A E 138, 139, 141, 300
Franklin 32, 33, 74, 80
Freund, A P H 'Harold' 121, 156, *249*, 250

Gabriel 64, 65
Garing, W C 125
Gasmata 142, 150, 158, 180, 190
Gavutu Island *206*, 207, 218, 219
Gazelle Peninsula 136, 137
Geidans, Patricia (née Latimer) 295
Geidans, Peter 295
George V 21
German New Guinea (see also New Guinea, Papua New Guinea) 62
Getting, Frank Edmond 'Hungry' 23, 36, 39, 42, 50, *163*
Gill, George Hermon 277
Gill, James Connal Howard vi, *112*, 122, 126, 127, 132, 133, 134, 136, 137, 138, 139, 141, 142, 143, 144, 145, 157, 158, 179, 191, 203, 204, 245, 293, 296, 297,
Gilling, Lloyd Falconer 36, 39, 47, *163*
Gizo 120, 227
Gnair 156
Goad, Jack 155
Gold Ridge 208, 226, 236
Good, Percy *183*, 186, 187, 188, 189, 191, 289, 300
Gona 239
Grampus 229, 232
Grand Fleet 39, 44, 45, 46
Grant, Duncan 22, 28, 29, 32, 33
Gregory, Henry 84, 85, 88, 134, 160
Guadalcanal vii, ix, 128, 184, 201, *206*, *217*, 207–237, 239, 248, 256, 258, 265–283, 287
Guasopa Harbour 257

Hall, William 23
Halligan, Reg 56, 58, 108, 285
Halsey, William 'Bull' *174*, 236, 270, 284, 288
Hamilton, H 204, 243

Hamilton, Mac 153, 245, 257, 261
Hanisch Harbour 158
Hardie, Andrew 37
Harding, K 223
Harris, 'Bucky' 270
Harris, G C 'Blue' viii, *112*, 155, 156, 160, 205, *249*, 250, 253, 276, 300
Harris Navy 155, 156, 157, 204
Harris, Ted 144
Hay, Ken Dalrymple *206*, 208, 226, 236, 237
Henderson Field 221, 222, 270
Henderson, Frank 147
Henry Reid Bay 139
Hirst, Paul Hugil 36, 39, 51, *163*
HMAS *Albatross* 93
HMAS *Anzac* 50, 51
HMAS *Australia* 29
HMAS *Brisbane* 51
HMAS *Encounter* 29
HMAS *Lusair* 278
HMAS *Madang* 297
HMAS *Melbourne* 29, 54
HMAS *Moreton* 275, 278
HMAS *Platypus* 50
HMAS *Samarai* 297
HMAS *Swordsman* 49, 51
HMAS *Sydney* 50, 123
HMS *Canada* 39, 40, 41, 42, 43, 44, 45, 47, 48, 54
HMS *Glorious* 39, 42, 45
HMS *Nimrod* 52
HMS *Prince* 45, 57
HMS *Resolution* 45
HMS *Spencer* 48
HMS *Sybille* 48, 49
HMS *Vanguard* 44
Holland, Frank 142, 145, 151, 160
Horton, Dick ix, 218, 224, 225, 226, 233, 291
Howells, Elmer Benjamin 36, *163*
Hughes, Billy 109
Hunt, R B A 118, 122

311

Huon Peninsula 88, 248

Iboki Plantation 145, 156, 158
Ind, Allison 201, 202
Inus Plantation 185, 186, 210, 213
Itebi 71
Itni River 250
Iwi 141

Japandai 65, 66
Jervis, C C *112*, 120, 179, 190, 300
Jervis Bay 22, 31, 32, 33, 34, 38, 55, 56
Johann Albrecht Harbour 253
Josselyn, Henry ix, 218, 224, 225, 229, 231, 232, 265

Kahili 234, 235
Kainantu 101
Kairiru 79
Kalai Mission 141, 142, 143
Kalas 135, 137
Kanakas (see South Sea Islanders)
Karawari 68
Karkar Island 104
Karlai 139
Kasileia 140
Kataku 216
Kavieng 119, 125, 132, 180, 190, 192, 193, 194, 195, 196, 199, 216, 248
Keenan, Jack 229, 232, 265, 269
Kennedy, Donald Gilbert ix, *171*, *217*, 209, 210, 211, 222, 227, 228
Kennedy, John F 293
Kentish, Leonard 300
Kerschbaum, Father 71
Kessa Plantation 186, 187, 188
Kieta 74, 119, 120, 182, 184, 185, 212, 213, 216, 268
Kimlin, Peyton James 36, 39, 52, *163*

Knight, G T 141, 143, 144, 159, 300
Koch, Harold *170*, 204, 241, 242
Kokoda 159, 239
Kroening, Dr 184, 185
Kruger, Paul 18, 38
Kuester, Gus 156
Kunua Plantation 212
Kuper, Geoffrey 227
Kyle, Alan Fairlie 'Bill' ix, 84, 88, 89, 99, 100, 101, *112*, 121, *170*, 180, 191, 194, 195, 196, 197, 198, 199, 204, 300

Lady Betty 92
Lae 85, 90, 95, 115, 131, 146, 155, 156, 158, 181, 190, 248, *249*, 250, 255, 259, 278
Lagui 214
Lakatoi 146, 157, 158, 160
Lamingi 136, 137
Lamont S 120, 138, 144, 145, 159, 179, 190, 300
Langemar River 99
Langiona 152
Lark Force 131, 133, 160
Larkins, Frank Lockwood 23, 26, 29, 32, 33, 34, 36, 50, *163*
Lassul Bay 150
Latimer, Emma Caroline 'Lassie' (née Feldt) 11, 18, 19, 20, 26, 27, 28, 31, *163*, 285
Latimer, William Alexander Fleming 31
Laurabada 158, 159
Lavoro Plantation 209
Laws, D A 153, 259, 260, 300
Laycock, Gordon 288, 290
League of Nations 62
Leahy, Mick 99
Leahy, Pat 99
Lecky, John Valentine Stuart 'Jack' 36, *163*

Levein, Cecil John 94, 95, 96, 100
Ley, Jimmy 42, 44
Lockhart, G 127
Lolobau 146, 147
Long Island 252
Long, Rupert Basil Michel 'Cocky' vi, viii, 23, 36, 50, 114, 115, 116, 117, 119, 120, 122, 123, 124, 126, 159, *163*, *167*, 189, 190, 200, 204, 223, 224, 255, 258, 269, 274, 277, 282, 288, 289, 290, 291, 292
Looker, C 251
Lukis, F A 125, 192
Lunga ix, 208, 209, 211, 215, 221, 223, 226, 228, 231, 233, 234, 255, 265, 271

MacArthur, Douglas 200, 234, 245, 273, 280, 282
MacDonald, Gerry 103
Macfarlan, Donald ix, 126, 127, 128, 187, *206*, 207, 208, 211, 215, 226, 234, 274
Mackenzie, Hugh Alexander 'Macka' viii, ix, 23, 36, 39, 51, 92, *112*, 124, 125, 126, 127, 128, 132, 133, 134, 135, 136, 137, 141, 142, 143, 144, 145, 159, *163*, *169*, *170*, 179, 190, 191, 204, *206*, *217*, 218, 221, 222, 223, 224, 225, 226, 228, 229, 236, 237, 241, 255, 256, 258, 266, 267, 268, 270, 271, 274, 279, 282, 286, 287, 290, 298
Mackie, John 182, 184, 186, 210, 213, 234, 267, 268, 269
Maclaine, J D 85
Madang vi, 56, *60*, 62, 67, 68, 74, 83, 88, 102, 103, 104, 105, 106, 107, 108,

INDEX

120, 121, 131, 145, 156, 157, *175*, 248, 250, 258, 259, 278, 288, 289, 290, 291, 292, 297
Magai 118
Maierhofer, Johan 141, 143
Maka Island 119
Malabonga 132, 134
Malahuka 151, 153, 154
Malaita Island 207, 208, 209, 218, 271
Malaita 119
Malu 65
Mamarega 214
Mambare River ix, 246
Manus *60*, 62, 64, 77, 119
Marai 137, 138, 140
Marcena 58, 62
Marchant, William 207, 208, 218, 226
Marienburg 64, 71
Markham River Valley 85, 86, 88, 101, 158, 260
Marshall Islands 62
Marsland, G H 'Rod' 146, 147, 148, 149, 150, 151, 157, 158, 160, *170*, 204, 241, 242, 243
Mason, Bill 153
Mason, Cecil John 197, 198, 199, 204, 300
Mason, Joe 153
Mason, Paul Edward Allen ix, *112*, *169*, 182, 185, 186, 189, 191, 192, 213, 214, 216, *217*, 219, 220, 227, 233, 234, 268, 270, 289
Matahai 210
Matchin Bay 210
Matty Island (see Wuvulu Island)
Mavolo River 140
McCarthy, Keith viii, 99, 105, *112*, 133, 140, 142, 143, 145, 146, 147, 148, 149, 150, 151, 152, 153, 154, 155, 156, 157, 158, 159, 160, *169*, 180, 191, 204, 241, 242, 245, 253,

256, 257, 261, 262, 263, 274, 276, 296,
McCauley, Molly 274
McDonald, J H 132, 180, 196, 198
McGilvery, Harry 85, 94
McKay, Jock 103, 104
McManus, James Cathal Boyd *173*, 274, 275, 276, 291
McNicoll, Walter 105, 118
McQuarrie, Hector 220
Medic 16
Meggi 124
Melville, Jack 81
Merle-Smith, Van 200, 243, 275
Merrylees, J I 182, 185
Metlik 194
Milim 143
Millar, C J 246
Miller, H W 241
Milne Bay ix, 239, 240, 243, 256, 257
Misetiwai 141, 142, 143
Mitchell, Jean 94
Mitchell, Eric *112*, 180, 189, 191, 192, 300
Miwo River 216
Molika River 214
Mollison, P J 204, 241, 242, 243
Money, Bill 156
Monk, William 23
Montevideo Maru 160
Montoro 64, 71, 102
Morgan, Charles 32
Morobe *60*, 62, 88, 96, 105, 247
Mt Tuangi 132
Muliama 196, 198
Munda 228
Mundi Mundi Plantation 231
Murray, Harry 196
Murray, Hubert 61
Murray, K L 'Paddy' 125, 203, 204, 242, 245
Muschu 79
Mutapina Point 214

MV *Leander* 119
MV *Macdhui* 108, 159

Namatanai 81, 118, 119, 180, 194
Nautilus 267
Naval Intelligence viii, 114, 115, 201, 223
Neil, Normie 107
Netherland Indies 61
Neumann, Vic 155, 156, *249*, 250, 251, 252, 253
New Britain *60*, 62, 124, 131, 145, 146, 149, 154, 155, 156, 180, 245, 250, 261, 278, 282, 286, 291, 293
New Georgia Islands 207, 221, 227, 228
New Georgia Sound (see also The Slot) 207
New Guinea Volunteer Rifles (NGVR) 131, 132, 261
New Hebrides (see also Vanuatu) 54, 116, 122, 123, 197, 211, 236
New Ireland *60*, 62, 118, 120, 179, 190, 194, 197, 199
Newman, Jack Bolton 26, 33, 36, 39, 50, *163*
Niall, H R 121
Ninigo Islands 204
Nissan Island 75, 120, *172*, 179
Nixon, Richard 288
Noakes, Lyndon Charles ix, *170*, 246, 247
Norfolk Island 55, 56, 57
'Norland' 1, 14, 30, *161*, *162*
North East (NE) Area 116, 117, 120, 124, 125, 132, 188, 200, 202, 273
Noumea 55, 204, 236, 270
Nubia 121
Nubia 121
Nugget 184, 188
Numa Numa 119, 184, 186

313

Nurse, Edwin Scott 'Eddy' 33, 34, 36, 39, 50, *163*

Obst, Adolph 155, 156, *249*, 250, 251, 252, 300
Ogilvie, L 223, 224, 225
Olander, A R 'Bert' 151, 153, 158, 160, *249*, 250, 253, 254
Open Bay 145
Oro Bay 243, 245, 251
Osborne House (Aus) 22, 29
Osborne House (UK) 21, 22, 24
Otibandi 99
Owen, Bill 144, 159
Owen Stanley Range 239, 240

Page, Cornelius Lyons 'Con' *112*, 131, 132, 180, 189, 190, 191, 192, 193, 194, 199, 300
Page, Harold 62, 160
Pak Island 119
Palmalmal 142, 144, 159, 241
Palmer, Edward 144
Paluma ix, *172*, 239–243, 256, 257, 261, 272
Parer, K 120
Paterson, J H 127, 155, 251
Pearce, George 58, 108
Pearl Harbor 128, 131, 218, 219, 220
Pentland, Jerry 85
Pigibut Plantation 189
Pioneer Class (see also Royal Australian Naval College) 1, 29, 32, 33, 36, 37, 42, 43, 48, 50, 51, 52, 56, *163*, *164*, 278, 287
Playfair code 118, 157, 241
Pondo Plantation 148, 149, 150, 152, 153, 154
Pope, Cuthbert 23
Porapora 212, 218, 219, 267, 268, 269

Port Moresby 61, 114, 115, 116, 118, 120, 121, 122, 123, 124, 125, 126, 127, 128, 148, 149, 151, 155, 157, 158, 159, 168, 179, 180, 181, 182, 191, 195, 205, 210, 211, 212, 215, 216, 218, 220, 239, 242, 243, 245, 251, 253, 256, 260, 262, 274
Potsdam Haven 71, 80
Pryce-Jones, I 258, 274
Pule, Daniel 221
Pursehouse, L *112*, 180, *249*, 250, 254, 279, 300

Queen Carola Harbour 187, 188, 210

Rabaul viii, 30, 55, 58, 62, 63, 74, 76, 81, 91, 92, 98, 118, 119, 120, 122, 123, 126, 127, 131–160, 179, 180, 181, 182, 184, 189, 190, 194, 195, 196, 197, 204, 205, 216, 219, 222, 240, 245, 248, 259, 287, 288, 293
Radke, Ted 156
Rai Coast 104, 105, 205, 248, 250, 256, 259
Ramada 225, 226
Ramu River 101, 106, 258, 260
Read, William John 'Jack' ix, 103, *112*, *169*, 182, 183, *183*, 184, 185, 186, 187, 188, 189, 191, 192, 210, 211, 212, 214, 215, 216, *217*, 218, 219, 220, 222, 227, 233, 234, 235, 266, 267, 268, 269, 270, 289, 297
Reid, Roger 52
Reilly, Winn Locker 36, 39, 56, *163*
Rein Bay 145
Reye, Ada Bothilda 'Paddy' 'Pat' (née Feldt) 12, 18, 19, 49, 53, 54, 102, *162*, *163*, 285
Reye, Albert James 'Jim' 49, 53
Reye, Eric James 53
Rhoades, Frederick Ashton 'Snowy' ix, *170*, *206*, 209, 211, 225, 226, 234, 289, 297
RMS *Omrah* 37, 38
Roberts, Caleb Grafton 200
Roberts, Tom 200
Robinson, Alf 139, 140, 143
Robinson, Eric 'Wobbie' 75, 256, 289
Robinson, RA 'Robbie' 204, 241, 242, 256, 270
Rooke Island 121, 248
Rohrlach, Dave 155
Ross, Alan 101
Rowlands, Ned 101
Royal Australian Naval College (see also Jervis Bay, Osborne House and Pioneer Class) 1, 19, 20, 31
Royal Naval College 21
Royal Sovereign 39
Russell Islands 207, 233

Sadleir, Cyril Arthur Roy 36, 50, *163*
Saidor 205, 251, 253, 259
Salamaua 83, 84, 85, 86, 87, 88, 89, 91, 92, 93, 94, 95, 98, 99, 101, 102, 120, 121, 131, 146, 147, 153, 158, 180, 181, 190, 246, 248, *249*, 255, 258, 259, 261, 293, 294
Samarai 55, 61, 181
San Cristobal 119, 207, 208
Sanpun 141, 142
Santa Isabel Island 207, 209, 210, 227
Santo 236
Sattelberg 250, 254
Savo Island 209, 211, 235
Scanlan, John 131, 132, 133, 138

INDEX

Schroeder, Lafe *206*, 209, 211, 225, 226
Searle, L H 246
Segi 222, 227, 228, 231
Seleo 77
Sepik *60*, 62, 65, 73, *166*
Sepik River 64, 67, 69, 71, 72, 74, 77, 80, 103, 257, 260, 262, 263
Seton, C W *170*, 229, 232, 265
Sewa 240
Sexton, T W 208
Sexton, W O 139
Shortland Islands 189, 229, 232, 233, 265, 270
Showers, Henry Arthur 'Harry' 36, 39, 50, *163*
Siassi 121
Simberi Island 190, 193
Simons, Charles 45, 57, 58
Sinclair, B A 85
Sio 250, 276
Sly, D I 186, 187, 234, 267
Smit, Bert 153
Smith, David 'Mick' 153
Smith, Ivan 134, 137, 138, 139, 142
Sohano Island 182, 184, 212
Solomon Islands vii, ix, 54, 62, 76, 116, 117, 119, 121, 122, 123, 126, 182, 203, 207–237, 256, 257, 258, 265–283
Soraken 75, 184, 212
Sorem 187
South Sea Islanders ('Kanakas') 6, 10, 11, 12, 13, 16, 55
Squires, W H 'Dickie' *112*, 180, 191, 300
SS *Almora* 4
SS *Mégantic* 52
SS *Nestor* 53
SS *Orsova* 54
St George's Channel 195, 196
Stonehaven, Lady 93
Stonehaven, Lord 93
SumSum 137

Surprise Creek 97

Tabar Island 131, 132, 180, 189, 190, 192, 193
Tabararoi 214
Tadji 120, 121
Talasea 74, 124, 133, 142, 145, 146, 147, 154, 155, 156, 248, 250
Talmage, Jack 193, 194, 199, 300
Tanambogo Island 127, *206*, 207, 208, 209, 218, 219
Tangarare Mission 226
Tatau Island 190, 193
Taungi 134
Taylor, J L 263
Teop Harbour 267, 270
The Slot (see also New Georgia Sound) ix, 207, 227, 229, 232, 265, 292
Thompson, Horace John Harold 33, 36, 39, 51, *163*
Thomson, Drummond 184, 185
Thousand Ships Bay 210
Thursday Island 123, 126, 240
Tikopia 54
Timperley, Alan 159
Trobriand Islands 136, 142, 158, 159, 179, 256
Tokidoro, Nelson 147, 148
Tokiplau, Joseph 147, 151, 152
Tokyo Express 227, 265
Tol Plantation 138–151
Toma 128, 132, 133, 134, 146
Toriu River 148
Totol 156
Townsend, W L 'Kassa' 64, 66, 67, 80, 94, 120, 155, 156
Train, Gordon 204, 221, 222, 223, 225, 270, 300
Trist, Les 99
Tulagi Island vii, ix, 54, 119, 120, 126, 127, 132, 187, 188, *206*, 207, 208, 210, 211, 215, 216, 218, 219, 220, 271
Tulgai 119
Tupling, W 204, 205, *249*, 250, 253, 254, 300
Twining, Merrill 215

Ubili 146
Ulawa Island 119
Ululpatur 118
Umboi 155
USS *Gato* 269
USS *Guardship* 270
USS *Sturgeon* 160
USS *Yorktown* 211
Utapua 54

Vallentine, Harry Bertram 36, *163*
Valoka 145
Vandegrift, Alexander 'Archie' 215, 225, 226, 237, 265
Vanikoro Island 54, 119, 120, 209
Vanimo 77
Vanuatu (see also New Hebrides) 54
Veale, Lionel 243, 257, 261, 262
Veale Reef 243
Vella Lavelle Islands 207, 257, 261, 262
Vial, Leah 180, 181, 258, 300
Victory 5
Vila 54, 126, 127, 208, 209, 210, 218, 224, 236
Viru Harbour 227, 228
Vitiaz Straits 250
Volupai 250
Vouza, Jacob 220, 221
Vungana 223

Waddell, Nick 218, 229, 232, 265
Wade, Thomas 119
Waitavolo 139, 140, 141
Walindi 156

315

Walstab, John 63, 64, 65, 66, 67, 69, 74, 93, 103, 133
Wamput River 99, 108
Wanderer 75
Wanliss, Col 91
Waria River 88, 247
Warum 79
Waterfall Bay 137, 142, 144, 159
Watkins, Llewellyn Leigh 36, 39, 50, 52, 56, *163*
Watson, Hugh 47
Watts, Adrian Joseph Beachleigh 36, *163*
Watut River 88, 96, 98, 99
Wau 85, 86, 89, 93, 95, 98, 106, 107, 108, 109, 110, 115, 294, 298
Western Highlands *60*, 62

Wewak 64, 77, 79, 80, 81, 104, 120, 121, 248, 250, 257, 260, 261, 263
White Australia Policy 16
White, Cyril Brudenell 102
White, Hugh 49
Whittaker, George 103
Wickham, Harry 228
Wide Bay (NG) 137, 139, 142, 145
Willaumez Peninsula 145, 146, 151
Williams, H L *170*, 246
Williamson, Adolphus 'Partridge' 46, 47
Willoughby, Charles 200, 202, 245
Wisdom, Evan 58, 62, 63, 71, 74, 103

Witu Island 146, 156, 157, 158, 248, 250, 251, 253
Woodlark Island 256, 257
Woodroffe, J L *112*, 179, 190, 198, 199, 204, 300
Wright, Malcolm *170*, 203, 297
Wuluwut River 140
Wuvulu (Matty) Island 74, 205

Yambon 65, 66
Yauwika, Sergeant *171*, 184, 185, 219, 234, 267, 279, 289

Zenag Gap 87

ABOUT THE AUTHOR

Betty Lee is a retired medical practitioner living in Brisbane with her partner and adult son. She has a daughter living in New South Wales. Betty is a great niece of Eric Feldt and is sorry that she never met him. She grew up in country Queensland, living next door to her grandmother, who was affectionately known as Nana by many in the small town, and who was Eric's sister. The family tended not to discuss the past or family history. Apart from the mention that Eric had been Head of the Coastwatchers in New Guinea during the Second World War, little else was said.

Betty attended Somerville House and The Women's College in Brisbane and graduated from the University of Queensland. She has been a keen bridge player and together with her partner has represented Queensland in interstate competitions several times. In her late teen or early adult years she read Eric's *The Coast Watchers* and was impressed and moved by the story and his writing ability.

In 1978 she and her then husband and two children went on a cruise to the Pacific Islands which was chosen because it included a visit to the Coastwatchers Memorial in Madang.

One of the first things Betty did upon retiring was to read *The Coast Watchers* again. She also became interested in family history. Being contacted by Vice Admiral Peter Jones, who was looking for information from the families of the first ever cadet shipmen of the Royal Australian Navy, was the beginning of finding out about what a truly talented and remarkable man Eric Feldt was. Her admiration and pride in Eric and the Coastwatchers has been magnified, as has the feeling of enormous gratitude towards them.